Family Assessment Handbook

Family Assessment Handbook

AN INTRODUCTORY GUIDE TO FAMILY ASSESSMENT AND INTERVENTION

Second Edition

Barbara Thomlison
FLORIDA INTERNATIONAL UNIVERSITY

THOMSON

BROOKS/COLE

Australia • Brazil • Canada • Mexico • Singapore • Spain • United Kingdom • United States

THOMSON
BROOKS/COLE

Family Assessment Handbook: An Introductory Guide to Family Assessment and Intervention, **Second Edition**

Barbara Thomlison

Senior Acquisitions Editor: Marquita Flemming
Assistant Editor: Alma Dea Michelena
Technology Project Manager: Inna Fedoseyeva
Marketing Manager: Meghan McCullough
Senior Marketing Communications Manager:
    Tami Strang
Project Manager, Editorial Production:
    Rita Jaramillo
Creative Director: Rob Hugel
Art Director: Vernon Boes
Print Buyer: Doreen Suruki

Permissions Editor: Roberta Broyer
Production Service: International Typesetting
    and Composition
Copy Editor: Meg McDonald
Cover Designer: Tessa Avila
Cover Photos: Corbis, Getty Images
Cover Printer: Edwards Brothers
Compositor: International Typesetting
    and Composition
Printer: Edwards Brothers

Printed in the United States of America
2 3 4 5 6 7 10 09 08 07

Library of Congress Control Number: 2006920896

ISBN-13: 978-0-495-09096-0
ISBN-10: 0-495-09096-4

Thomson Higher Education
10 Davis Drive
Belmont, CA 94002-3098
USA

For more information about our products, contact us at:
Thomson Learning Academic Resource Center
1-800-423-0563

For permission to use material from this text or product, submit a request online at **http://www. thomsonrights.com**.

Any additional questions about permissions can be submitted by e-mail to **thomsonrights@thomson.com**.

To my family Ray, Lynn and Breanne—with love.

To Bailey. The little dog with a big heart for making friends and pleasing everyone he met. Your achievements were great; more frequent flyer miles than most people, and a meritorious degree from university.

To Madison—aka "Big nose" The big dog with a giant sense of humor. Turkey dinner in our family will never be the same without you. You live on through Lexington and Avenue.

Brief Contents

Contents

CHAPTER EIGHT

Linking Assessment and Intervention   95

Part Three: Practicing Family Assessment: Case Studies

CHAPTER NINE

The Del Sol Family: Marital Conflict and Parenting Concerns   105

Preface

Family assessment activities are one of the most common elements of daily practice engaged in by every practitioner. It is not possible to understand and appreciate the difficulties families experience without exploring and assessing their strengths and abilities to discover their resources for focusing on solutions. Of course, there are many models of family practice, but most practitioners do not adhere to a specific model, and they essentially approach families with the idea of identifying interventions to improve individual and family functioning. Many new and promising programs and technologies are increasingly available to improve family practice. All families have the right to receive effective interventions; and to this end, the *Family Assessment Handbook* describes a variety of practice-, evidence-, and consensus-based approaches that can be used in various settings.

Preserving the original integrity of the *Family Assessment Handbook,* the second edition contains several new features: chapter additions and revisions; an extra chapter on issues facing families with an older adult living with them; further evidence-based interventions; updated assessment technologies; three additional cases for study; and revised learning activities. The book uniquely balances theory, clinical application, and self-assessment. It is intended to provide a broad, evidence-supported approach to a family system framework, to planning contextually sensitive interventions for problems of families. Essentially the organizing principles in this book describe the ecological perspective to assessment-based decision making for evidence-supported interventions to meet the needs of families. In this approach no single specific model is advocated; however, assessment and intervention tools presented are aimed either at promoting family strengths or at alleviating consequences of common problems in families. This book assumes, also, that practitioners are motivated to use tools that are recognized as a best practice for strengthening families while supporting parents' skills and motivation for change. Evidence-supported, family-centered interventions are associated with improvements in child developmental status, parenting skill, and family relationships as well as enhancing the interrelationships among individuals, families, and their social and environmental relationships.

Recognizing that skills for working with families are not developed solely from reading, the author encourages practitioners to evaluate the family systems of which they are part and to practice the concepts by case study and discussion using the eight cases provided. Skill development results from actual work with families across settings. Each new encounter is a learning experience, so each encounter with a family should introduce new learning to understanding the family as a unique system. Expertise also flourishes under the guidance and consultation of quality supervision.

The second edition of the book continues to offer a beginning perspective to practitioners who must develop a practical understanding of families and the relevant multiple systems critical to understanding, preventing, and treating family problems. Regardless of the issues and concerns, families are the key agents of change, and family practitioners are strategically positioned to help families by using brief, time-limited, and effective family interventions in practice.

To the Student and Instructor

The purpose of this book is to give students introductory knowledge and skills for the assessment of family functioning and guidelines for clinical assessment and intervention planning. Students, beginning practitioners, and instructors can facilitate learning through the case studies and activities, which are intended to stimulate learning and thinking and the integration of theory and practice. Activities have been field-tested with students and are designed to stimulate self-awareness, critical thinking, and classroom discussion. The practice guidelines offer information for use in treatment decision-making stages for the most common family problems. Cases need to be individualized, and the selected empirically supported treatments and interventions presented are those found to be most useful across different cultural milieus, settings, and populations. In addition, assessment is viewed from a developmentally informed perspective, and the practitioner specifically is viewed as part of the interplay of systems interacting with the family system.

Eight case studies are included that focus on particular populations and issues of family functioning. Students should think of themselves as the practitioner in the case and address the assessment from that perspective. The family journal assists students in learning more about their values, morals, beliefs, and personal family system functioning. All of the cases, activities, and concepts emphasize the complex interplay of multisystems. The clinical issues and conceptual approach are intended to address professionals working in settings requiring a time-limited practice context, yet needing an effective approach to changing social environments with ethnically and culturally diverse families. The questions and activities are designed to stimulate thinking about the issues, the assessment, and decisions in each case. Apart from the study activities with each case, other activities include:

- Students can role-play clients and practitioner in the cases.
- Students can write an assessment for each case.
- Students can go to the Internet and identify empirically supported evidence for clinical interventions in the cases.
- Students can develop a treatment plan for each case.
- Students can identify empirically based research studies for the problems in the cases.
- Students can change the ethnicity of the families and develop culturally appropriate interventions for the cases.
- Students can locate treatment manuals by exploring the Internet.

Organization of the Book

The book has three interrelated teaching and learning units. For reinforcement of theory and concepts, activities are provided in each chapter to enhance learning. Learning activities can be used as separate teaching assignments, in small groups, or as self-directed assignments.

The activities could also apply to either the student's family journal or one of the cases. There are three parts to the book:

- *Part One* includes three chapters addressing the foundations for family assessment and intervention and reviews theory, concepts, and context for assessment and intervention planning. Chapter three in this part focuses on assessing your family and it can be used throughout the course as students write in a journal daily aspects of their family life. Self-assessment and critical thinking using a family journal approach illustrates the impact of various systems on individual behavior, thinking, and bias. Each student can explore his or her family system through the family journal, learning through self-reflection how family environments influence the individual. Critically reflecting on their family histories and beliefs helps students understand how these factors influence perceptions, values, attitudes, and responses to the families seeking service from them. By examining their family membership, family of origin, and their current family dynamics, students will understand the development and maintenance of their patterns of interaction, the uniqueness and diversity of their families. In this way students learn the systemic approach and the myriad issues for assessment and planning in family practice by learning more about themselves within the context of their family experiences. Every family has a unique story.

- *Part Two* addresses the assessment process and intervention planning teaching family systems theory, family life development and locating evidence-based interventions for practice. Five chapters emphasize family strengths and coping in response to stress and demands in their environments. Diversity and difference is highlighted as the foundation of family strengths with the family as the expert for solving their situation. Family systems theory serves as the base for working with families and their needs. To reflect current thinking students will learn how to locate evidence-based practices for selected but common problems families experience in most communities.

- *Part Three* includes eight case studies illustrating the interplay of family systems, needs, culture and diversity that occurs among families and their situations. Family case studies are designed to take students through the process of assessment and intervention planning while at the same time dealing with ethical dilemmas.

The case studies are derived from the author's practice experiences and those of practice and academic collaborators Jennifer Becker, Marian Dumaine, and Denise Gammonley. Case studies are used to

- Assess unique family issues and concerns.
- Practice family interviewing skills through group role simulations.
- Assess family systems for strengths and resources in planning for interventions.
- Reinforce theory and concepts of multisystemic family assessment.
- Practice organizing information by writing a professional family assessment report.
- Increase students' awareness of their strengths and skills for helping.
- Present ethical challenges and ethical decision-making.
- Identify evidence-based interventions that are appropriate to the family problems, resources, and culture.

Finally, the book is written in an informal manner to complement a variety of teaching and preferred learning approaches of instructors and students. Through reading, discovery, and active learning students gain confidence and understanding of family assessment and intervention by exploring their family experiences. To use the activities and family journal effectively, students need to be in a climate of trust and know that there are no right answers or easy predictable solutions—only that a thorough search for evidence-based information for practice is considered the best practice. Differences among families are seen as strengths and an opportunity to promote resilience.

Acknowledgments

The second edition of *Family Assessment* could not have evolved without the efforts and assistance of a number of people who helped make this a successful project. In particular, I have always found the staff at Brooks/Cole to encourage and support creative ideas. I am grateful for the exceptional support from Lisa Gebo, Caroline Concilla, and Alma Dea Michelena for helpful advice and assistance at every call. You are an exceptional team, and I thank you once again. I would like to thank the contributors, Dr. Denise Gammonley, Dr. Marian Dumaine, and Jennifer Becker, for sharing family stories from their practice. I am fortunate you wanted to share your family practice cases with students and instructors. Finally, a special acknowledgment and appreciation is extended to the Killam Trust Foundation, for awarding me a Killam Resident Fellowship for the original manuscript development.

I am also grateful to the following people who reviewed the book:

Daniel L. Yazak, Montana State University, Billings
Brenda Smith, University of Cincinnati
Cheryl Mimbs, Southeast Missouri State University

▼▼▼

CHAPTER ONE

The Context for Family Work

Each family is unique, and individuals develop within their families responding distinctively to the common and not-so-common influences and experiences that embrace and shape the family environment. Families are composed of many interrelated and meaningful parts interacting with each other. Consider, though, how the various rules, traditions, communication and language patterns, gender roles, and cultural and religious ideas influence differences within individual development in families. No two individuals or families will evolve in exactly the same way. Each family will have a unique circumstance for development and change. As a result, it is essential to have an organizing framework to help us understand a family, a family's unique circumstance, why a problem exists, and what is necessary to foster resilience and change.

The following chapters present the context for helping families and a framework of ideas and concepts for understanding families as a system. Having a family orientation is somewhat different from therapeutic work with individuals, groups, and communities. As you read this book, you will see this more clearly as you learn how to think differently when working with families and develop solutions with families that reflect what families need and want. Essential skills for formulating an assessment and intervention plans for family practice are presented within the context of families, their environments, and their social situations as well as the context of professional family practice.

Assessing and evaluating families and their situations and formulating goals can be daunting for any family practitioner, but especially if you are a novice practitioner. Your enthusiasm and optimism for helping families are the first requirement, and perhaps of equal importance will be the need to consider the family as *partners* in the process of change. Why is this important? Families know what they want and need, and in this respect families are the experts about their situations. This position empowers clients as competent to enable them to find solutions to their life troubles. Your role is to motivate, facilitate, and collaborate with them to achieve the goals needed for building solutions to their difficulties. With this in mind, you can develop confidence and competence about these tasks if you follow a systematic, best-evidence-supported practice approach to help you plan assessment and intervention strategies.

Gaining confidence in conducting a family assessment begins with understanding the context of family functioning before you address family issues. Viewing the family as a system influenced by many factors will direct you to identifying problematic areas, assessing the strengths and abilities of both the individual members and the family as a system. Once you know the circumstances that influence the helping process for families, you should be able to provide effective interventions.

A family systems approach is less individually oriented than other helping or therapeutic approaches: It treats the family as a unit. In this context practitioners view a family as a system experiencing various issues and problems within itself and with the systems with which it interacts. Even so, the individual family members and their actions must be considered, and the impact of various systems—especially the family system—on individual behavior is of primary importance. Because the family environment is a central influence on individual family members, family experiences play a critical role in causing, promoting, or reinforcing troubling behaviors of children, adolescents, and adults. Therefore, it is important to develop interventions targeted to parents, siblings, and the entire family unit.

However, families are not the only influence shaping family members' beliefs and behavior. Others such as peers, teachers, coaches, child care providers, neighbors, and community members often influence how a family member thinks, feels, and behaves. Family interventions to prevent, reduce, or remediate problems frequently need to be complemented by interventions carried out in these other systems or settings that impact family members, such as a child care setting, a school, or another community service system.

Interventions designed to change the beliefs, attitudes, or behaviors of family units are often challenging, and in some situations they are costly. A single intervention conducted in isolation is not likely to solve a number of family problems, and the most effective approaches include several types of interventions and strategies that complement one another. Even these may fail to reach some families and individuals most in need. Often interventions are introduced in advanced stages of family problems when they are more difficult to change. Carefully consider your skill level, expertise, resources, and community support when selecting interventions. Above all, make sure the interventions you select fit together for addressing the family troubles. Keep in mind that families need to be informed and involved in deciding which intervention to use, and you may need to modify an intervention to make it appropriate to the circumstances, culture, and community. The context of assessing and planning for family interventions is critical.

Family Defined

As diverse structures and definitions of *family* evolve from gender role shifts and changing attitudes in society, there are debates about what constitutes a family and how *family intervention, family practice,* and *family therapy* are defined. Some models of family treatment define *family* differentially, such as rigidly adhering to treating the entire family unit; other approaches are more flexible, treating the family unit while working individually with various family members. You need to know how you define *family* at both the personal level and the professional level. Are these definitions the same? Your definition influences how you approach the assessment process and intervention choices. Essentially, family treatment involves family members, and a broad definition of *family* and *family intervention* is applied in this book. However, intervention choices in this book are primarily influenced by the quality of knowledge and research about a family problem.

Families consist of people who have a common history, experience a degree of emotional bonding, and share goals and activities. Family issues and concerns may include physical survival, social protection, education, and development. They may involve acceptance, nurturance, approval, belonging, identity, and support and growth of individuals and family members. The members may or may not be biologically related; the bonds that unite them may or may not be legal ties. Theirs is a shared experience marked by the social and psychological interdependence that is characteristic of all family relationships. The family must also be seen within the context of other systems it interacts with such as those of the community, school, workplace, church, culture, race, social class, and beliefs.

The very notion of *family* conjures up memories, feelings, and experiences for each of us. Everyone has a different definition of *family* and a different family experience. Here are the defining characteristics used in this book:

- Families share a sense of history.
- Families have some degree of emotional bonding.
- Families engage in direction and goals for the future.
- Families may or may not be biologically related.
- Families may or may not have legal ties.

The bonds between family members are powerful, existing through time and often with long-term significance. Most family systems contain members who are biologically related and bound in some form of legal contract. Children become part of a family through birth, adoption, foster care, or other guardianship arrangements. Other family units whose commitments are firm, whose goals are defined, and who share a sense of history are interdependent but may not be legally or biologically related. Family members may have a broad definition of who constitutes their family. Knowing whom the various members consider to be their family is important for the practitioner.

Successful families depend on individuals and the family unit to fulfill many of the social and psychological needs of the group as a whole and of individual members. When families are unable to successfully reach this goal or parts of the goal, the practitioner, as an intervener, can be an important service.

Family Context

Helping families does not involve only the family unit. This unit must be placed in a broader context, and that context includes you as the helping practitioner. Your experience with your own family and your opinions and beliefs will affect how you relate to the families who come to you for help. It is essential, therefore, that you spend some time learning about yourself before you start working with families. In addition to having self-knowledge, you must be prepared to deal with areas that can be troubling in their ambiguity. Among the issues that arise in working with families are those that pose ethical concerns. Given the influence that practitioners have on families, they must approach ethical decisions in practice carefully, drawing on theories of ethics, codes of professional conduct, family practice theory, cultural context, evidence-supported practice, their professional identity, and public policy guidelines. Ethics and self-understanding are both involved in how you present yourself to others and the way you understand yourself and others. The inner dimensions of who you are affect your professional practice and lead to a number of implications regarding your interactions with families and the context of professional practice. For example, how do you effectively work with families who present spiritual ideas and religious beliefs that are different than yours or may even conflict with your own belief systems? How do you assist families who believe that corporal punishment is acceptable discipline for children or have specific ideas about the roles and responsibilities of women and working outside the home? These are some examples of many discrepancies you may encounter.

Personal and professional values and ethical standards are important in understanding who you are. Perhaps you have not given much thought to what values you hold and how these values affect the way you will practice with families. *Values* are the principles and standards of conduct that you deem good, right, or desirable. These ideals are embedded in your communication, behavior, or interaction with families. They are part of the social norms you acquire and include culturally guided likes and dislikes that are part of you. Every time you think in terms of *should,* the behavior you are considering is based on a value or norm. Values may be personal to you; part of the dominant culture; or drawn from your ethnic, racial, or specific community or cultural group belief system. Values also come from your professional affiliation and education. The purpose of understanding yourself and your values is to understand how these ideals influence your thinking and behavior with families. They also influence the way families experience you; therefore, they cannot be viewed in isolation from the context of family systems.

Family assessment involves determining *with* the family its members' strengths and concerns. This means you must attempt to understand the behavior of family members as a family system within the context of your profession, the practice setting that employs you, and your personal values, ethics, and family system. Ethical standards are the system of moral prescriptions or ways of acting that express your values. These standards will guide you as you work with families.

Beliefs, Preferences, and Facts

Beliefs are assumptions about what is true or false and may or may not be testable (Gibbs & Gambrill, 1999). *Assumptions* guide your personal actions and shape your thinking; they are an expression of your convictions. *Preferences* speak to your *values* about many issues and are not a matter of determining what is right or wrong, true or false. *Facts,* on the other hand, are subject to evaluation and testing and have a scientific basis or other evidence-supported claim. Critical reflection lets you consider your beliefs and preferences and separate this information from facts. The benefits of critical thinking include learning about alternatives and enhancing the quality of your decision-making skills in work with families (Gibbs & Gambrill, 1999). Such reflection allows you to discard irrelevant, misleading, and inappropriate sources of information that may be harmful to families.

When assessing family distress and functioning, you have five major sources of ethical and value-based knowledge to consult. These areas are (1) personal beliefs, (2) family beliefs, (3) professional beliefs, (4) practice setting beliefs, and (5) legal requirements. Each of these carries certain obligations that should be familiar to you before you work with families.

Personal Beliefs

Practitioners who are involved with parents and children bring their own experiences and biases to their work. They will be immersed in family matters at both the personal or subjective levels and the professional or more objective levels. By examining your personal beliefs or views and underlying assumptions about children, parents, and families, you will have a framework within which you can compare your own values and the various ways others think about the often value-laden area of child care and family life. Beliefs also influence your views of family functioning, family distress, and choice of intervention strategies as well as how you define successful outcomes for the family and individual family members. Your personal beliefs may additionally affect your willingness to comply with the policies of your practice setting and with professional standards of conduct and ethical practice.

A major reason for examining your personal beliefs before working with families is to identify potentially biased attitudes and behavior in yourself that may become barriers to family work. Problems of families often bring practitioners face-to-face with family behaviors and attitudes that have brought harm to them or others. In examining your underlying assumptions about children, parents, and families, consider the "shoulds" you have about children and parents. For example, where child abuse has occurred, a parent says, "Whipping a child is good for him. How else will he learn?" You, on the other hand, have seen the resulting marks on the child and ask yourself "Should this child remain in the home?" Although your personal beliefs and values suggest the child will continue to be harmed if corporal punishment is continually used, legislation and policy will guide your decision; and despite your personal beliefs, leaving the child in the family unit may entitle the family to primary support services and other interventions.

Self-understanding involves examining your family context: It is in the context of family that you form many of your values and ethical stances. Keeping personal feelings and needs separate from professional relations is necessary to avoid negatively impacting the families that you help. You must ask whether your personal values create barriers to working with particular families or particular problems of families and whether they affect your choice of intervention strategies. Practice models vary according to who is held responsible for problems and who is responsible for the solutions, and your values may affect your preference for one or another model. For example, empowerment models of intervention focus on solution aspects but not necessarily on responsibility for problem creation. Collaborative approaches will be more comfortable for families and practitioners who perceive each other as partners in solving problems and where strengths and competence are kept in the forefront. For other situations, families and practitioners may be more comfortable with an "expert" model of intervention, such as those based on the medical model—particularly when serious and persistent mental health issues are evident.

Family problems and solutions are complex, and strategies for combating them must not be based on personal preferences. Interventions need to be guided by evidence-supported studies from research. This is information derived from rigorous evaluations of intervention studies reported in peer-reviewed literature for a particular problem. Best practice interventions can also include promising practices not yet scientifically proven but recommended on the basis of community experts. What matters most is that practitioners use the best available research, combined with clinical expertise and client values, in making informed assessment and intervention decision making (Gibbs, 2003; Sackett, Strauss, Richardson, Rosenberg, & Haynes, 2000). Part of your assessment process with families is to begin with a careful assessment and to place the need for information into an answerable question before you track down the best available evidence to answer that question (Gibbs, 2003). For example, what psychosocial interventions reduce parenting problems with preschool children? Together with the family, you will critically appraise the best information currently available from both the literature and the practices that meet the community's and family's values, needs, and objectives.

Values or beliefs influence how practitioners interpret the family's problems. That is, practitioners' assumptions about the causes and change potential of the family's problems can shape their intervention choices. How practitioners respond to family problems, as well as issues of confidentiality, family self-determination, and family structure, are influenced by personal and professional ethics, values, and obligations. Continue to monitor personal feelings about individuals and families you are working with to ensure you do not unfairly impede them in their goals.

Family Beliefs

Family values and beliefs are the ideas, opinions, and assumptions held by individuals and families. Values and beliefs are unique to each individual and family. Although a family may share values and attitudes with the dominant culture and specific subcultures with which they identify, how they express or translate these values within their own family will be specific to the family. Cultural genograms and ecomaps (see Chapter 5) are initial tools to assess family beliefs. Exploring family rules and traditions will provide more in-depth knowledge of the family belief system. Asking questions of family members about the "shoulds" held by the family will help access family rules concerning discipline, structure, and communication. Discussing support networks with a family helps you learn about the nature of exchanges the family members have with others outside their immediate unit.

In working with families you may seek solutions within their belief system framework, or you may work to change or shift some values where harm or safety issues are obvious. This is a delicate undertaking and must be approached with diligence and care. You as the intervener are in a position to influence family behavior and beliefs, and you must guard against imposing your own beliefs. Contracting and setting specific objectives must be agreed upon with the family before undertaking change, unless of course it is a matter of safety.

Professional Beliefs

The common base of social work values or professional beliefs has been written about extensively and can be synthesized under the following principles:

- Respect the individual worth and dignity of families.
- Value the individuals' and family's capacity for change while respecting the family's right to self-determination.
- As a professional, recognize that family empowerment is a highly valued objective. This enables families to access needed information, services, and resources through equal opportunity and meaningful participation in decision making.
- Confidentiality is paramount, although there are limits to confidentiality that must form part of informed consent.
- Informed consent documents are an integral part of contracting with families. Behaving in a trustworthy manner is required.
- Practice within your areas of competence and expertise. Accountability to families and the profession must be observed (Gambrill, 1997; Reamer, 1995).

All activities during assessment, formulating goals, and evaluating families must be rooted in professional values that allow you to offer service to families with a maximum of skill and respect while tailoring interventions to their unique culture and needs. Professional values help us to avoid stereotyping families based on certain characteristics or consumer groups while appreciating their differences.

Practice Setting Beliefs

Values of agencies and organizations influence such factors as the practice setting's mission, policies, and procedures. These in turn directly affect who is served and how. Policies regarding eligibility for service greatly impact program and case decision levels. Personal and professional values may conflict with practice setting directives, especially in areas of service priorities and program development. The practice setting culture and even physical arrangements reflect organizational values. For example, a cramped, cluttered space may give families a sense that they are not valued, or a lack of available evening appointment times may give families a sense that they are not valued. The amount of autonomy staff members are given in making decisions with families will be reflected in how decisions are made. Empowered practitioners may feel better able to facilitate family empowerment.

Practice settings have working relationships among other practice settings. Often families are involved with multiple interveners, and the highest standards of collaboration must be adhered to by all human service professionals. One valuable source for guiding practice in this area is the Campbell Collaboration Principles (http://campbell.gse.upenn.edu/). The Campbell Collaboration provides exceptional systematic reviews focusing on the fields of social work, education, and crime and based on best practices in developed principles of collaboration. To ensure the highest possible standards are employed with the community, the partnership, and the participants, several guiding principles on which to base work with others are presented:

1. Collaborate both internally and externally to foster good communication and open decision making and teamwork.
2. Build on the enthusiasm of individuals by involving supporting people of different skills and backgrounds.
3. Avoid unnecessary duplication by good management and coordination to ensure economy of effort.
4. Minimize bias through a variety of approaches such as abiding by high standards of scientific evidence, ensuring broad participation, and avoiding conflicts of interest.

5. Strive for relevance by promoting the assessment of policies and practices using outcomes that matter to people.
6. Promote access by wide dissemination of the outputs of the literature search, taking advantage of strategic alliances.
7. Ensure quality by being open and responsive to feedback to ensure quality improvement (www.campbellcollaboration.org/FraAbout.html).

The Campbell Collaboration Web site is a good source for the best available information about selected psychosocial and health problems for summaries of solutions to intervention questions. Other Internet pages are also helpful.

Legal Requirements

All jurisdictions in North America have legal requirements regarding limits to confidentiality. You will need to know and explain to families, as part of the original contracting for services, that confidentiality may not apply in instances such as reporting child abuse, reporting the potential of a family member to harm self or others, or responding to a court order requesting release of family records.

Many legal concerns cannot be covered in this chapter (see Reamer, 1995), but the impact of the federal law known as the Health Insurance Portability and Accountability Act, or HIPAA (PL 104-191), is perhaps most relevant to you. Briefly, HIPAA establishes a minimum protection of a client's medical records, which are defined as any recording of any kind, that identify the recipient's past, present, or future conditions or who is receiving medical, behavioral, and many social services. This includes written and electronic records and oral communication (Corcoran, Gorin & Moniz, 2005). HIPAA is designed to protect the privacy of clients and specifically prohibits disclosure of any identifiable information without written consent from the consumer. HIPAA also allows consumers access to their records, regardless of whether the clients are uninsured or covered by a private insurance company or Medicare and Medicaid programs (Thomlison & Corcoran, in press). The release of information is lawful if three conditions are met: (1) the client agrees in writing, (2) the disclosure is in the best interest of the client in bettering treatment, and (3) only the minimally necessary information is disclosed. To summarize, the impact of HIPAA will include obtaining written permission for release of information, allowing your clients fairly complete access to all the records you keep and those of your supervisor, and influencing how and with whom you communicate, such as on the cell phone. So this is an important legal requirement for practitioners in many fields.

Other regulations may also be in effect, such as managed care policies concerning documentation for services. You need to learn what legal and licensing regulations you work under for ethical documentation of family practice.

Maintaining Ethical Standards

Beyond professional and legal regulations, practitioners must take care in how they use information, as well as their power and influence with families. The pressure to make ethical judgments can be overwhelming, not only for students and novices but also for skilled and experienced practitioners. Two major issues will be considered in this section: (1) the importance of ethical decision making and (2) confidentiality and the application of ethical principles to practice dilemmas.

Ethical Decision-Making Protocol

Practitioners need to develop an awareness of and sensitivity to ethical decision making. Tensions between personal beliefs and the profession's espoused values may lead to ethical dilemmas for practitioners. These tensions underlie many ethical practice decisions and dilemmas. There are no simple answers to these situations, and there is no agreement whether personal or professional values should take precedence. When values conflict, practitioners must weigh the competing obligations of the family, the employer, the profession, and third parties against the requirements of their own conscience. Practitioners must continually examine their personal beliefs as well as how those values influence their understanding of family problems, system problems, the application of knowledge, and strategies for intervention.

You need to keep in mind families' rights and well-being to make decisions based on the ethics of the profession. Remember, ethical action includes commission (what was done) and omission (what was not done). Failing to act may be overlooked when assessing a course of action. Ethical decisions must be made in a rational manner that is comprehensible to others, including families, colleagues, employers, and professional associations.

Despite careful planning, ethical conflicts will arise. Gambrill (1997) and Reamer (1995) discuss at length crucial and ethical thinking and actions. Many situations arise that present an ethical dilemma in working with families in distress. Consider the following factors in ethical decision making:

- The family's interests, rights, and values.
- The interests and rights of others involved in the situation (such as individual family members versus the family system).
- Your professional code of ethics and how this relates to the situation.
- Your personal values and ethical stance.
- Practice setting policies and procedures that relate to the situation.
- The legal and licensing regulations and implications of each intervention decision (Gambrill, 1997).

Gibbs and Gambrill (1999, p. 190) provide a checklist of ethical concerns that may help guide your ethical decision making. Use of this protocol becomes necessary when several ethical guidelines conflict and thus the potential solutions are imperfect and often unsatisfactory. Sometimes dilemmas can be avoided through careful planning and good assessment procedures. For example, use clear and understandable language to inform families of the purpose of proposed services, as well as the risks related to them. Some examples are limits to available services, relevant costs, reasonable alternatives to service, appeal procedures, and families' right to refuse or withdraw from treatment; these must be presented to families during the engagement process.

Practitioners' standards of practice, knowledge, and skills are the foundation of ethical practice. Careful application will help practitioners avoid potentially serious situations such as the following:

1. Misdiagnosing the seriousness of an adolescent's depression, which could lead to the young person's suicide.
2. Underevaluating the potential of further assault by a violence-prone partner in supporting a woman's decision to remain in a highly dangerous domestic situation.
3. Making an incorrect assessment of an adoptive home leading to an adoption breakdown and subsequent maladaptive behaviors for the child involved.
4. An error in judgment that leaves an infant in a situation where abuse might occur, leading to the child's serious injury and death.

In such contexts, quality of service and quality of care must be maintained so that a situation of unethical conduct or incompetence is avoided.

Confidentiality Concerns

Historically, professionals such as social workers and others have developed guidelines to help practitioners make sound, ethical decisions. National bodies such as the National Association of Social Workers (NASW) have developed codes of ethics. These codes are written to address practice settings, practice issues, and problems practitioners face every day. The codes do not prescribe explicitly the professional behavior required. Often competence guidelines are developed to provide more detailed descriptions of professional behavior to be used in various

A. Keeping confidentiality.
   1. Limits on confidentiality are described.
   2. Confidentiality is maintained unless there are concerns about harm to others.
B. Selecting objectives.
   3. Objectives focused on result in real-life gains for clients.
   4. Objectives are related to the key concerns of clients.
C. Selecting methods.
   5. Assessment methods relied on provide accurate, relevant information.
   6. Intervention methods selected are likely to attain outcomes that clients value.
   7. Assessment, intervention, and evaluation methods are acceptable to clients and to significant others.
D. Fully informing clients.
   8. Clients are given an accurate description of the accuracy of assessment methods used.
   9. Clients receive accurate estimates of the likely success of recommended procedures.
   10. Alternative methods and their likely consequences are described.
   11. Clear descriptions of the cost, time, and effort involved in a suggested method are presented in language intelligible to clients.
   12. An accurate description and the likelihood of side effects (both positive and negative) of suggested services are provided.
   13. An accurate description of the helper's competence to offer needed services is provided.
   14. Appropriate arrangements are made to involve others in decisions when clients cannot give informed consent.
E. Being competent.
   15. Helpers are competent to use the assessment measures they rely on.
   16. Helpers are competent to use the intervention methods they rely on.
F. Being accountable.
   17. Arrangements are made for ongoing feedback about progress using valid progress indicators.
G. Encouraging a culture of thoughtfulness.
   18. Positive feedback is provided to colleagues for the critical evaluation of claims and arguments.
   19. Efforts are made to change agency procedures and policies that decrease the likelihood of providing evidence-based practice.

Figure 1.1. Checklist of Ethical Concerns (*Source:* From *Critical Thinking for Social Workers: Exercises for the Helping Professions,* revised edition, by L. Gibbs and E. Gambrill, p. 190. Copyright ©1999 Pine Forge Press. Reprinted by permission.)

settings for reasonable practice. Specific conduct in specific circumstances is often required as noted in the following discussion of common concerns.

Legal Obligations   The limits of confidentiality—such as when a practitioner has a legal obligation to report a situation, even against the family's wishes—need to be spelled out clearly to families at the onset of contact. Do not wait until a situation arises. Stress that confidentiality cannot be maintained under conditions outlined in legal statutes or when there are compelling professional reasons for breaking it. State these conditions in the first contact with families. Examples include laws mandating the reporting of child abuse, child neglect, and elder abuse. The limits of confidentiality are described to the family with assurance that confidentiality will be maintained unless there are concerns about harm or safety.

Fully Informing Families   Families have a right to truthful information about matters relevant to their treatment and welfare. They should be fully informed about assessment methods, and any interventions selected need to reflect the outcomes the family wants. Families should receive clear descriptions of the cost, time, and effort involved in the treatment process (Gibbs & Gambrill, 1999).

Obligation to Adhere to Regulations   The desire to protect families from harm may raise some issues related to paternalism in practice. Forcing a family to accept services against its wishes is an example of paternalism. Protecting families from themselves when they fail to exercise "good" judgment raises concerns about self-determination and informed consent. Sometimes the practitioner believes that harm to the family may result if the helper adheres to policies and regulations. Examples of this may include the legal mandate to report child abuse or practice setting policy to report income or assets for determining the level or costs of services. The issue is one of protecting the family's welfare and deciding whether this justifies not adhering to legal requirements or practice setting policies.

Service Limitations   Once you have decided what services the family requires, you will face considerations about the types of services, the duration, and the intensity of services needed. You will likely make these decisions based on the family's needs, ability to pay, or other criteria, such as needs for growth, change, safety, and stability. Most families benefit from a set of integrated services tailored to their individual needs, so multiple interventions may be required.

Practitioners may face different kinds of dilemmas in managed care agencies or in organizations that have constraints on the amount of services they can offer. Many publicly funded agencies are limited in the support or services they can provide because of financial constraints. Therefore, hard choices must be made about the number of families served and how these families are selected. Sometimes practitioners may disagree with agency decisions when they believe services are denied to families they see as being in great need. What then? What do practitioners do? They cannot serve families who are not approved for services by the practitioner's employing agency. Do they try to change the decision at the agency level? These are ethical dilemmas for the practitioner.

Coordinating multiple interventions is more likely to address a number of needs and will stand a better chance of making a difference to the family than will a single intervention. This makes sense from the ecological and systems perspective as well as from the point of view of service provision, particularly when service constraints are present and the practitioner can develop formal, professional services with less traditional resources. The practitioner's willingness to ensure an appropriate response to the family that is unique to its needs and priorities should be the practice guideline when both services and opportunities are limited.

Summary

- Families are unique systems of influence.
- Families must be informed and involved as full partners in the change process.
- The context of working with families includes a complex interplay of environmental factors, personal beliefs, and social, ethical, and cultural values as influences on practice.
- Environmental influences play a critical role in impacting various individual and family behaviors.
- Practitioners must be competent in understanding family difficulties and in their ability to skillfully consider methods of change.
- Practitioners must consider each family's personal beliefs and preferences in assessment and intervention planning.
- Practitioners implement their obligations under practice setting beliefs, as well as professional and ethical standards.

Learning Activities

Activity 1.1 Sharing Views on Family

1. Students will introduce themselves to the class within the context of their families by addressing the following:
   a. Who are the members of your family?
   b. In your view, what does *family* mean to you?
   c. What is the single most important message you received from your family?
   d. What is your definition of *family*?
2. Note common key ideas and themes that emerged from the presentations on a flip chart or the board.
3. When you have completed this activity, examine the common and uncommon experiences among the families. What did you learn that was new or surprising from other students' family experiences?
4. How similar to or different are families from your definition of *family*?
5. What are the implications of your family experience for working with families? What bias do you need to be aware of that may influence your practice?
6. What are your thoughts about what constitutes an ideal family?

Activity 1.2 My Family Journal: My Family Experience — Beliefs and Preferences

Self-awareness is important to working with other families. Therefore, it is necessary to reflect on your family experiences and how these will impact practice. You draw your values and ethical stances from the context of family experiences. Write your response in the spaces provided here and then discuss your responses with classmates.

Identify 10 things you learned from your family that will make you a good practitioner and how these can influence you in helping families:

1. From my family I learned that _____
   How will this influence you in practice with a family? _____
2. From my family experience I learned that _____
   How will this influence you in practice with a family? _____
3. Continue to develop your list.

Activity 1.3 Yellowbird Family Case

The task is to read the Yellowbird Family Case Study (Chapter 11) and think about the ethical conflicts in the case and how these might be handled. Identify a dilemma in the case and address the situation by answering the following questions:

1. Describe a confidentiality dilemma in the case.
2. Is the value of self-determination relevant to this case, and if so, how?
3. Identify the values and beliefs about how this family operates or functions.
4. Describe the competing values in this case.
5. Identify other examples in the case that may involve competing personal and professional values dilemmas.
6. In class, role-play for 15 minutes the first meeting with the Yellowbird family presenting the issue of confidentiality. Then evaluate the case using Figure 1.1, Checklist of Ethical Concerns (Gibbs & Gambrill, 1999). What difficulties did you encounter in applying these principles to the case?

CHAPTER TWO

A Framework for Understanding the Family

Many books address the various aspects of conducting a family assessment. The practice aspects of conducting an assessment are the focus of this book. To enhance the quality of the assessment process and findings, you must accept four guidelines for gathering information about a family and its members:

1. Good assessment information results from a planned or systematic approach to the family and the family situation.
2. To make profound changes in the life of an individual, child, or family, the most effective strategy engages the family as an active partner in the process. Family systems thinking and planning are necessary when change is needed in the environment (Huffman, Mehlinger, & Kerivan, 2000).
3. Family experiences play a critical role in causing, promoting, or reinforcing behaviors and competencies (Corcoran, 2000). For example, it has been found that children with early cognitive, social, and behavioral difficulties are known to have increased rates of conduct problems through their teenage years. Understanding this will allow us to examine the child's early behaviors within the environmental context that puts this child at risk for getting off track in school, with peer relationships, and with self-control.
4. Use the empirical literature to guide decision making when recommending and selecting interventions for change. Although it is tempting and may even be more expedient to bypass empirical information about the effectiveness of different clinical interventions, it is now considered an ethical and professional obligation to seek the best available evidence, appraise its credibility and applicability in terms of your client's circumstances, values, and preferences, and apply it as a first choice treatment (McNeece & Thyer, 2004).

Considerable information relating to effective psychosocial interventions and their direct application to family practice will be found. Starting with these assumptions will help you organize your thinking for the kinds of questions that are likely to effect change in the family. The assumptions with which practitioners view the child, family, and environment will set the theoretical framework for thinking about resources for intervention and change.

Families and Environments

To understand the complexities of the family's environment and situation, practitioners need a guiding framework that provides direction and focus for practice (Rothery, 1999). Viewing the family in the context of its environments is important if you are to learn how families, individuals, and environments change. The environment where the child and family develop informs us about their strengths, supports, emerging competencies, stresses, and needs. Examining environments the family interacts with tells us about members' adaptation to stresses, needs, and problems. Focusing on environments where individuals and families develop and interact is identified as a multisystem perspective. This perspective offers an opportunity to examine or assess the adequacy of the many relationships that link individuals with their environments (Rothery, 1999). Furthermore, it helps us distinguish the strengths and coping abilities and patterns families have shown in the past when conflict and stress were not present in their environmental interactions.

Thinking from a multisystem perspective about family assessment and intervention is a sound, effective way to approach the family's unique situation. Each family system will have its own developmental pattern and interactional system. Common patterns can be identified, but essentially family systems are distinctive. Thinking in a multisystem framework is the first step to getting started and determining creative approaches to family circumstances. Research shows that it is also necessary to have authentic and active family involvement to ensure that appropriate resources and interventions are connected to the problem-solving process. This can be one of the most challenging aspects of assessment. Solutions must fit the family situation. Engaging the family at the beginning gives you the best opportunity to systematically and comprehensively respond to the diversity of family need.

How will you know the family is involved and engaged in problem solving? Although there is limited research addressing predictors of family participation in family therapy, a few investigations have had success in retaining parents and families (Barth et al., 2005; Haggerty et al., 2002; Webster-Stratton, 1992, 1997). These have notably used cognitive behavioral parent training components in family work to reduce risk factors and enhance protective factors for maladaptive child and family functioning. As noted earlier, family factors play a central role in protective factors for children's developmental outcomes; similarly, family factors play a role in participation in treatment. Engaging families in treatment requires attention simultaneously to the needs of multiple individuals, as well as the systemic process or family environment that governs family interaction. There are sophisticated scales to measures family engagement (Alexander & Luborsky, 1986) and the helping alliance; but for the beginning practitioner, evidence of family engagement can be seen in family members attending meetings with the practitioner, participating in meetings, relating or feeling connected to the practitioner, participating toward the helping goals and objectives, and adopting the contract for service (M. MacGowan, personal communication). The nature and quality of family involvement will vary depending on many factors, but it is necessary to think about how each family is organized and functioning to understand how its members will be involved and engaged in the process of change.

Getting Started

Family life and family functioning are incredibly complex processes that cannot be understood through a single observation or encounter. Consider the following example. If you look at a photograph of a family engaged in an activity such as playing a game, watching TV, or eating a meal, what could you say about the people? Although you would have a snapshot of data, you could say a great deal about what you think you know. The difficulty is that you may misinterpret what you see because of viewing that family from your own life experiences, events, values, and cultural beliefs, as well as personal and professional knowledge. Depending on your point of view, values, or theoretical understanding, you can make many statements based on that photograph, but they will only be conjecture or hypothesizing based on limited information. It is a good place to start, but there is a great deal more to learn because a family in action, sitting with you, can provide far more information both in terms of the family interactions and their processes. As a practitioner you need to make sense of this complex information, and understanding the dynamic interplay of families as a system helps reduce the complexity.

Whether novice or expert in working with families, you can begin to make guesses or hypotheses about what it might be like to be a part of the family in that photograph. From looking at it, you might say the family members appear loving, lonely, or distant from each other by noting their physical positions and emotional or facial expressions. You might note whether individuals are touching, holding, or gesturing to another. However, you are still just making assumptions based on that one moment. What you infer about the family will to a large extent be influenced by how you think and what you are thinking.

Other sources of information are necessary. Knowledge of family functioning is needed to extend your understanding of what is happening. Knowledge about family theory is another source, as is knowledge about your own family experiences. Potentially all knowledge sources are helpful. And the knowledge, skills, values, and attitudes related to your thinking affect your practice decisions with families. Being aware of what you know, don't know, and need to know helps you reflect on your actions.

Gibbs and Gambrill (1999, p. 4) address the importance of critical thinking for family practice decisions. Critical thinking shapes the assessment and intervention process. The following questions are suggested as a framework to evaluate your initial thinking about a family:

1. What assumptions am I making about this family?
2. What am I taking for granted about this family?
3. What data, facts, information, and observations am I using to arrive at my point of view about this family?
4. How am I interpreting the information about this family?
5. What conclusions am I coming to about this family?

Practitioners use many criteria to evaluate what they think and see and the action they will take. Avoiding cognitive biases will help you avoid making unsound practice decisions and the tendency to accept initial assumptions without question and to believe that causes are similar to their effects (Gibbs & Gambrill, 1999). There are many ways of thinking and arriving at conclusions. Being aware of the sources of information or knowledge helps you avoid biases, reaching the wrong conclusions, or making unsound decisions about a family and their situation.

Family Engagement

Families seeking the services of a practitioner vary greatly, as will the kind of issues they want help for and the type of change desired. Some of the ways they will differ include family structure, developmental life stage, ethnicity, race, and their functional abilities due to the nature of their troubles and troubling behaviors. Some families require considerable help, whereas others need less. Some will ask for service; others will not be as forthcoming and may even be referred to you by a court. Regardless of the types of services or issues families are seeking help with, they want to know that you will be of assistance in designing interventions to promote solving their problems confidently and competently.

Engaging the family in the process of change is paramount. The focus of concern with a family begins with the practitioner's behavior and the family response. A relationship is needed between the two systems, and this connecting of the practitioner with the family system is referred to as *joining the family* or the *therapeutic alliance*. It is an alliance and connection of the two systems, not just the individuals. All members of this joined system can influence the change process. Therefore, the first encounters are crucial and will determine the nature and process of what evolves and unfolds in the helping relationship.

Through this helping relationship the practitioner begins to develop an understanding and complete, coherent story of a family and its struggles and demands. That is, what is the current situation and what is needed to make a difference for the family? Relationship building engages the family so the practitioner can build a knowledge base for understanding how a family responds to demands from the various environments as well as providing ideas about what supports it needs and the strengths it has within its system and surrounding network. The basis for helping to reduce the complexity is to understand families as social systems that are interacting with multiple systems both among the family members and between the family members and others. The resulting information helps us decide what intervention is needed to generate particular results (Corcoran, 2000; Rothery & Enns, 2001; Weiss, 1995).

Failure to adequately engage and retain families in interventions is a serious problem. Little research is available to guide practice on how to engage and retain families. Family factors play a central role in engaging many families, particularly in the presence of parenting stress, child conduct disorders, adverse parenting practices, parental mental illness, economic factors, and immigration and legal issues (Robbins, Alexander, Turner, & Perez, 2003). Identifying family protective factors and strengths early in the engagement phase will enhance family continuation in treatment. These findings highlight the importance of the family–practitioner alliance in family work. Data from research studies suggest that providing interventions to improve parenting practices, at the earliest signs of risk factors for child behavior problems, improves child and family outcomes (Olds, 2002).

The processes of family engagement and participation vary, but some practitioners use specific strategies such as contracts and rewards and culturally specific content (Webster-Stratton, 1998), consistent staff (Olds, 2002), and alliance building between parents and staff to develop readiness to change (Fisher & Chamberlain, 2000). Risk factors for family treatment dropout are negative parenting practices, child behavior problems, language barriers, and cultural mismatch between parent group leaders and participants, as well as parental perception of low intervention relevance and beliefs about their parenting competencies and the causes of their children's behavior (Burns, Hoagwood, & Maultsby, 1998; Webster-Stratton & Taylor, 2001). Family engagement is related to how and when families are involved rather than the particular type of service received (Burns, Hoagwood, & Maultsby, 1998; Olds, 2002; Fisher & Chamberlain, 2000).

Family engagement is often complicated by the fact that family members are engaging with multiple systems, and efforts to involve another service may confound intervention with you. The effectiveness of interventions is highly dependent on parent cooperation, enthusiasm, motivation, and sustained effort (Burns, Hoagwood, & Maultsby, 1998). Practitioners interview families in every type of organization and environment and work with a variety of family structures, problems, and issues. Each of these settings will have a somewhat different set of criteria for engaging families and conducting family interviews as well as different data or information to be collected. However, some common elements to consider about families for assessment apply regardless of the setting or mandate for service.

Guiding Principles of Assessment

Deciding what intervention to use develops directly from the context of assessment. Consequently, the practitioner must consider a number of issues about the assessment process. Culture and beliefs of the agency, the practitioner, and the family influence every aspect of practice and must be reflected in assessment and intervention choices. Assessments outline a treatment approach in which target problems are linked to goals, family strengths, and specific treatment steps. A frequently encountered difficulty is that many families seeking help come from backgrounds and experiences different from those of practitioners, which makes family engagement for service a formidable task. As a first and most important step, practitioners must recognize the need for sensitive and responsive assessment approaches. Second, they must understand the purpose, key concepts, and assumptions of family functioning. Life functioning can be assessed across various domains, and families can assess their progress toward these goals.

Approaches to Using Evidence-Based Assessment

Practitioners have an obligation to attend to issues of quality in assessment, using sound theoretical frameworks, systematic approaches to interviewing, and standardized instruments and techniques to gather data. Also, they must be aware of where good assessment leads: to interventions that are appropriate for addressing the family's problems and that have good prospects for producing positive outcomes. Therefore, practitioners must be mindful of guidelines for the assessment process. Principles for blending practice and science for sensitive and responsive family assessment include the following:

1. Families have the right to receive the most effective available service to prevent or reduce distress and improve functioning. This requires practitioners to keep abreast of current intervention research on outcome effectiveness (Corcoran, 2003; McNeece & Thyer, 2004).

2. When family assessment is well defined and when interventions are used that are based on current best evidence from scientific research that supports the use of certain treatments or interventions, the outcome is more likely to be positive (Corcoran, 1992; Gibbs & Gambrill, 1999; Thomlison, 1984).

3. "Clients should be offered as a first choice treatment, interventions with some significant degree of empirical support, where such knowledge exists, and only provided other treatments after such first choice treatments have been given a legitimate trial and shown not to be efficacious" (Thyer, in Thyer & Wodarski, 1998, p. 16).

4. No one study, no matter how carefully done or how positive the results, is considered evidence by itself. A group of well-done studies with similar findings is needed to come to the conclusion that there is good evidence for a particular approach (Hughes, 1999).

5. It is best to focus on characteristics of individuals and families that are prosocial, resilient, or adaptive—those that are generally regarded as competencies rather than pathologies. Social skills, communication, and learning styles are promising targets of intervention and lend themselves to enhancement (Fantuzzo, McDermott, & Lutz, 1999).

6. Sensitive and responsive assessment requires practitioners to widen the scope of their assessment to attend to the various developmental and ecological factors with greater precision for more culturally diverse populations (Fantuzzo, McDermott, & Lutz, 1999).

7. Assessment needs to be taken at multiple points in time to develop an adequate understanding of supports and resources for intervention for diverse populations, such as highly stressed and low-income families and those who are at disproportionate risk for victimization (Ammerman & Hersen, 1999).

8. An evidence-based approach to assessment begins with careful assessment, setting clear and measurable goals and reflecting an individualized intervention plan, that monitors progress toward the goals, modifying the approach as needed (McNeece & Thyer, 2004).

Family assessment is conceptually anchored in the ecological family systems framework. This general unifying perspective emphasizes the "goodness of fit" between individuals, families, and their environments, and it examines how people adapt to the stresses in their social and physical environments (Rothery & Enns, 2001). When we adapt well to these demands and needs, families flourish; and when there is difficulty responding effectively, disorganization results. Lack of personal and familial resources are primary reasons families have difficulty responding favorably to stress and demands in their environments. Other factors include family experiences and resilience. "These differences are attributable to mediating factors, primarily personal and familial beliefs, values, competencies, and skills. They are also powerfully influenced by context" (Rothery & Enns, p. 4). The knowledge base underlying the multisystemic framework is supported by strong research evidence as well as expert opinion (Henggeler, Schoenwald, Bordin, Rowland, & Cunningham, 1998). Therefore, multisystemic core concepts form a sound basis for assessment and intervention for families and family circumstances.

Elements of Assessment

The importance of high-quality assessment is underscored by today's practice context, where service trends toward time-limited, brief treatments and evidence-supported practice, incorporating family-centered approaches. It is therefore essential for practitioners to view the goal of assessment as a brief strategy that is comprehensive and systematically focused and that views evaluation as essential (Corcoran, 1992; Thyer & Wodarski, 1998). The ultimate goal of assessment is to make resource and intervention decisions that address family functioning and the environments impacting the lives of families. The framework for assessment should be open to change as new information is presented or new situations emerge.

Purpose of Assessment

Assessment determines family resources or strengths to address the family concerns. Making sense of data through assessment has these three specific functions:

1. *Understanding the family issues:* Assessment provides a framework for defining and conceptualizing family issues, although it can never explain all family phenomena. Assessment informs you about the family adaptive responses to the stresses and demands in the environment.

2. *Planning for interventions:* Assessment assists in organizing and synthesizing family information to provide a focus for intervention. Understanding the linkages and inter-dependent relationships a family has with other systems shows how much these systems affect each other. The appropriateness of a specific intervention to address families' stresses and demands can then be determined, and strengthening the formal and informal supports in the lives of families becomes possible.

3. *Identifying needed family supports and resources:* Assessment provides a framework to identify what outcomes are desired. Exploring with the family their need for support and resources improves outcomes of service. After the initial contact for service, the first task a practitioner is likely to have with a family is usually a formal assessment of needs. Rothery and Enns (2001) have identified four general areas in which families may need supports and resources:

   a. *Concrete, instrumental support:* Basic goods, material, and financial aspects necessary to cope with everyday demands of life. Finding adequate accommodation, child care, or items such as a refrigerator focuses on such needs. Formal agencies and extended family and friends are possible resources for these needs.

   b. *Information, knowledge, and skills:* Information and knowledge that families need if they are to make informed decisions about options or alternatives available to them. Examples are information about parenting a child with troubling behaviors, preparing for employment, caring for a child's medical condition, entering a substance abuse treatment program, or leaving a violent partner. Educational focused programs are a source of formal assistance, while peers, family, colleagues, and friends are examples of informal resources to address this type of need.

   c. *Emotional supports:* These are important to daily functioning. If such relationships are maladaptive, absent, or stressed, then families do not feel supported, understood, or safe. Counseling that focuses on therapeutic relationships will be required if family members are to change their experiences.

   d. *Affiliational supports:* These are important to provide families with a sense of belonging in the family network, neighborhood, and community. The opportunity to have meaningful social roles is necessary for validation. Friends and relatives are important.

Exploring these areas of support and how they are reflected in the family's circumstances provides the initial information for framing a family's situation and experiences. Through the interviewing process, you and the family learn about the behavior and social functioning of the children and the family in their environmental context and discover and highlight their strengths and concerns. This entails a process of fact finding and organizing information about the issues and concerns of the family. Interviews and other assessment tools will be used to collect this information about the family concerns, strengths, and functioning. Assessment is viewed as both an ongoing process and a product (Hepworth, Rooney, & Larsen, 1997).

The Assessment Process

The assessment process includes gathering, analyzing, and synthesizing relevant data about the child and family context not only to identify the stresses and problems and resulting adaptation, but also to evaluate strengths and resources. The setting, the family's problems, and the practitioner's role and orientation to the information collection task will determine the nature of the assessment process. Emphasis is on discovering strengths. The practitioner will look for characteristics that are prosocial: positive coping skills, resilient or adaptive skills, ways the family has solved previous problems. These are family competencies and strengths that can help the family toward effective outcomes. Focusing on the social skills, communication methods, and learning styles of the family is often wise because they lend themselves relatively easily to positive change (Corcoran, 2000; Fantuzzo, McDermott, & Lutz, 1997).

As mentioned earlier, building a relationship with family members is essential if the practitioner is to obtain high-quality information. At the beginning of family contact, rapport is established through the interview process. Practitioners need effective communication skills to accomplish this. Apart from the reasons a family is seeking assistance, families must be active participants in the change process, but seeking help is not easy for most people. Talking about your private family troubles to a stranger creates anxieties about what will happen. Families will be worried about how you will view them and their current reactions to stresses and difficulties. They will also be concerned about your thoughts and reactions to their differences from you in gender, class, race, and cultural practices. The practitioner's tone of acceptance in this initial contact is critical to establishing rapport and building the necessary relationship and alliance with the family.

The most credible information will be obtained by interviewing the family in their natural environments. Assessing the family in their home environment provides an opportunity to observe their interactions within that context. It will diminish, but not alleviate, the family reactions, anxieties, and feelings about help. Assessing families in an office places them in an unfamiliar setting in which to interact with you. In the home context you can see the impact of problems on the family and the influence of family interaction and relationships on the problems. Interviewing in the family home gives you access to the interaction of people, places, times, and contexts that are the sources and the solutions of family functioning (Bronfenbrenner, 1979; Whittaker, Schinke, & Gilchrist, 1986). Home visit strategies have been identified as especially effective in addressing various parenting and parent–child health, behavioral, social, and emotional problems. Early family support and education interventions have shown evidence of positive impact, particularly with families of young children (Corcoran, 2003; Olds, 2002).

Therefore, to understand a family's functioning, it is essential to use assessment strategies that take into account the people, individuals, and environments influencing them. Furthermore, the context in which a family is functioning determines whether the family's functioning is adaptive or maladaptive. The impact of culture is an example where language barriers or different cultural meanings of a particular situation can have varied interpretations if viewed outside the family home and neighborhood. These issues are particularly salient when assessing parent and child concerns. Parental expectations of children's behavior vary by neighborhood and ethnicity (Fantuzzo, McDermott, & Lutz, 1999). Expectations influence perceptions and interpretations of children's behaviors. Families living in neighborhoods with increased violence are more likely to encourage children to physically defend themselves, which increases their aggressive behavior. Assessment in the home setting enhances the quality of the information obtained in this example.

The Framework

The developmental–ecological perspective emphasizes the importance of human development in the context in which the development occurs, and it seeks to understand human development in terms of changes over time (Cicchetti & Lynch, 1993). The situation must be understood within the context of the dynamic and continuous development—was it typical or atypical? This reflects the adaptation or maladaption of various behaviors in individuals and families.

The ecological perspective shows us the general and specific risk and protective factors to understand the multiple influences within the child, parent, family, and broader social context associated with problem development (Fraser, Kirby, & Smokowski, 2004). Behavior is viewed as the result of interactions among risk and protective factors, which influence the onset, development, and maintenance of problem behaviors within the context of various life settings. Interactions are further complicated because these factors are embedded in systems at many different levels in the environments and across multiple systems. Assessment of the risk factors provides "points of entry" for intervention; the goal of intervention is to reduce the effect of the specifically targeted risk factors, noting that intervention strategies will not affect all risk conditions (Fraser, 2004). Interventions might target various situational experiences such as corporal punishment in child abuse or nurturing in parent–child interactions. Home visits allow optimal viewing of the developmental ecological interactions occurring in individual and their families.

Assessment Tools

Assessment tools are used to gather pertinent information about a family. Some are more complex and superior than others and require considerable skill and knowledge about a specific area. An example of an assessment tool used by advanced practitioners is the *Diagnostic and Statistical Manual for Mental Disorders (DSM-IV)* (American Psychiatric Association, 1994), used for a clinical diagnosis in mental health of adults and children. Other methods and tools require less skill. Although there is a need for high-quality assessment information to inform intervention strategies, beginning practitioners should use tools geared to their skill and competence level, moving to more sophisticated methods and measures as their skill increases.

Assessment strategies vary, but all family assessment processes should take into account how children, adults, and families function in their multiple and simultaneous environments—how they interact and experience each situation. The type of assessment needed will affect outcome. There will be variation between qualitative and quantitative assessment. Children and individuals with specific difficulties need specific assessment tools. For example, you may be interested in a parent's attitude toward a child and a child's attitude toward a parent. Tools specifically developed for this problem assessment are found in the Hudson (1982) *Clinical Measurement Package;* in Corcoran and Fischer (2000) *Measures for Clinical Practice: A Sourcebook;* and Jordan & Franklin (2003) *Clinical Assessment for Social Workers.* Qualitative and quantitative approaches may both be appropriate. It depends on the situation, the problem, and the skills of the practitioner. For example, observation is a qualitative approach to assessment, but observation and use of a standardized questionnaire or checklist provide an enriched assessment with more extensive information. Regardless of the method of data collection, the practitioner treats the family as the experts on their situation, obtaining data through collaboration, respect, and cooperation.

Practitioners need to use multiple methods of obtaining data, and they should use tools that are well known and theoretically sound in construction. These tools help practitioners measure family functioning across domains—for example, the frequency of family conflict or the type of parental functioning—and provide a more objective assessment of a family-specific problem. The findings serve as the basis for identifying the plan for change. Practitioners need to use assessment techniques in which they are skilled and that they are competent to administer. A compendium of brief assessment tools relevant for today's practice context is available in the work of Corcoran and Fischer (2000), which provides a comprehensive review of standardized measures for clinical practice with children, adults, and families for various problems. Information often needed for family functioning that a practitioner may measure includes social support, attitudes to a child or spouse, emotional closeness, and level of stress. These tools and measures are rapid assessment instruments and require only a brief time to administer. Beginning practitioners will probably use one or a combination of the assessment types described here:

1. *Interviewing techniques:* Interviewing is probably the most frequently used method to gather information. Most practitioners use this qualitative form of data collection because it can readily reveal the context and meaning for the family's situation. "Interviewing is a highly personal, interpretive, reflective, and elaborative" process (Jordan & Franklin, 2003 p.146). Questions are asked and answered, and from this interchange the practitioner extracts meaning about the family. Questions are asked to focus on what families want to change about their situation. Your role is to help convert these wishes into clearly identified goals. When family members are seen as a group the practitioner can gain understanding of the family structure, dynamics, power, and interaction. Such an interview provides information about family functioning and shows the practitioner where intervention can change the patterns of the family system.

   Interviews can be structured, semistructured, or open-ended. Structured interviews have formulated questions that are asked by the practitioner, who follows the set questions. Semistructured interviews also have a list of questions, but they serve as beginning points from which the practitioner can branch out, following leads suggested by the answers. Open-ended interviews do not have a predetermined set of questions, and the practitioner can ask questions as they arise in the meeting and probe for further responses. All forms of interviews have specific purposes which the practitioner must stay within.

2. *Mapping and graphic techniques:* The most common tools to use in this category are the ecomap, genogram, a social network map (see Chapter 6), and the social support grid. The ecomap is a pictorial view of family contacts with others outside the family, including organizations, agencies, and involvement with others. The genogram is a picture of the family constellation; when multiple generations are included, this tool affords an overview of the family internal and external structures as well as its context—the boundaries and composition. The social network map presents a view of the family environment and the people, organizations, and groups that support the family. Examples of the ecomap, genogram, and social network map and grid are found in Chapter 6 with a discussion of how to use these assessment tools. The social support grid expands our understanding of the family's ecomap. Mapping family supports explores sources of strength and assistance and identifies critical resources and types of support available for each family member. You will systematically identify the types of concrete, instrumental, and affective supports available to help the family. Completing the social support grid with the family may generate information you can use to make the family feel more hopeful; the exercise may even uncover resources to explore further. The goal is to gather sufficient information to show the family that there is real support available in their environment even if they have not tapped it deeply, and to mobilize encouragement and motivation for designing the service plan. What kinds of informational, emotional, and affiliational supports are present? What is needed? These are the questions to explore in developing the social support grid.

3. Time lines can also be used to map the critical events and conditions in the life cycle of the family or one of its members. The unit of attention for the time line could focus on a child, family, or events in the family. Sequences of events are chronologically organized and graphically represented through these time lines. This allows for the tracking of events over time and viewing the order in which events occurred as separate or layered.

4. *Family scales:* These are standardized measures that assess family functioning. Corcoran and Fischer (2000) provide a complete, valid, reliable list of rapid assessment tools, including many self-anchored rating scales. Examples of family scales appear in Chapter 6.

5. *Observational techniques:* These are tasks or assignments the family completes while the practitioner observes. Family roles, power, interaction, and decision making are usually observed. Role-plays or simulations are used to enact a family situation or a dyadic

situation, such as by having members reenact a family conflict or verbal exchange to gain greater information about and understanding of a situation or issue. Learning new skills and being persuaded of their usefulness requires practicing them. Structuring opportunities to practice skills teaches family members to interact and allows the practitioner to review their progress by giving feedback.

Assessment determines the family's resources, difficulties, stressors, and reactions, as well as strengths and factors related to resilience. It is an intervention in the family system. The family is viewed as the expert and is engaged to work on the chosen area of concern; in this way a strength-based focus directs the solution.

Writing the Assessment Report

The product of assessment is usually a written report summarizing the family members' issues and their strengths and resources (Hepworth, Rooney, Dewberry Rooney, Strom-Gottfried, & Larson, 2006). With data organized by headings, reports integrate the practitioner's impressions, information from the interviews, and any assessment measures used to summarize family, marital, individual, and social functioning. Done correctly, a report summarizes the data obtained about individuals and family interactions and presents a rich framework for facilitating interventions to promote change. The report also includes a plan for providing resources and change-focused strategies.

The assessment report is difficult for many practitioners to write because it is not an essay, but a *synthesis* of the data collected. An example of a family situation assessment report can be seen in Chapter 13, The Sherman Family, Applying for Adoption. Note that specific areas about the family functioning are reported and described. The writer has synthesized the facts and impressions into a coherent description of strengths and resources, presenting the family's coping abilities individually as well as describing the environmental strengths and resources such as housing, employment, and support through social networks.

Different types of assessment focus and present information for different purposes. A psychosocial assessment is different from a functional or behavioral assessment. The data gathering process and focus for different types of assessment differ. All assessments, however, have a multiple-purpose focus, which is gathering information from multiple sources or systems. The guiding principle in determining the balance of information required from the family, and the supports for prevention of problems, should be based on minimal intrusion into the family system but inclusiveness of the systems to meet the assessed needs for positive family outcomes. Although there is no single way to conduct a family assessment, there is also no one way to write the assessment report.

Summary

It is useful for practitioners to adopt a clear conceptual multisystemic framework for viewing the family and its functioning. Systemic thinking helps this process because it allows the practitioner to examine data and information about family relationships that impact the family. This framework also helps the practitioner understand the influence of the individual and other systems on the family. Families are both the source of as well as the solution to their problems and concerns. Identifying family strengths is an essential part of assessment. The following assumptions are key to assessing families:

- Believe that each family member has potential for positive development.
- Assume that all family members have inner competence or strength.
- Adopt the belief that all families have strengths.
- Assume that focusing on strengths leads to finding more strengths.
- Realize that family-generated solutions to problems are the ones that are most effective and long-lasting (Thomlison & Thomlison, 1996).

Learning Activities

Activity 2.1 Finding Strengths and Resources

Students work in pairs and interview their partners for 20 minutes. Reverse the interview process for another 20 minutes. Students should share their answers with the class for a discussion of identifying strengths for change-focused solutions.

1. Ask your partner how he or she solved problems in the past. Focus on getting details about any inner and or outer resources the person used to solve or reduce the problems. Write down your findings of the strengths and resources of the person interviewed. Now reverse the interview process and repeat the exercise. When both interviews are complete, share the strengths and approaches to solving problems that were identified. How are individuals similar in their approach to solving problems? Identify characteristics people use to reduce their problems.
2. Why it is important to use a strength-based approach when working with families?
3. What are some issues that arise when using a problem-focused approach?
4. List strengths you would look for in a family.

Activity 2.2 Family Engagement Qualities

Write a summary of the personal and evidenced-based qualities for assessment you have. Begin by describing what you have experienced in your family, done in the past, inherited, or learned from reading about families that will make you a good family practitioner. What unique characteristics do you bring to this process that facilitate family engagement? How did you learn this about yourself? Then identify from empirical literature two or three research studies about the qualities of effective therapists or practitioners. Write an integrative summary comparing and contrasting your personal qualities with the evidence-based qualities. What conclusions can be drawn? Be sure to append the articles as part of this paper.

Activity 2.3 The Jacques Family Case Study

Read the Jacques Family Case (Chapter 15) and write your responses to the following questions:

1. What assumptions are you making about this family?
2. What are you taking for granted about this family?
3. What data, facts, information, and observations are you using to arrive at my point of view about this family?
4. How are you interpreting the information about this family?
5. What conclusions are you coming to about this family?
6. How would you go about engaging the family in treatment?
7. What parts of the family system would you work with?
8. Create a plan for engaging the family.
9. Identify cultural variables that may affect the quality of communication and family engagement. How would you address these challenges?

▼▼▼

CHAPTER THREE

Assessing Your Family and Critical Thinking

Assessing Your Family Experiences

You would think it would be easy to explore yourself, but really it's one of the hardest things to do. . . . This program teaches you about caring and helping in every aspect. It lets you understand yourself so that when you are out into the practice settings, you can understand how the families are feeling.

—Student

This chapter is quite different from most in this book. It focuses on applying family systems learning to your own family life experiences so you can learn about and better understand yourself within the context of your family. Writing about your family forms a different kind of context for learning. Learning also comes through your experiences and applying theory to these. Through assessing your family system and critically reflecting on events and situations, you also learn about other families. You will learn several things:

- To integrate family content knowledge with your life experiences to assist in your understanding of family dynamics.
- To examine the process of a family—your own—in order to understand the family as a constantly changing system influencing belief systems, behaviors, and relationships.
- To build on what you bring from your family experiences, personalize your approach to practice and learning, and understand the diversity of ideas and outcomes when applying the family assessment process to practice.

A picture is worth a thousand words, and a good example is even better. Learning about families requires moving from what you know to more detailed challenges and requirements for greater depth of knowledge. Focusing on our own families teaches us to be more sensitive to the diverse family processes and outcomes that we encounter in practice. Self-assessment and critical thinking about your family system can illustrate clearly how and why the family assessment process is a dynamic entity of multiple processes. It also can show you that reaching new heights in understanding a family requires us to seek new levels of understanding about our own families.

Because *critical thinking* is often defined in many ways, clarification of this concept is important. Although it is often defined as a questioning approach to issues, a broader meaning is more useful to practitioners, such as the one used by Paul and Binker (1990; and applied to learning by Paul and Elder (2004). "The art of thinking about your thinking while you are thinking in order to make your thinking better: more clear, more accurate, or more defensible" (p. 643).

This chapter is a major assignment to be completed throughout the family course and is a supplement to the various topics in family assessment and interventions. It will give you a tool for examining yourself and reflecting on how the values, beliefs, rules, rituals, and traditions of your own family shaped your behavior and thinking in adulthood. Personal views and stories shape how you see and experience others. Moreover, your family belief systems influence your interactions with other families and can be a source of bias in your practice. It is hoped that by examining these family influences you will learn from this critical thinking process and thereby be in a better position to understand other families. To gain the most understanding from this chapter you must be honest about yourself and your family life. Keeping a family journal is one of the best tools to discover your own family influences.

Journal Writing

The journal, or directed diary, is a writing tool for learning about yourself. It can be simple or complicated. Above all, it is a tool for critical thinking. The journal is an ancient tool that goes back to the 10th century, when Japanese ladies of the court used their "pillow books" to reflect on life and love. During the 17th century Protestants and Puritans applauded the self-discipline of diary keeping. As a student, journal writing will help you recount events and thoughts about growing up in your family. You can retrace the subjective, lived meaning (Reimer, Thomlison, & Bradshaw, 1999, p. 140).

Writing a journal is somewhat different from keeping a diary. Responding to the journal questions in this chapter, you will focus primarily on external and internal events and structures influencing you and your family. Through self-examination and reflection, you will find that journal writing is a safe place to raise issues, address your fears and concerns, and come to understand how these events and family stories shaped the adult person you have become.

Journal writing is a useful analytical tool. The purpose of recounting through writing what happened in the family is to focus or reflect on the significance of activities or events as they relate to learning to work with families. Although recounting significant and meaningful events are important, it is the process of writing and reflecting on those events and understanding differently now as an adult that is most meaningful. Through directed journal questions, areas of family life can be reviewed in an effort to construct and deconstruct information to help you understand how families are formed and what maintains their dynamics. It also helps us to understand rights and responsibilities of families, uniqueness in families, and ways our values are formed. Through the process of thinking critically by journal writing, you can search for details of events, patterns, and themes, all of which impact self-awareness. The classic analytical framework of "who, why, when, where, what, and how" is always useful in reaching conclusions about what you are learning about your family. In turn, this will be relevant to your learning needs.

Why Critical Thinking?

According to Paul and Elder (2004), if you question information, conclusions, and points of view, you improve your learning. Striving to think beneath the surface of what may seem obvious in your reading, writing, speaking and listening helps us become effective problem solvers. "Critical thinking is a process . . . that entails effective communication, problem-solving abilities, and a commitment to overcome our native egocentrism and sociocentrism" (p. 1). The objective of journaling is to stimulate you to apply critical thinking about yourself in the context of your family and to consider how those early experiences affect your current personal and professional relationships. Applying family systems principles, assumptions, and concepts to your own life can be self-revealing and informative as a tool for improving the quality of your life.

Essentially you will discover that journal writing involves much more than the writing and appraisal of thoughts and events in your family's life. The role of writing a journal involves the careful examination and evaluation of beliefs, feelings, and actions. Well-reasoned thinking is a creative form of understanding your purpose and learning about yourself.

How to Start Writing a Journal

The secret to writing about your family is to simply start. What matters is that you begin to put your thoughts, ideas, and feelings on paper in response to the assigned questions later in this chapter. This is a purposeful process designed to clarify thinking and form a baseline against which you can measure changes in yourself. For example, how do you communicate with your parents? Do you feel comfortable when you communicate with families? Do you feel anxious when dealing with parent–child conflicts? Do you feel uncomfortable approaching women about family finances? Are you proud of your relationship skills with adolescents? These feelings and thoughts are likely related to your family experiences; therefore, you need to become aware of these relationships so they do not inappropriately influence your work with families. Each time you write you appraise your thinking. You will want to review your responses for themes, ideas, and patterns. Do you need to examine an experience from another point of view? From the parent's perspective? From a sibling's perspective? Analyzing experiences provides depth, breadth, and greater understanding to the complexities of a situation. As well, you will need to consider what the events meant and how you felt about them. Keeping a journal is a way of organizing and summarizing thoughts. Read your entries aloud as a form of feedback.

What Will You Learn?

Keeping a journal will teach you about self-assessment for self-improvement. Through journal writing you will discover assumptions, alternative explanations, and biases about yourself as a developing professional. You will also take an objective look at your abilities and strengths. From this self-discovery process you will uncover thinking and learning styles, attitudes, and strategies associated with yourself as a developing professional. Self-assessment is viewed as an opportunity for learning. Each time you appraise your thinking you are also helping your families in valuable ways. Reviewing your life history and seemingly inconsequential events and skills is worth considering. Which experiences taught you a memorable lesson? What subjects were you good at in school? What painful experiences have you endured? What can you learn from these experiences that will assist you in working with families? Critically thinking about your abilities, experiences, and skills will help you face the challenges you in working successfully with families and their painful situations.

Some guidelines for analyzing and critically thinking about your journal responses to the family questions include these:

- Think in terms of opposites.
- Explore feelings by considering different views from different perspectives.
- Focus on problem finding and problem solving.
- Emphasize understanding.
- Question practices, rules, and thinking about family life.
- Reflect on experiences or events.
- Recognize the affective or emotional influences.
- Recognize attitudes and values associated with cognitive biases.
- Reflect on self-awareness by asking, What do I believe? Why do I believe that? Do I have a vested interest in this issue?

- Identify recurrent patterns of interaction.
- Differentiate fact from opinion: How could I verify or test that?
- Connect with your current beliefs and thinking (Reimer, Thomlison, Bradshaw, 1999, p. 141).

Writing is a learning tool for heightening and refining the process of reflection. The purpose of writing about the events and experiences from your family is to think about their meaning for you as a student learner and developing professional. The more you become aware of the significance of these developing experiences, the more you will be able to tap your inner strengths and capacities. The focus will be on your unfolding awareness of self and the meaning, values, and interrelationships you are discovering in your analysis. Reflection promotes inner or emotional awareness. It is a cognition process. In fact, writing is what compels us to reflect rather than ruminate. Reflecting on your experiences enables you to draw on inherent resources. Journal writing can generate positive thoughts and give you a clearer sense of self. These entries help you use your strengths in improving your practice.

Now that you understand the purpose of writing a journal, you are ready to engage in family exploration. It is hoped that you will elaborate on your ideas, beliefs, and attitudes about content and process from multiple perspectives. Accomplishing this task requires you to be both honest and willing to write with integrity. Remember to write respecting confidentiality within your own family constellation.

Learning Activities

Activity 3.1: Self-Defense — Weekly Course Journal Entry

You will keep a journal throughout this course with no fewer than 14 entries. The journal entry should be a weekly account of your interactions, thoughts, or events that reflects your understanding of the strengths and resilience in your family. How do these observations and experiences help your personal and professional development? Each entry should describe the interaction or event and appraise the factors that are most important each week. Your final entry should consist of an integration of yourself and the insights that you discovered, as well as your understanding of how this impacts your professional family practice.

Activity 3.2: Exploring Your Family and Your Development

The questions that follow are designed to stimulate your thinking and learning and help you get in touch with your inner resources and the factors affecting your ideas about families. The assignment is to be written and handed in to your instructor and should demonstrate critical thinking. In other words, use the guidelines in this chapter to identify themes, patterns, and self-understanding and the impact your family has had on your own development.

1. *Family of origin structure, roles, and expectations:* Describe your family system by examining the family structure, roles, and expectations of the membership of your family. Include your family of origin experience of marriage, separation, divorce, and multigenerational family connection.
   a. What expectations do you have about your family structure for the future? Describe your thoughts about marriage, separation, and divorce, and multigenerational families.
   b. Write about a special situation or event that impacted your family structure, role(s), or expectations that occurred during your childhood.
   c. What do you consider unique about your family or characteristics about your family?
   d. What do you think was the most meaningful influence from your family?
   e. What role did you play growing up in your family? What role do you currently play in your family? Is there another role you would prefer? Why?

2. *Your understanding of gender, culture, and ethnicity:* Describe and give examples of gender roles in your family of origin. What behaviors were expected from or associated with males and females during childhood, adolescence, and young adulthood? Describe any other influences on gender behavior in your family.

   a. Draw a three-generation family genogram depicting culture and ethnicity. To understand the role of uniqueness and culture in the formation and development of the family system, place cultural symbols on the genogram. Mark your genogram with appropriate data and symbols using a legend. Colors can be used. Write an assessment focused on gender roles, culture, and ethnicity for your family. The genogram and reports can be discussed and shared in class.

   b. What messages did your family express about people who are different from the racial or ethnic orientation of your family or of different sexual orientation? About roles of women and men? The place of children? Who is defined as an outsider and insider and how they are treated? What impact have these messages had on how you view yourself?

   c. Identify some of the biases, prejudices, and stereotypes you learned from your family of origin about socioeconomics, ethnicity, types of work, handling money, and education.

3. *Social network map and grid:* Assess your family system and its social network map. Draw a family social network map and complete the social network grid (Chapter 6). Write a summary narrative of the strengths and resources of your family.

4. *Family rituals, traditions, and transitions:*

   a. Identify a ritual in your family and why it occurred. Design a new ritual to change the family pattern of behavior. How would you initiate or assist a family in developing a ritual?

   b. Identify a tradition in your family and how it evolved. How does this tradition affect you?

   c. Identify a transition and how it was handled in your family.

   d. Identify a tradition that needs to be changed in your family. How would that help your family?

   e. How would your family be different without rituals and traditions?

5. *Family connections:* Think about your family relationships and the significance of these relationships.

   a. Who in your family had a strong influence on your development?

   b. How did you feel about being cared for by people other than your parents?

   c. What was your relationship with extended family members such as aunts, uncles, and cousins?

   d. What role did your grandparents play in your life?

   e. Did your family have a problem (such as mental illness, unemployment, or poverty)? How was that understood in your family?

   f. What rules and expectations were present for boys and girls? What form of discipline was used in your family most often? Was the discipline the same for girls and boys?

   g. Who participated in the decision-making process?

   h. What types of rewards were given for family and individual successes?

   i. Describe what you hope may be the same or different in your future family compared to your family of origin.

6. *Family support systems:*

   a. What kinds of environmental strengths and resources did your family use?

   b. How was stress handled in your family? Can you identify patterns or attitudes associate with stress? Were they apparent in more than one generation? How do you handle stress?

   c. Whom did your family turn to for help when support was needed?

   d. Who in the family did you turn to for help? Who helped you solve problems?

e. What obstacles (internal and external to your family) prevented access to environmental resources?

f. What did your family understand about the environment?

g. What resources were needed or required that were lacking in the environment?

h. Identify your family strengths.

7. *The family assessment report:* Develop a family assessment report following the suggestions and headings in Chapter 7. You may wish to add other headings to include relevant information. There are many ways to organize a family assessment report and they are usually tailored to fit the issues, agency or purpose for which the report is to be used. Appraise your family system and its functioning. What intervention do you think is warranted to address family issues? Describe the intervention.

8. Identify ten lessons learned from your family experience that can be guidelines for practice with families.

Activity 3.3: My Social History

Interview a family member to obtain the following information about yourself:

1. Who provided the information? Describe the interview time, place, and atmosphere. Did new information emerge? If so, describe.

2. Provide your birth information include your birth weight, time, date, city, country, and name as spelled out on your birth certificate.

3. List your mother's name, age, and occupation; your father's name, age, and occupation; and your siblings' names and ages.

4. Are you aware of any key information about your parents that was notable at the time of your birth?

5. Describe yourself physically at birth.

6. Describe your personal qualities. Who in your family do you most resemble?

7. Do you remember any messages from parents from your childhood?

8. Describe your relationship with siblings and their whereabouts.

9. Did your family move? What were the reasons for the moves? What was the most significant aspect of these moves?

10. Identify any significant relationships in childhood—adults, friends, teachers, pets, and so on—that influenced you.

11. How were you described as a child in terms of attitude, behaviors, talents, and abilities? What activities were you involved in as a child?

12. What special moments are you most proud of and least proud of?

13. Describe your childhood schooling experience and how this affects your learning today. Identify a memorable moment.

14. Did you have any birth, health, medical, or developmental concerns or hospitalizations?

15. What are your strengths and self-perception?

16. Include a picture of yourself as a child, and comment on it.

Activity 3.4: Seeking Help

To work as a family practitioner, you must be aware of your own personal issues about receiving and seeking help. Your *thoughts, feelings, and experiences* about asking for and receiving help from others influence how you will relate to families who need your help. Consider the following three types of help-seeking situations and write your thoughts, feelings, and reactions to seeking help:

1. Describe a recent situation in which you *asked for and received help:*

    a. What were your feelings about asking for help?

    b. What were your thoughts about asking for help?

c. What actions did you take in seeking help?

d. What would you do differently next time?

2. Describe a recent situation in which you *asked for help and the person did not give help:*
   a. What were your feelings about asking for help and not receiving it?
   b. Did you receive no help or just not any help that was useful for you?
   c. What were your thoughts about asking for help and not receiving it?
   d. What actions did you take in seeking help? What did you do after not receiving help from this person?
   e. What would you do differently next time?

3. Describe a recent situation in which you *needed help but did not ask or ask directly for help:*
   a. What were your feelings about not asking for help?
   b. What were your thoughts about not asking for help?
   c. What did you do instead of seeking help?
   d. What would you do differently next time?

Students: Look at the similarities and differences between your thoughts and feelings in these situations. Reexamine your actions taken as well. What is different about these situations? Do you tend to ask directly in some situations but not in others? Do you subtly expect people who know you to "read your mind" and anticipate your needs and meanings? (Examining the relationships between your thoughts, feelings, and actions is based on cognitive–behavioral theory.)

▼▼▼

The Family System

A family system is probably the most basic unit to which anyone belongs. It determines nationality, ethnic group, and the kind of community in which we grow to adulthood. It plays a part in social and economic status, religious affiliation, and even occupation. It provides roots; it defines attitudes and values; and it is a large part of who we are. The ability of parents to develop a sense of security, self, and family identity for children is critical to the children's developmental outcomes. Most important, perhaps, a family provides a sense of belonging. This sense of belonging shapes both attitudes and behavior. Individual outcomes, as a result of quality parenting and family care, show the impact that continuity of family relationships and attachments have on one's developmental history. When one or both parents raise a child continuously, giving him or her good physical, social, and emotional care, that child feels loved and valued.

Intervention is influenced by views held about families by both the practitioner and the family. Practitioners have personal and professional beliefs about families (see Chapter 1), and these beliefs influence how assessment and intervention are implemented. For example, is an assessment done in the agency setting or in the family home environment? Is an intervention selected based on what we know about its effectiveness or because its use is the common practice of the agency? All of the practices are influenced by the personal, professional, and practice beliefs of service systems. Most important, families hold views about themselves and their family life, and it is difficult to understand the factors that bring a family for help if the family beliefs, attitudes, and sense of belonging are not explored. For example, a practitioner's belief about parenting in single-parent households may influence how she or he receives, perceives, and treats a family. A practitioner who believes alcoholism is a consequence of personal weakness will likely respond differently to a family experiencing alcoholism than to a family experiencing the effects of a stroke if the practitioner also believes the stroke is beyond the control of the individual or family. Thinking about whom a family consists of and exploring with a family what ideas and attitudes affect the issues in the family are the beginning point of family assessment.

Family

The family is a vastly different unit today from what it was 20 or 30 years ago. The "typical" family unit consisted then of a legally married man and woman living together with their mutual children—possibly with a grandparent in the household and an uncle or aunt nearby. Today we recognize a vast number of other family types, all of which may consider themselves normal. Many families, no matter what form they take or lifestyle they pursue, experience concerns, difficulties, and problems.

Various family structures have both liberating features and new stresses concerning choices for individuals. In the past, family roles and boundaries were relatively clear-cut and rigid. Today family structures "mirror the openness, complexity, and diversity of our contemporary lifestyles" (Elkind, 1994, p. 1). Roles and boundaries are far more fluid and flexible now, and the family is also more vulnerable to pressures from the outside now than in the past. Consequently it is important to think of families in a different light.

The clearly defined roles and boundaries of the idealized family—a household with two married parents and their children—were especially beneficial to children and adolescents, offering well-defined limits and standards. Children and youth could afford to focus on the demands and conflicts of growing up. This helped some parents as well. For other parents, the roles were confining and demeaning for both men and women. Women were discouraged from careers outside the home, and men were often stressed by the sole breadwinner role. Couples stayed together until the children were independent, which sometimes meant forever. Elkind (1994) notes that families' strong boundaries served the needs of the children more than the needs of the parents. Given today's diverse family forms, parental needs may be better served than those of children.

Research reveals several shifts impacting family life and functioning. Families now live in more stressful environments. One in four young children lives in poverty (Stormshak, Kaminski, & Goodman, 2002), and there is more homelessness, single-parent households, exposure to family, street, and neighborhood violence, illegal drugs, and life-threatening illnesses such as AIDS. Other stressors on children include (1) living with a parent who is distressed and at a distance from extended family assistance and support; (2) living with a parent who is depressed; (3) living in a family where the parent(s) work extended hours, making parents often unavailable; (4) living with a parent who provides inadequate linguistic and/or cognitive stimulation; and (5) living in neighborhoods with few community supports and resources (Thomlison & Craig, 2005, p. 328.).

Acculturation stress and discrimination also contribute to family stress. Whether caused by religious, ethnic, cultural, gender, or family background factors, increasing racial and ethnic diversity of the population impacts family functioning and development of children (Fraser, Kirby, & Smokowski, 2004; Kumpfer, Molgaard, & Spoth, 1996). Nevertheless, these structural factors tend to be correlated with family dysfunction and poor child developmental outcomes. Parents (88%) believe now that parenting is more difficult than it was for previous generations, and 86% of parents are unsure of the appropriate parenting practices to use with their children. They believe children have less moral and religious training (53%), less supervision and discipline (56%), and are being raised in highly stressed family environments by distressed parents (The National Commission on Children's National Survey, 1991). For example, poverty and other social and cultural risks may increase family stress, leading to inconsistent parenting and poor child-rearing practices, and placing children at risk of social, emotional, behavioral, educational, and other developmental difficulties. Keep in mind, however, that many children in these circumstances are not at risk and are healthy due to their family strengths and resilience.

A new imbalance has been created with the loosening of roles and boundaries. Parents have greater relief from earlier confines, but children and adolescents experience greater stresses growing up when family rules, boundaries, and values are ambiguous, uncertain, and ever-changing. Societal forces associated with the sexual revolution that has taken place during the past decades are changing and equalizing the roles and responsibilities that were once gender-associated.

Couples, families, and children have had to change their living styles. As you assess a family, you must consider roles and role conflict as causes of stress in individual and family functioning. You must also take into account the role of culture in determining and defining roles and responsibilities in the family. Each culture has different expectations and ideas concerning male–female roles and parent–child roles, and these must be reflected in your assessment.

Perhaps it is an oversimplification to attribute many of the problems children and their families experience to the changing family balance, but this highlights what practitioners and social workers need to address in assessing family functioning. Assessment should focus on reducing family stresses of both parents and children, not just the parents. This in turn enhances the resources of family members and the family as a social system. Examining the family member boundaries becomes a critical task of the practitioner in determining family interaction patterns, roles, and power and parenting issues. One of the first objectives in assessment is to identify the patterns of interaction among family members and the roles and power assumed by individuals.

The stable and harmonious family is something of a myth (Allender et al., 1997; Elkind, 1994). Change and stress are experienced in all families. The developmental life cycle of families can be interrupted by divorce, separation, and remarriage, and all families regardless of structure experience multiple stressors as they transition from one stage of family development to the next. Stressors are related to anxiety-provoking events as the family moves through time, coping with predictable or normal family stages and events and unpredictable, traumatic ones. The way families address change and stress determines their level of adaptation or adjustment for continuing to perform family functions. How a family handles stress will be affected by the family and will affect the family. Stress and coping are a normal occurrence in families, and new experiences and information from various systems can work to resolve many family issues. Practitioners need to balance the family views, needs, and situation with the range of systems interacting with the family. Preventing compromises in development and strengthening competencies in individuals and the family system as a whole are required. This is an example of systemic thinking illustrating the ecological or multisystemic perspective.

Theoretical Basis for Family Assessment

Multisystemic family practice is influenced by the many ideas and values that are at the core of social work theory and the practice of helping families. An integrative practice framework encompasses basic social work values and provides a critical appraisal of the various environments or social systems that surround children and families. Certain key assumptions and concepts are important to organizing information for assessments and for designing services.

Key Assumptions
Family systems practice requires you to (1) build on the resources within the family and community, (2) focus attention on the family–environment interactions, and (3) recognize the effects of environmental factors on family and child functioning. Families are not homogeneous groups. Each perspective in a family will be unique. Begin with an examination of the family relationships and the dynamics of family circumstances. What happens between individuals in a family influences family functioning and outcomes. Three influential components are (1) family relationship patterns, (2) family characteristics, and (3) sources of stress.

Family Relationship Patterns Families establish relationships, develop patterns, and create ways of organizing themselves that are unique to every family unit. Family patterns are seen in the quality of parent–child transactions, the experiences of families with their members, and the quality of health and safety provided by each family to its members. How a family goes about organizing itself and meeting the needs of its members is as important as who does this and what is accomplished in the process.

The quality of family relationships contributes to the social and emotional competence of children, which is central to positive developmental outcomes and functioning (Huffman, Mehlinger, & Kerivan, 2000). Children's social and emotional competence will affect their later academic, behavioral, and social functioning. Parents and consistent caregivers play a protective role in developing social and emotional competence in children. Therefore, understanding the family relationship patterns and ways of interacting is important to the outcomes of both children and parents.

Family Characteristics   Family characteristics, such as the personal characteristics of parents, their family of origin experiences (historical events and current connections), and resources such as competencies, social support, and material support, will influence or interfere with the family carrying out the family patterns. Individuals and extended family systems have a direct and indirect influence in how a family carries out its functions. Families are products of early experiences, learning, and systemic current influences. These are both positive and negative influences and contribute to the development of resilience in families.

Sources of Stress   Stressors or demands on parental resources also positively or negatively influence the family's ability to function optimally. Stressors may be risk factors that the family is unable to overcome and therefore may lead to poor outcomes. When stressors are overcome, protective factors develop based on a positive experience, and families develop resilience in coping with environmental stressors and demands. The strength of the multisystemic perspective is that it relies on assisting families in addressing their priorities in the context of their existing and potential relationships with available and accessible community resources and sources of support. As a result, focusing on family strengths encourages the development of family and individual resilience and increases the opportunity for good outcomes.

The framework for family practice is summarized as follows:

1. *Emotional connections:* Families are bound by strong emotional ties, a sense of belonging, and a passion for being involved in one another's lives. Understanding family behavior and functioning in this context exerts a strong role in determining what assistance a family needs to address its concerns, stressors, or situational difficulties. Changing the systems that interact with families changes families.
2. *Family as a resource:* All families have strengths, often unappreciated or unrealized. Drawing on the family as a resource also makes full use of the family's inner resources. Understanding the complexity of the family environment requires you to understand the uniqueness of families while understanding the intricacies of their situations. The family is the primary nurturing unit for individual well-being and the source for the development of competence and resilience. Each family is unique. Families are not a homogeneous group.
3. *Family-centered approach:* Family-centered practices focus on relationships, interaction, and reciprocity. Information is learned about how family members impact and influence each other. The family determines changes in family members. Family members are the experts on their circumstances and experiences. Practitioner expertise helps families manage the change process (Wright, Watson, & Bell, 1996).

Key Concepts

Understanding the significance of the environmental context of the family system is the key to assessing family process and outcomes. Focus on the family as a social system rather than on just the individual member systems in the family. Explore how each environment or system interacts to produce the dynamics within families and between families and their environments (Mattaini, 1999). In trying to explain why individuals act in the family as they do, practitioners know that the behavior of one family member is highly influenced by the behavior of other family members and the family's environment. In fact, all behaviors in a family are systematically influenced and related to one another. When one part of the system changes, this produces change in other parts of that system. Interactions provide information.

Patterns of interacting are unique to each family system. Invisible boundaries delineate the family from other environments or systems but allow transactions with these systems (Minuchin, 1974). The family members interact with each other in ways that allow the best adaptation possible to a complex environment of family stress and conflict. Minuchin (1974) notes that families are often resistant to change while they are in a constant battle to achieve balance. This can be a complex situation when you think about the family and environmental stress identified earlier in this chapter.

Adaptation and flexibility are necessary for change. When the structure of the family system changes, the family is transformed, and family members are altered accordingly. Families adapt and change according to both internal and external conditions from the multiple systems impinging on them. As a result, each person's experiences change. When families are inflexible and unable to adapt, maladaptive patterns emerge.

Five concepts are basic to understanding the family as a system:

1. The family as a system is greater than the sum of its individual systems.
2. The family system performs functions.
3. The family system develops system and subsystem boundaries.
4. The family system evolves constantly, creating a balance between change and stability.
5. Family behaviors are best understood from a circular causality rather than linear causality.

These concepts are important to assessment and will provide meaningful information about the members of the family and how they are connected to one another.

Concept 1
The family as a system is greater than the sum of its individual systems.

This concept is especially useful in applications to practice because of two assumptions:

1. The parts are related to one another such that any change in one part will affect the others.
2. Each part is related to one or more other parts in a reasonably stable way during any particular time.

Recognizing that all behaviors in a family are systematically related to one another tells us that it is important that practitioners see all members of families to know how they work and to understand the individual components or parts of that system. In other words, you must look beyond the individual in trying to explain the individual's behavior. You will understand the behavior, feelings, or functioning of a child or spouse if you understand the family as a whole. You do this by observing and hearing the interactions among family members, which is a richer context than just talking to individual family members. Who talks to whom? When does this occur? For example, if Martin, age 10, is stealing from other children at school, you can try to understand the behavior simply in terms of Martin's motives, impulses, or other reasons. Or you can consider factors beyond the child and look at the larger context, his family, in an attempt to understand how the behavior is an expression of his family system. If you can figure out how Martin's behavior is systematically related to the other parts of the family, you can change Martin's behavior by changing some aspects of the family's behavior, not just by trying to change the child. Martin's father may be ignoring him except when he is in trouble, and Martin's mother may also be ignoring him and spending more time with his infant sister. Perhaps Martin's mother is depressed since the birth of his sibling. You may learn that Martin's behavior changed only since the birth of his sibling. It is possible that Martin has few friends at school and his behavior is an attempt to be part of a friendship group. Martin, to get his father's attention and his mother's time, steals from other children at school. One way to stop the thefts would be to encourage the father and mother to find ways to spend more time with Martin, thus fulfilling his needs.

Remember the large wooden doll with many dolls inside it, each doll within another? Family systems are similarly embedded within other systems. It is useful to view the family as nested within parts of larger systems, such as the extended family, neighborhood, clan, or community and work and social communities. Practitioners visualize this relationship between individuals, families, and their connections with others outside the families by drawing a set of circles called an *ecomap*. The circles outside the family can be depicted as larger or smaller, depending on the relationship of the family with these systems. When assessing families it is often initially helpful to draw an ecomap. In Chapter 6 the ecomap is applied to assessment. The ecomap is a graphic tool that helps us look at the interacting factors that make up the total family environment. It gives us a picture or overview of the family in its situation and environment. It illustrates the "nested" or interconnected systems. Interfaces between the family and the community, its members and others can be depicted in the ecomap. The strength of contacts with other systems is also shown graphically (see Chapter 6).

Concept 2
The family system performs functions.

A family has multiple purposes but essentially develops skills or competencies in its members for productive membership with other societal networks and participation in meaningful community life. Through its social network, the family processes information, makes decisions, engages in productive and expansive activities, and provides for individual growth and development. As a psychological environment the family provides its members with a sense of belonging and connectedness to each other. Attachment or emotional closeness develops and is integral to the survival of the unit and the development of social and emotional competence of individuals. Through its communication processes, the family shapes behavior, beliefs, and values of its members through acceptance, disapproval, attachment, and bonding. This is accomplished through caring for and nurturing members yet assisting them to retain separate identities.

Concept 3
The family system develops system and subsystem boundaries.

Boundaries are invisible demarcations or dividers between family members or among parts of the system such as between parents and children or between the family and the community (Minuchin, 1974). Boundaries define separateness and autonomy in a family and its subsystems. Examining and defining boundaries in families is important. Boundaries can be created around belief systems, ideas, or roles. This suggests that some family members participate in some of the systems and not in others. Some members participate in multiple roles. Functions often define the boundaries, such as parent–child subsystems. Understanding normative family functions makes it possible to construct or strengthen boundaries when necessary, such as when disruption occurs because of lack of clarity in the distinctions between subsystems. Families will differ in how individuals are assigned to specific subsystems or how easily individuals can move from one subsystem to another.

Boundaries are permeable and regulate contact between systems. Boundaries that exist between family members are described as rigid to diffuse depending on how open (permeable) and closed the boundaries are. In general, the greater the clarity and distinction between boundaries in a family system, the more effective the family functioning. Boundaries that are too rigid discourage closeness among member and outside systems. Families with overly rigid boundaries are often referred to as *disengaged families*. This family system characteristic limits warmth, affection, and nurturing, but it does foster independence. Families with diffuse boundaries are enmeshed with one another and offer mutual support but at the expense of independence and autonomy. Enmeshed families are loving and considerate, but their members may have difficulty in their relationships with others outside the family (Nichols & Schwarz, 2005).

Most families have qualities of both boundary types at some point in time and under some circumstances. Of course, boundaries change across the lifespan. Healthy boundaries allow members to shift and change as needed. When working with families it is useful during assessment to consider the following questions about boundaries:

- Who is a member of this family system?
- What key systems are involved with this family?
- What large systems does this family belong to?
- What parts of this family system boundaries need to change?

Mapping techniques (see Chapter 6) called genograms and ecomaps provide a conceptual view of family systems and subsystems interacting with the family. These tools help practitioners and families to see the various systems and boundaries the family interacts with, such as spouse subsystem, parent–child subsystem, and family–community subsystem. Constructing a visual model of the family's structure, interaction, and functioning gives both you and the family a more complete picture of the family system and its social environment. From these visual tools practitioners can focus the inquiry or questions of assessment. Chapter 6 contains further discussion of these assessment tools.

Family structure is maintained by the boundary interactions of systems. There is a hierarchy of systems in families such as parent–child, marital, spousal, and sibling subsystems. These smaller units, which operate within the larger context of family, are organized to perform certain functions. Any number of subsystems can operate within a family, and any individual may be a member of more than one subsystem. Boundaries operate between individuals or subsystems; they regulate the amount of contact that the individual or subsystems have with each other (Nichols & Schwarz, 2005). Adaptive or effective family functioning is encouraged by clear boundaries, which encourage independence but provide an appropriate amount of affiliation (Nichols & Schwartz, 2005).

One important system function that allows families to follow general rules is the innate power hierarchy within the family, which mandates that parents have more authority than children within the adaptive and well-functioning family (Minuchin, 1974). Family expectations emerge from the constant negotiation and interaction of subsystems. Consider the parenting subsystems, for example, in the Greene family. There are two adults—Mr. Greene and his wife—a former husband, and two children from the former marriage. In this family the spousal subsystem is composed of Mr. and Mrs. Greene. The parent subsystem is organized to permit Mrs. Greene and her mother to fulfill the parenting functions. Mr. Greene and the children's father do not perform in this capacity. In assessing this arrangement, the important criterion is how effectively this arrangement meets the family's overall needs and the needs of the children. The Greenes may function well in the described arrangement. One would expect such an arrangement to produce problems, however, particularly if Mr. Greene and the children's biological father refused to accept the arrangements and interacted with the children in a way to produce conflict with Mrs. Greene and her mother. Similarly, problems could emerge if the new spouse, Mr. Greene, began to take on parenting functions and the mother–grandmother parenting subsystem failed to accept him in this role. This lack of clarity could be expected to produce problems until a new parenting arrangement was sorted out.

Families differ by their position along a continuum from boundaries that are too rigidly closed to those that are too easily crossed. Minuchin (1974) uses the terms *enmeshment* and *disengagement* respectively to refer to rigid or diffuse boundaries. Boundary problems occur when the family system rigidly adheres to one of these extremes. This is seen, for example, when parents in an enmeshed family may become tremendously upset because a child does not eat dessert. On the other hand, the parents in a disengaged family may feel unconcerned about a child's dislike of school. The child may complain or show troubling behavior, but tensions likely will emerge in various parts of the family system and systems outside the family.

Subsystems where boundaries are ill defined or too loose show comparable difficulties in families. Consider a family in which one or both of the parents have problems such as mental illness or alcoholism. In these situations one or more of the children often assume parenting functions when the parent is unavailable. Boundaries are assessed for their permeability and limiting factors. If boundaries are too permeable, the family identity and integrity are weak, and the practitioner needs to strengthen the boundaries. If boundaries are too rigid, the family will need assistance to allow new information and communication to flow into it for optimal development and functioning. In each family there will be unique boundaries, beliefs, and expectations surrounding various subsystems and role functioning and interactions with the larger systems. A great deal of family work centers on boundaries and boundary shifting.

Concept 4
The family system evolves constantly, creating a balance between change and stability.

Family systems are in a constant state of flux, shifting and changing with each interaction and achieving a balance within them. Change is both normal and necessary, but there is a tendency to perceive change as negative. Prolonged change in some families may lead to instability in the system. Temporary change may cause disruption briefly, as when a parent is hospitalized, but most family systems return to normal after such a short disruption. When sustained change occurs in a family, there is a shift to a new balance, and then reorganization. An accident, a death, a birth, a job change, reduced income, or illnesses are some events in the lives of families causing change and reorganization. Although most families will reorganize to handle the changes, some families will not be able to adjust for lack of resources or other reasons and will need to find solutions outside the family. Practitioners help families find ways to obtain a balance and equilibrium, usually by identifying resources and solutions to their needs.

Concept 5
Family behaviors are best understood from a circular causality rather than linear causality.

Parts of the family system interact to serve a particular function. The structure of these connections forms patterns. Linear patterns are limited to sequences such as

$$A \longrightarrow B \longrightarrow C$$

In this example A causes B, which results in C. Many events are linear in cause and effect, but not much information will be learned from linear interaction. When practitioners consider behavior and family communication from a circular perspective, information they learn will generally be more accurate. In family systems circular patterns are formed and a closed recursive loop is the interaction pattern that is observed, such as this:

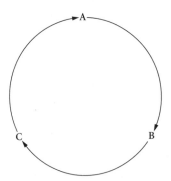

In this example, A and B interact to result in C, which in turn causes A—and a circular pattern emerges. The system is mutually reinforcing. The cyclic nature of these mutually reinforcing and influencing interactions can be positive or negative. When these interactions are negative, families find themselves locked into rigid patterns that can be difficult to change without new interactions outside the family system. The timing and meaning give relevance to these patterns, and the relationships are reciprocal (Tomm & Sanders, 1983).

Circularity is perhaps the most important concept in family interviewing. When practitioners ask questions of a linear nature, these are descriptive. Information is limited and marginally helpful when these questions are asked. For example, a linear question is, Does Dad worry about Mom having another stroke? Circular questions produce much greater information in family interviewing—information that is explored from a *difference* point of view. For example, What is the problem in the family now? What is the main concern about Mom now? What problem does this pose for the children? How is this different than before? Who agrees with you about this problem? What does her behavior mean to you?

By exploring differences among the family members, practitioners can identify specific behaviors perceived as problematic. *Explore differences between perceptions, objects, events, meanings, and ideas* (Franklin & Jordan, 1999). Each member of the family mutually contributes to the adaptive and maladaptive family interaction. Each person's behavior influences that of the other. The perception of each family member is valued and important in helping families construct a new way of viewing each other so they can break out of their maladaptive cycle. Families, who rarely understand the cycles of their interaction, need assistance to move from the linear to the circular perspective of causation. Franklin & Jordan (1999, p. 345) illustrate examples of a sequence for circular questions for general situations, such as those shown in Table 4.1.

Helping families to change is not always an easy task, and it can be complicated. Family members' vision of possible outcomes may not always be consistent, and trying to identify a common and shared outcome among members is important to this process. Describing concerns is easy, but finding a shared vision requires the practitioner to help the family understand how the current situation differs from the desired goal state and to clarify the necessary steps to move from one to the other (Mattaini, 1999).

Family Development

Theories and concepts of family development contribute to understanding family functioning by considering developmental issues, stress, coping and adaptations, and cognitive development. Families, in general, move through certain stages, performing a number of tasks and key processes. The literature identifies different stages emerging for single-parent, divorced or remarried, adoptive, and various other family structures. Although it is not necessarily meant to portray all families, the mainstream family development framework (Carter & McGoldrick, 2005; Wright & Leahey, 1994) is a useful way to look at what is happening in a family. Determine the stage the family is experiencing and the tasks associated with that stage; then decide whether the attachments emerging are adaptive or maladaptive for family members.

Stages

The following developmental stages are presented only as a guide and may not be relevant for every family. The developmental stages families transition through are these:

- *Single young adult:* Launch single young adult—differentiate self from family of origin.
- *Couple stage:* Marriage and joining of families—establish a couple identity through negotiating issues, rules, and traditions.
- *Childbearing and preschool children stage:* Introduction of children into the family. The couple joins in child rearing, financial, and household tasks. Realign relationships with extended family to include parenting and grandparenting roles.
- *School-age children:* Period when children are in school—kindergarten through high school.
- *Families with adolescents:* Shift in parent–child relationships to permit adolescents to move in and out of the system. Begin shift toward joint caring for aging members.
- *Launching children:* Renegotiate marital system as a dyad. Develop adult-to-adult relationships with grown children and parents.

Table 4.1 Examples of Circular Questions

Exploring Present Situation	Exploring Past Situation	Exploring Future or Hypothetical Situation
Who does what when?	Who did what then?	What would she do differently if she did (not) do this?
Then what happens?	What solutions were tried?	
What next?		
Where is she when this happens?		
What does she do?		
Then what do they do?		
Who notices first?		
What does she respond?		
When she does not do that, what happens?		
Exploring Difference	**Exploring Difference**	**Exploring Difference**
Has it always been this way?	How was it different?	How would it be different if she were to do this?
	When was it different?	
	What else was different then?	
	How does that differ from how it is now?	
	Was it then more or less than it is now?	
Agreement/Disagreement	**Agreement/Disagreement**	**Agreement/Disagreement**
Who agrees with you that this is how it happens?	Who agrees with you?	Who would agree with you that this is probably what would happen?
Explanation/Meaning	**Explanation/Meaning**	**Explanation/Meaning**
What is your explanation for this?	How do you explain this change?	Why do you believe this would happen?
What does this mean to you?	What does this change (or lack of change) mean to you?	How do you think your wife would explain it?
		What would this mean to you?

- *Parents in middle age:* Maintain own or couple functioning and beginning interest in physiological decline. Deal with loss of spouse, siblings, and peers.
- *Aging parents:* Generally deal with a slower life pace. Almost all retired, and many adjusting to some physiological slowing. But aging parental roles are changing as adults live longer and have new opportunities to pursue.

Tasks

As an ever-changing system, families master the tasks and stresses associated with each phase, developing resilience, strengths, and competencies. When tasks are not successfully carried out or are impeded, difficulties can occur, creating stressors and disruptions. For example, parents may have fears about an adolescent moving out of the home to college. Conflicts may arise between the adolescent and parents, and the parents may prevent the young adult from leaving home, seeking freedom, and self-direction. This may delay the young adult's development.

A crisis can impact family development. The unexpected birth of a child to an adolescent child in the family is an example. A crisis can be overcome, or it can be so traumatic that the family never returns to its former competent level of functioning. Events can impact family structure and family membership and tasks at every stage.

Attachments

Each family will be unique in terms of the relational processes experienced. Relationship patterns in the family system expand and contract at various stages, realigning over the life span as members come and go and move through their personal development. Exploring family connections or attachments gives a picture of the quality of interpersonal relationships within the family. The type or quality of emotional attachments established with family members is likely to determine the kinds of relationships established later in life with others, including spouses and children (DeMaria, Weeks, & Hof, 1999; Minuchin, 1974). The quality of family relational experiences provides a secure base for family functioning, especially patterns of closeness and distance.

Family Structure

One common family type is the single-parent family. This currently prevalent family structure is typically formed either by a never-married mother or through unscheduled transitions such as divorce or death. Father-led households are less common, and the major distinguishing feature between the two households is the disparity in household income. Young never-married mothers with small children are among the poorest families today. Increasingly, single people, male or female, gay or straight, are adopting children to form families. Such families are still few, but they face considerable stressors from the environment.

Remarried, blended, or stepfamilies are perhaps one of the most common forms of changing family structure. Stepfamilies will go through restructuring family boundaries as they address issues of parenting, power, and intergenerational issues (Carter & McGoldrick, 2005). Multiple internal and external stressors often accompany stepfamilies as parents work through agreements for the new family on issues such as parenting, discipline, visitation, alliances, and supports. There are issues associated with loss and change experiences for the children and families of origin. Parental responsiveness, rules and routines, and competing behaviors among the children and parents often create conflict for all the families. For an in-depth discussion of the family life cycle stages, see Carter and McGoldrick (2005).

Family Culture

Culture impacts a family's structural, developmental, and functional aspects. *Culture* refers to the distinct way the family behaves, thinks, and communicates, permeating its customs, beliefs, and values (Cross, Bazron, Dennis, & Isaacs, 1989).

Practitioners need to have self-awareness of their own cultural orientation and its impact on families. In their interactions with families, there will be dynamics that practitioners must acknowledge, adjust to, and accept. This self-awareness will be helpful as practitioners work with the family's natural and informal supports and helping networks within the community. Included among these are neighborhoods, schools, churches, faith-based organizations, and other institutions.

Emphasis should be placed on the strengths inherent in all cultures and ways to use these strengths for the unique needs, treatment issues, and concerns of families. The focus should not be on advocating for alternative family remedies, but rather on working with families and their circumstances, valuing diversity and respecting its worth. The implications for practice are that families' differences are as important as similarities. All families share common basic needs, but there are differences in how families of various cultures meet those needs. Each culture finds some behaviors, interactions, or values more important or desirable than others, and knowing this can help you interact more successfully with differing cultures. Awareness and acceptance of differences in communication, life view, and definitions of health and family are critical to the successful delivery of interventions (Cross, Bazron, Dennis, & Isaacs, 1989).

Guiding principles for working with families of various cultures include these:

1. Respect the unique, culturally defined needs of various populations.
2. Acknowledge the role that culture plays in shaping behaviors, values, and view of the society.
3. Recognize that primary sources of support for minority populations are natural helping systems such as churches, community leaders, extended family members, healers, and others.
4. Acknowledge differences in the concepts of *family* and *community* among various cultures and even subgroups within cultures.
5. Remember that minority populations are usually best served by people who are part of that culture.
6. When working with minority families, know that process is as important as outcome. Recognize that using the best of both worlds enhances the capacity of both family and practitioner.
7. Understand and recognize when values of minority families are in conflict with dominant society values.
8. Practice with the knowledge that some behaviors are adjustments to being different (Cross, Bazron, Dennis, & Isaacs, 1989; Okun, 1996).

Acknowledging cultural differences and being aware of how they affect the helping process is the starting point for discussion with culturally different families. You will need to adapt your assessment approaches because the dynamics of difference can be most problematic at this stage (McGill, 1992). For example, Latino children may have caretakers whom they refer to as "mom" and "dad" who may not legally be guardians. Indian mothers may leave younger children in care of older children as a commonly accepted practice in their communities. In black families, a man may not be an official part of the household even though he is an integral part of the family system. Furthermore, time concepts may be different, and formal appointments may not be accepted or understood. Work hours, spiritual practices, or family obligations may conflict with traditional practices of agencies and organizations for home visit appointments. Each of these situations could be interpreted as weakness or family maladaption if the practitioner is not sensitive to cultural behaviors of the family. Determining what is normative in the context of the family's culture is necessary for accurate assessment information.

The use of evaluation measures needs to be carefully considered because tools may be biased by misinterpretations of language usage. The key to successful assessment and intervention is the ability to communicate respect and separate the cultural factors from social and economic factors (McGill, 1992). In an effort to simplify the complexity of working in a multicultural context, McGill (1992) and DeMaria, Weeks, and Hof (1999) suggest the following questions to ask families for cultural information as a way to understand needs and concerns:

1. Where did this family come from?
2. When did they come to this country?
3. What were the circumstances that brought them to this country?
4. What is important to this family?
5. Who are the current members of this family?
6. What kind of people would they describe themselves as?
7. How do family members describe themselves racially?
8. How do you define yourself?
9. What good and bad things have happened to them over time?

10. What were or are the group's experiences with oppression?
11. What lessons have they learned from their experiences?
12. What are the ways in which pride and shame issues are shown in this family?

These questions examine the family experiences both within the family and through the members' larger group and community experiences and biases. Knowledge and understanding of the family's collective story of how they have been coping with life events and how they have responded to pain and troubles can emerge. The practitioner hears the context of the family concerns, and meaning becomes clearer. Genograms and ecomaps (see Chapter 6) can offer a graphic way to capture the family unit's cultural story while encouraging a systematic view of the family and its functioning. The use of the genogram determines the family structure by generation and kin relationships in a culturally sensitive context.

Family Beliefs

Family beliefs are the attitudes and expectations that influence various areas of family functioning. Identifying and clarifying the beliefs held in families helps families and practitioners understand the interactions and alliances formed in families. This explains family behaviors and informs us about family functioning. Beliefs and assumptions develop from family experiences and are intricately connected to behavior.

Over time, family members may have learned rules and beliefs that are not necessarily accurate, and these may have led to the development of myths. A family myth is a false belief that justifies and sustains ongoing patterns of interaction that are generally not positive (Wright & Leahey, 1994, p. 63). Family exchanges are shaped by these unwritten rules or beliefs about events and situations. Helping family members articulate their beliefs and examine them is an important intervention. For example, family members may believe they cannot disagree with mother because she may become depressed again and end up in the hospital. Therefore, family members remain silent and apprehensive about talking about differences of opinion and collude in silence. The result of the silence is that tension builds and family members feel "they walk on eggs" trying not to upset mother. The children resent mother's unstable health, and father is angry for having to speak for the children. In this example the practitioner must articulate the rules and then check out the beliefs with each family member, asking, What happens when people in this family disagree with mother? What would happen to mother if you expressed your thoughts and feelings? Identifying beliefs can increase or decrease solution options when problems arise. Different views need to be tolerated in families. How families adapt to various stressors depends on the beliefs they hold; and in the same way, the beliefs of the practitioner about the family and their stressors profoundly affect how the family is approached by, engaged by, and receives services from the practitioner.

Family Traditions and Rituals

Families have a wide range of traditions (beliefs and behaviors) shaped by culture and experience. Traditions have benefits for families, and they may also be debilitating. They are customary ways of doing things or ways of behaving, thinking, or feeling that are patterned and learned from family and culture (Rothery & Enns, 2001). Traditions structure behavior, and the assumptions underlying them shape individual and family perceptions and behaviors in predictable ways.

> People come to relationships with traditions they have accumulated throughout life, and these will shape their response to the challenges that any new relationship represents. Rules about closeness and distance, about how to treat each other's vulnerability, about nurturing, support, feelings, power, having fun, food, sex, money, religion, holidays—these and many more are powerful determinants of the quality of our relationships (Rothery & Enns, 2001, p. 219).

Traditions normally are supportive, nurturing, celebratory, or growth enhancing. Understanding the assumptions that support or inhibit traditions tells us how effective family boundaries are and how well they meet needs and problem-solving demands. Effective traditions nurture and sustain families in meaningful and continuous ways. Traditions may also work against family members, or there may be a lack of traditions for coping in a family. For example, if George grew up in a family that valued early leaving and autonomy, he may grow impatient with his son Marc, creating conflict in their relationship, if he views Marc as lazy and dependent on the family. On the other hand, if George grew up in a family that made independence difficult, he will have a different response to Marc. Exploring family traditions (beliefs and experiences) about these situations uncovers role behaviors, assumptions, and cultural expectations about what and who supports and constrains change. Some families may need to develop traditions to assist in effectively managing issues and situations. They may need to learn how to celebrate closeness, collaborate over tasks, or nurture children and adults. Such acts can create intimacy, pride, and sense of belonging to important life events.

Traditions and rituals can block individuals' healthy development and reinforce the need for rebellion in response to rigidity, but they can also draw the family together in an opportunity to celebrate events. Families can be understood in the rituals and traditions that arise from their religions, culture, and racial identify. How are important times, events, and situations recognized and celebrated? Meaning is attached to these events for a family through special foods, family humor, and getting together and celebrating.

Families who make opportunities to join together in traditions have a sense of commitment and emotional bonding. When this is lacking, a practitioner's intervention may be needed to help a family create a ritual that prescribes a specific act for family members to perform designed for changing the family system's rules. The ritual calls the family to join in new combinations or alliances not generally found in the existing family system. Various levels of importance with family systems are tied to beliefs, roles, rituals, and traditions, such as Christmas, Hanukkah, and Ramadan. Here is an example of a ritual in therapy from Sargeant (1985):

> The husband of a married couple had an extramarital affair. In order to move forward with the wife who found it difficult to forgive the husband, the practitioner designed a ritual. The couple needed to leave the "old marriage" and start a "new marriage." The couple referred to their need to bury the old and to begin anew. The practitioner noted the lack of transition between the old and the new and presented the ritual as that transition. The ritual included acknowledging both the good and the dysfunctional aspects of the old relationship. For this couple, the ritual provided a way of leaving the "old" marriage behind and beginning to focus energies on rebuilding a more workable relationship. This is significant as frequently with this type of presenting concern, couples become stuck on the ability of one spouse to forgive the other, rather than on the ability and commitment to rebuilding. It is important to note that this provides one point of redirection but is not the sum total of the work the couple invests in.

For rituals and traditions to have family meaning and significance, they must be *repeated* and must be "coordinated in order to provide a sense of predictability, connections, and a way to enact values" (Doherty, 1997, as cited in DeMaria, Weeks, & Hof, 1999, p. 183).

Questions to ask families about rituals and traditions include these:

- How does this family celebrate rituals of *connection?* Consider family meals, bedtimes, daily leaving and coming home, holidays, weekday rituals, couple rituals, child rituals.
- How does this family *observe* these rituals of celebration? Consider birthdays, school success, holidays, religious passage, births, marriages, and other meaningful passages (DeMaria, Weeks, & Hof, 1999, p. 183).

Rituals and traditions may influence roles within the family; therefore, it is important to conceptualize rituals from a family perspective rather than from the viewpoint of the individual. Rituals are used to break rigidity and to reinforce boundaries of a family system. To change the family system's rules, practitioners use the technique of designing a family ritual to prescribe clear expectations for actions. They teach families to establish a new pattern of thinking, feeling, acting, and problem solving when problem-solving abilities are limited.

Transitions such as parenthood, divorce, adolescence, reunions, and graduations may need to be marked by rituals.

Family Functioning

Families function on many different levels and have needs ranging from basic to complex, covering the spectrum from physical needs, such as food and shelter, to self-actualization. Assessment examines how a family fulfills certain common needs by asking about roles, tasks, and responsibilities. Determining whether basic functions of minimal safety, stability, and nurturing occur in the family is the first step. Once basic functioning is understood, the practitioner determines the adequacy of boundaries—parenting and authority. Do the parents set and maintain limits for the family members? Are the limits sufficient for the situation? If not, is stability of the whole family system threatened? A summary of family functioning roles and tasks, and the interventions that can be helpful, is presented in Table 4.2: Basic Family Functioning Needs and Resources (Kirkpatrick & Holland, 2006). Common issues often center on the needs identified in this table.

A basic family function is to provide food, shelter, safety or protection, health, and nurturance for its members. A family that is functioning well will provide the following:

- *Stability and safety for the child and family:* Families provide a continuous caring and nurturing environment necessary for children to develop family identity and a sense of belonging where attachments are formed. Children must feel and be safe in the family environment. Stability is also related to providing financial security. Families must have adequate financial resources to continuously secure food and shelter.
- *Heath and education:* Families safeguard health and provide nutrition for healthy growth and learning. Families also teach morality, respect, public acceptability, self-care, socialization, and social roles.
- *Competence:* Families provide emotional support so that social and emotional competence of its members can emerge. The family is also a source of self-esteem, motivation for achievement, and work orientation for its members; it gives them religious and spiritual orientation, family ties, and values.

Family functioning reflects the rigidity and maintenance of boundaries, relational patterns, family of origin experience, and the current context, including cultural and value orientations of the family. Table 4.2 offers guidelines to practitioners in assessing family functioning issues and determining the interventions that can address these.

In addition, adaptive family functioning includes good communication among family members and low levels of family conflict (Green & Werner, 1996). An important component of good communication is the degree to which family members are open, honest, self-revealing, and direct with each other. How open families are in expressing feelings, including anger and conflict, indicates the degree of expressiveness. Families with a full range of expression of feelings, from happiness to sadness to anger, are healthy. Families with rigid patterns of emotional expression within a narrow range are considered unhealthy. Verbal and nonverbal family communication patterns are relevant to assessment.

Family functioning is also influenced by power and control in the family system. Power and control are exhibited in various ways. Instrumental means include the use of objects or privileges—for example, television, toys, and movies. Psychological power and control refer to communication and feelings to influence behaviors such as praise, criticism, and imposition of guilt. Corporal control includes physical punishment, hugging, and spanking. Positive and negative control and influence operate in all families, and examining the rules and how they are enforced, and by whom, establishes the appropriateness and consistency with which power and control are used in the family (Wright & Leahey, 1994).

Finally, alliances, coalitions, or triangles also describe family relationships. These family patterns may be healthy or problematic. Some examples of power, control, and alliances are these:

- *Complementary alliance,* such as a mother and child subsystem: unequal.
- *Symmetrical alliance,* such as between spouses: equal.

Table 4.2 Basic Family Functioning Needs and Resources

Issue	Family Tasks	Intervention Strategy	Intervention Technique
Level 1 **Physical and Life Sustaining** Food, shelter, protection, medical care, nurturance	Ability to carry out and manage all nurturing needs and provide food, shelter, safety, medical care, and minimal nurturance	**Focus on Strengths** Focus on family strengths, not problems; obtain support to enhance family capacity to meet basic level 1 needs, build family resilience, build positive response to stress	**Focus on Family/Community; Focus on Resources** • Family preservation • Case management • Support network • Parent teaching strategies
Level 2 Limits and safety	Sufficient authority to provide minimal structure, limits, and safety; structure and organization	**Focus on Strengths** Strengthen the parental/caretaking role; build coalition of those in charge to reestablish authority with those in need of control; increase clarity of expectations	**Focus on Parent/Couple; Some Family/Community** Parental coalitions; set limits; clear communication; social learning skills; behavior contracts; behavior reinforcers; task assignments
Level 3 Establish clear, appropriate, boundaries: family, individual, and generational	Clear and appropriate space and boundaries for individual, family, gernerational	**Focus on Boundaries** Focus on problems; clarify the ideal family structure, considering the ethnic and family expectations; establish generational clarity	**Focus Is Couple and Individual** Protect family and individual and generational boundaries; rebuild alliances; balance triangles; task assignment; communication skills
Level 4 Inner conflict; intimacy, self-actualization, insight	Issues of inner conflict, problems with intimacy, self-actualization of family members	**Focus on Problems** Clarify and resolve earlier trauma, gain understanding of history, focus on spiritual needs, promote insight	**Focus Is Individual** Narrative interventions; intergenerational information; family sculpture [MM1], spiritual growth

Source: A.C. Kilpatrick & P. Holland, Working with Families © 1995, Published by Allyn and Bacon, Boston, MA. copyright © 1995 by Pearson Education. Reprinted by permission of the publisher.

- *Triangle:* a third person is brought in to defuse high anxiety in a dyad. This dilutes high emotionality and anxiety.
- *Multimember coalitions:* alignment of members against a third.
- *Attachments:* strong emotional bonds between members.

Determining these connections and relationships in family systems is important to understanding their current functioning. These are essential assessment information sources.

A family can be skillful and powerful at drawing an outsider into its point of view. By using systems theory and concepts about family change, the practitioner can minimize this danger, knowing what to look for in terms of information while remaining relatively unaffected by the family dynamics. Not all information will fit the practice framework, and there is always a risk of ignoring important data. Nevertheless, to understand individual behavior within the context of family and its multiple systems, use the most relevant framework to make sense of what you are seeing and hearing.

Summary

- The framework for family practice is directed by thinking "family as context," informed by belief systems wherein the family is a special social environment conceptualized as consisting of multiple systems.
- Each system is interactive and interdependent with parts of itself and with other systems it relates to. People, or groups of people, and the multiple systems interacting with them mutually influence each other's behavior.
- A family is more than the sum of its individual parts. It is a unique system with particular responsibilities and functions. It is purposeful and receives input from the components or members of that system, as well as from the environment outside the system.
- A change affects all family members. The family is able or unable to create a balance between change and stability.
- Systems theory is complex and difficult to apply to real-life family situations. But it helps us understand families and their social environments and how to locate the place for intervention. It does not tell us which interventions to use, but evidence-supported practice assists with that decision (Fraser, 2004; Roberts & Yaeger, 2004; Williams & Ell, 1998).
- By approaching a complicated family situation from systems theory perspective, using this as the foundation for understanding the family, the practitioner can be somewhat more objective about the family issues.
- Utilizing a multiple systemic perspective toward family assessment and intervention addresses many important aspects in helping families and the systems interacting and supporting the individuals in families.
- Individual members' behavior influences other family members. Family members' behaviors are best understood as having a circular rather than a linear causality. Although not discussed here, feminist family therapists emphatically object to the notion of circular causality because it leads to blaming the victim as much as the perpetrator in families where there is violence and maltreatment (Goldner, Penn, Sheinberg, & Walker, 1990).
- Practitioners who see the family context as interactions of multiple systems—the family and its social environments—will be better able to build on strengths in families and promote family self-change, a notion critical to practice.

Learning Activities

Classroom Activity 4.1 Family Traditions and Rituals

Students should take 15 minutes to record answers to the following open-ended sentences regarding their family traditions. Have students share their responses in the classroom.

Which of the responses may most influence how you interact with a family? Are family beliefs and behavior similar or different among students?

1. In my family, everyone thought my mother was_____.
2. In my family, everyone thought my father was the one who_____.

3. In my family, I was the closest to_____.
4. In my family it was important to_____.
5. The greatest strength about my family _____.
6. I wish that my family_____.
7. I learned in my family that I will always_____.
8. I learned in my family that I will never_____.
9. Our family never talked about_____.
10. Disagreement in my family was handled by_____.

Classroom Activity 4.2 Family Development

Some family events are normative and experienced by all families, whereas others are unique historical events to a family. Normative transitions for families are starting kindergarten, starting school, getting married, and leaving home. Other events are specific to a family and can dramatically change the life course for a family, such as the death of a child, developing a life-threatening illness, an accident, receiving a substantial inheritance, loss of the home, or a tragic situation such as a fire.

1. Identify six normative family events in your family. How did these events impact individuals in your family and the family as a system?
2. Identify three unique nonnormative family events. How did these events impact individuals in your family and the family as a system?

Share these events with colleagues or your group.

Journal Activity 4.3 My Family Journal

1. What messages did you receive from family members about the importance or role of children?
2. Identify examples and the sources of the following family traditions:
   a. A ritual of emotional connection.
   b. A ritual of cultural belonging.
   c. A dilemma that has affected more than one generation in your family.
   d. A tradition that has been changed, altered, or corrected.
3. What is the importance of identifying traditions in your life? How do these traditions work for you and support the ways you cope with everyday life? How do these traditions work against you?

Case Study Activity 4.4

Read the Del Sol family case study (see Chapter 9) and complete the following questions based on the case information:

1. Describe the cultural affiliations that exist in the family.
2. Based on the cultural affiliations of this family, describe how you would approach assessment.
3. Based on this case, how do the traditions (beliefs and behaviors) influence self-esteem, marriage, parenting, sexuality, familial responsibility, and loyalties?
4. Design a family ritual to address a predictable family system pattern that needs to be changed. Identify the tradition that does not work, and then design the ritual.

▼▼▼

CHAPTER FIVE

Intergenerational Family System

Denise Gammonley
University of Central Florida

It is common to have a biological parent living in the household of an adult child, and when this is the case, the parent takes on many roles and functions in part or wholly. As an extended family member, the parent may have significant roles to play within the family. These roles may be supportive—necessary due to health or economic issues—or they may be related to culture and tradition; and potentially charged issues can be associated with rules and roles between the grandparents, parents, and their children. Family assessment and interventions targeted to meeting the needs of older adults require inclusion of the key concepts and assumptions of a family systems perspective. In addition to assessing the family as a complex social system, the practitioner must highlight the influence of intergenerational relationships and the transitions occurring in these relationships as a result of the aging process.

Assessing and treating families in which older adults play a significant role requires practitioners to have knowledge in several areas of aging and the influences and beliefs about how family members relate to elders and the aging process. First, aging-related developmental and health issues affect the functioning of families. Different cultures and families have varying expectations about the role, vitality, and vigor of an older adult in the family. Second, the life course developmental perspective is a tool for understanding evolving family cultures, belief systems, and family–environment interactions. Third, intergenerational relationship transitions impact family system boundaries and patterns of functioning. The grandparent's role will be shaped by culture and traditions and is of special significance in any change considerations. A key organizing framework applicable to assessing each of these critical areas is the practice concept "The family system evolves constantly, creating a balance between change and stability."

Successful functioning of families with older people concerns recognizing the changing individual and family boundaries, as well as the accommodations to independence and to their roles, structures, and responses to functional abilities. The normal aging process features changes in physical and mental health status, economic resources, outside family social connections, environmental demands, and new and relinquished opportunities, which all influence family functioning. Some biopsychosocial challenges that may have presented little difficulty to an older adult and family in earlier years may create new challenges in later life. An example of this would be a grandparent who had been effectively serving for many years in the role of primary caretaker to young children while the parents worked. If confronted with a disabling chronic health condition, such as a stroke limiting speech and mobility, the likelihood of this grandparent sustaining this role would be doubtful, and the structure of the family system would be altered and caregiving obligations shifted among family members.

It is necessary to tailor both assessment skills and interviewing techniques to elicit intergenerational patterns that help plan for services and support families with older adults. Using principles of evidence-based questioning and searching techniques will help support older adults in families.

Developmental Issues

An important distinction in assessing the impact of aging on family functioning is to keep in mind the difference between normative developmental transitions associated with growing older and disability associated with illnesses common in later life. Negative myths and stereotypes about growing older may influence family functioning in subtle or overt ways. Ageism among family members (including the older person) may limit expectations for the elder's capacity to continue providing instrumental, emotional, and social support, providing stability and safety for family members, and maintaining appropriate generational boundaries. If the family attributes troublesome behavior on the part of an elder to age when in fact it is a result of a chronic disease process, the family system may develop a rigid and ineffective pattern of responding to the situation. Potential consequences of rigid communication patterns might be failure to seek assistance outside the family system to determine the source of the troublesome behavior or to obtain necessary services to promote coping. Based on the principle of circular causality, consequences of these rigid communication patterns would influence each family member's behavior, perceptions, and feelings, making change more difficult. Whether due to normative transitions or disease and disability, all families with older members confront periods of transition requiring alterations in structure and functioning. Understanding the range of developmental issues experienced by older adults will ensure an adequate assessment of their impact on the family system.

Social Support and Engagement in the Community

Most older adults remain vibrant and productive members of their families and communities and have close, mutually supportive relationships with their family and friends (Hooyman & Kiyak, 2005; Carstensen, Isaacowitz, & Charles, 1999). Although the family is the primary source of support to an older person, an important principle of intergenerational family assessment is that support is also provided to younger family members by older adults (Hooyman & Kiyak, 2005). Productive engagement in the community through volunteerism, paid employment, or informal caregiving has been associated with improved well-being for older people (Morrow-Howell, Hinterlong, Rozario, & Tang, 2003). For that reason it is vital to maintain social support and engagement outside the family system.

Changes in Physical and Mental Health

The most common chronic conditions among people age 65+ are hypertension, heart disease, arthritis, and diabetes (Administration on Aging, 2004). Mild to moderate hearing loss, loss of visual acuity, and slower reaction times are familiar sensory changes associated with growing older. Despite the challenges imposed by these conditions, most older people adapt their functioning to allow independent living and continued full engagement in all activities. As a person gets older, the likelihood of acquiring one or more chronic conditions increases along with the likelihood of experiencing multiple conditions. Because chronic diseases are characterized by periods of remission and exacerbation, families are likely to confront transitions in response to fluctuations in health status. When an older person has a chronic condition that is deteriorating or is experiencing a decline in the ability to maintain or engage in activities of daily living, families experience a significant reduction in stability.

Mental health in later life is generally positive for older adults. Elders have lower rates of diagnosable psychiatric disorders compared to younger adults (U.S. Public Health Service, 1999). The prevalence of cognitive impairments, such as dementia, does increase as we get older; however, this is most frequent in the oldest 85+ age group. When mental health concerns affect families in later life, they are most often associated with the presence of dementia as a complication of a chronic physical condition or in response to loss.

Declining Functional Abilities

Increasing numbers of elders in the population make it likely that most families will have an older member who experiences declining ability at some point (Administration on Aging, 2004). In response to serious life-threatening illness like cancer or heart disease, or due to advanced age and deterioration of chronic illness or dementia, many intergenerational families assist elders when declining functional abilities prevent independence. This transition is likely to disrupt the pattern of relationships and role responsibilities within families. The process of recognizing a change in the elder's ability, attributing that change to declining functional ability, claiming authority to act on behalf of the elder, and then deciding to act is challenging for family members (Qualls, 2002). Deciding to take on a caregiving role and making decisions on behalf of a dependent elder requires negotiation among all members of an intergenerational family system.

Retirement

For most elders retirement presents an opportunity to redefine identity, explore personal interests, and take a larger role in supporting the extended family through grandparenting or other forms of informal support. Some older adults are "pushed" into retirement due to the onset of caregiving responsibilities for a dependent spouse or grandchild. Adjusting to retirement is a key developmental task requiring families to realign relationships and roles, such as with the retirement of the primary breadwinner. More older people are not retiring due to personal preference or social and economic concerns, and they continue to work full-time or part-time well into their 70s. Helping families realign home responsibilities to support the needs of the older worker may be a challenge in some cases. Assessing reasons for retirement and expected role transitions in families should be a part of intergenerational family assessment.

Widowhood

Loss of a spouse or significant other is a normative transition in later life that alters the family structure. Lack of support from family members is a risk factor for complicated grief and depression among older widows (Nuss & Zubenko, 1992). Helping multigenerational families adjust to the loss of a spouse requires assessment of power and decision-making authority roles prior to the loss, along with identification of new subsystems within a family. After the loss of a spouse these new subsystem boundaries may be more likely to cross generational lines, particularly if the bereaved is frail and of advanced age. In this case the transition to widowhood could have a particular effect on sibling relationships by creating alliances between some children with the widowed parent while remaining siblings form a coalition apart from this alliance.

Assessing Families Using the Life Course Perspective

Life course refers to the unique paths of development people take in varied environments, as well as their varied life experiences from birth to old age. This framework highlights changing roles and relationships affecting family functioning across age groups. People change biologically, psychologically, and socially as they grow older. In the assessment process, questions focus on the notion of linked lives and the emphasis on history as important factors contributing to divergent paths taken by individuals and families across the life span. Explore how relationships change across generations and over time as a result of parallel changes in the personal biography of individual and family members (Bengston & Allen, 1993; Elder, 1977). Table 5.1 presents the principles of life course family assessment.

Transitions and Trajectories

Trajectories are how events unfold over time during someone's life; they are essentially the sequence and chronology of events and provide a historical perspective to family development, individual transitions, and trajectories. For example, being forced to adopt or relinquish a valued role can have different influences on individuals depending on their exact trajectory. "Forced" retirement due to a severe chronic illness may affect the psychosocial functioning of an individual at age 40 quite differently than it does at age 62. Because of the notion of circular causality, any transition affecting an individual family member affects all family members. Life course adds to our understanding of this process by incorporating awareness of the potential for different outcomes of transitions based on the generational status of a family member. Table 5.2 applies the family life course perspective to understanding the linked lives of a four-generation family: Flossie, Jane, Carole, and Fran. Looking at Table 5.2, note how different transitions and trajectories influenced opportunities and choices for these women. Flossie is the grandmother; Jane, the mother; Carole, the granddaughter; and Fran, the great-granddaughter. Each was born in a unique year, a different time in history, and thus had different opportunities and constraints on her development.

Expected family roles and communication patterns shift in response to both normal aging and disease and disability. An important task for the family in later life is to realign boundaries and subsystems and to incorporate the social environment to promote optimal functioning of the elder. Settings where the family interacts with the environment may broaden to include organizations that promote the health and well-being of a frail and dependent elder, for example. Changes in residential status create a significant transition point for intergenerational families in later life. Retirement and widowhood are two additional transitions that affect families. For families with adequate socioeconomic resources, life course theory tells us that the long-term trajectory for a successful retirement begins early in life with adequate opportunities for education, employment, and optimal health. For many children and grandchildren supported by older family members who provide financial support or direct care, opportunities to return this support in the form of informal caregiving when the elder requires assistance are an expected part of family life. This kind of reciprocity between generations promotes healthy family functioning in successive generations of the family. Helping intergenerational families adapt to challenges imposed by both expected and unexpected transitions associated with normal aging and disability associated with chronic disease is a key component of family assessment.

Decision-Making Authority

No greater challenge affects the functioning of an intergenerational family than a shift in decision-making authority when an older adult loses capacity to make decisions due to impaired cognition or functional abilities. The notion of generational hierarchy, meaning the presumed authority of the oldest member of a family, must give way to authority invested in a new family

Table 5.1   Principles of Life Course Family Assessment

Life Course Concept	Definition and Key Principles for Family Assessment
Age stratification	A sociological paradigm linking changes in individual and family lives with changing social structures.
	Groups of people who differ in age confront unique challenges determined by their individual development and concurrent changes in society.
Human development over time	Contexts of family development over time.
	Individual time: As the individual grows and develops biologically, psychologically, and socially, family functioning is affected in a reciprocal fashion.
	Generational time: Families contain members from many generations. Members of the same generation share values and relationships. Family relationships across generations change over time. Expected roles and functions of families differ across generations.
	Historical time: Each member of a family comes from a unique birth cohort and experiences a different set of historical events during his or her life course. These experiences continuously alter family and individual relationships, roles, and values.
Cohorts	Groups of people who enter a similar experience at the same time. Birth cohorts (people born in the same period of time) become more heterogeneous with advancing age.
	Birth cohorts between family subsystems are unique. Each birth cohort experiences a unique set of historical events, role opportunities, and constraints.
Transitions	Important events that serve as markers to change the "state" of an individual and the family.
	Transitions become turning points for families. They may be expected or unexpected. To remain a fully functioning system, families must successfully resolve transitions.
Trajectories	Pathways of individual and family development. Common trajectories affecting families are relationships, educational attainment, chronic illness, and careers.
	Transitions may have different meaning for individuals depending on the particular trajectory.
	Family trajectories are determined by the place of the family in the larger social world, their generational time, and their historical time.

subsystem (Qualls, 2000). Negotiating these transitions is a process for families that begins when some members of the family system notice changes in the elders' functioning, suggesting impairment in judgment or physical capacity. The process is rarely clear-cut and frequently creates long-term struggles for families. The attachment history between the elder and potential new family decision maker influences the choice, as does the relationship between siblings.

Widowhood is another family transition that signals renegotiation of authority in families. Families who have successfully renegotiated the hierarchy of decision-making authority may face fewer difficulties when confronting-end-of life care decisions on behalf of an elder near death. This difficult transition for families will be helped further if open discussions of preferences for end-of-life care occur while an elder retains the capacity to participate. Solidifying these

Table 5.2   Intergenerational Family Life Course

Family Member	Individual and Family Time	Generational Time	Key Historical Influences
Flossie born 1911	Came of age in the 1920s High school graduate Married young, five children Untimely and sudden widow at age 40 Single, working mother 25+ years Lost one kidney at age 42 "Snowbird" in Florida, age 66 Lung cancer at age 85	The "Greatest Generation" 1911–1924	WW I and II Roaring Twenties Great Depression Atomic bomb
Jane born 1930	Married after high school; three children, two adopted Untimely and sudden widow, age 48 Severe blood clot at age 69 At 75 continues working part-time and provides part-time care for toddler grandson with impaired mother	The "Builders" or the "Silent" generation 1925–1945	WW II The Fabulous Fifties Cold War Civil rights
Carole born 1958	Nurse/caregiver to terminally ill father at age 20 Married after college and RN degree Four children: elementary school through college Completed graduate school when last child entered elementary school Employed full-time	Baby Boomer or the "Me" generation 1946–1964	Kennedy assassination Space race Energy crisis Vietnam War
Fran born 1981	Oldest of four siblings College junior; education major Studied abroad in India	Generation Y or Millennium Generation 1980–2000	Internet School shootings Globalization 9/11/01

discussions through the completion of an advance directive by members of all generations promotes solidarity and connection.

Caregiving for a Frail and Dependent Elder

Assuming primary hands-on caregiving responsibility for a dependent elder is a transition that may or may not be expected by a member of the family. In 25% of all U.S. households family caregivers for older adults are women (National Center on Women & Aging, 1997), often spouses or daughters. Taking on the role of caregiver has important consequences for women in midlife. Women in the caregiving role are more likely to take early retirement or be unable to work due to the demands of caregiving, which impacts their own career and retirement trajectory and frequently the educational trajectory of their children.

Families who have clearly defined primary decision makers are better able to manage the demands of caring for dependent elders with diseases like Alzheimer's (Lieberman & Fisher, 1999). Similarly, family caregivers who clearly define the boundaries of their roles and set limits on the amounts and types of care they provide are better able to sustain the caregiver role (Scharlach, 1987).

Facilitating Residential Transitions for Older Adults

The decision to move, especially for an older individual or couple who have resided in the same location for many years, can create considerable stress for all involved family members. Losses associated with giving up the family home as a defining place of family connection requires rituals of letting go, finding a new location that helps define the place of the family in the community, and creating new rituals to support adaptation. In families where the older adult plays a significant role as a caretaker for younger members, a parallel process occurs. Younger grandchildren who leave their residence with an impaired parent must adjust (along with their grandparents) to the stress of moving to a new home.

Managing Multiple Work–Family Obligations

Family members in what is called the "sandwich generation" face the challenge of childrearing while simultaneously providing for the needs of dependent elders. Increasingly employers provide assistance programs, workshops, and flexible leave policies to support these families. Incorporating careful evaluation of the availability of community supports through employers, schools, and other needed resources should be included in an intergenerational family assessment.

Engaging Older Adults in Intergenerational Family Assessment

Approach older adults as vital, important members of the family when discussing alternatives in realigning decision-making authority. Unlike conducting assessment with children, decisional capacity is presumed intact for an elder unless significant cognitive impairment warrants concern or previously determined legal incapacity exists. Efforts to help a decision-impaired elder regain capacity through medical interventions or other means should be attempted before excluding her or him from participation in an assessment.

Concerns about losing power in families, particularly for dependent and frail elders, require astute assessment and observation skills and the use of circular questioning to construct appropriate goals. By formulating feedback to the family through sharing information about the scope, purpose, and impact of the problem, you can help allay some concerns. Failure to pay attention to building on individual and family strengths can limit open discussion of many issues by (1) distorting the source of the problem, (2) distorting the severity of the problem, (3) lacking interest in acknowledging a problem, and (4) expressing anger or denial of increasing dependence (Herr & Weakland, 1979). Acknowledging the difficulty inherent in discussing changes in family relationships brought on by the aging process can normalize the process for families. Creating an atmosphere of shared learning and exploration can help defuse some anxiety. Tools such as intergenerational genograms, family time lines, and social network maps, involving each family member in their construction, can facilitate more open dialogue about sensitive issues.

Evidence-based Intervention Strategies

Literature evaluating the benefits of interventions and program outcomes to support family caregivers of dependent elders is widely disseminated in peer-reviewed journals. Similarly, a review of empirically oriented practice textbooks and evidence-based practice Web sites will reveal considerable information relating to effective psychosocial interventions directly applicable to practice with elders and families (McNeece & Thyer, 2004).

Substantial evidence supports the benefits of family psychoeducation interventions for intergenerational families affected by severe mental illness, a wide range of physical diseases, and stresses associated with long-term caregiving for elders with dementia (Botsford & Rule, 2004; Goodman, 2004; Toseland, McCallion, Smith & Banks, 2004). Specific outcomes of these interventions include greater family well-being and likelihood to plan for the future, increased caregiver knowledge, and reduced need for hospital care.

Following are some useful databases and organizational resources for beginning practitioners to access:

- *Family psychoeducation:* evidence-based practices shaping mental health services toward recovery: http://www.mentalhealth.samhsa.gov/cmhs/communitysupport/toolkits/family/. SAMHSA National Mental Health Information Center, Center for Mental Health Services. A toolkit for practitioners, program planners, and policy makers interested in implementing family psychoeducation in mental health settings.
- *The AgeLine Research Database:* http://www.aarp.org/research/ageline/. Produced by AARP, this database covers a wide range of books, journals, research reports, and audiovisual content in social gerontology including policy issues, consumer information, and content helpful for practitioners.
- *Caregiver well-being toolkit:* http://www.chcr.brown.edu/PCOC/familyburden.htm. Brown University's Center for Gerontology and Health Care Research compilation of validated measurement tools to assess caregiver functioning.
- *National Family Caregiver Support Program:* http://www.aoa.gov/prof/aoaprog/caregiver/caregiver.asp. Administration on Aging source for policy, program, and consumer information to support family caregivers.
- *Generations United:* http://www.gu.org/. National Center on Grandparents and Other Relatives Raising Children; includes links to model programs.
- *GenoWare:* http://www.genogram.org/. Online demo of genogram software.

Summary

- Expectations about the role, vitality, and vigor of older adults vary across families in diverse cultures and evolve as members confront expected and unanticipated life transitions.
- Assessment requires an understanding of the distinctions between changes occurring as part of normal aging, and changes resulting from disease processes in later life.
- Family boundaries and subsystems are often realigned in response to retirement, widowhood, caregiving responsibilities, residential transitions, and changes in decision-making authority.
- Maintaining a focus on the older adult as a vital family member and use of circular questioning techniques in an atmosphere of shared learning can help diffuse anxiety and facilitate discussion of sensitive issues.
- Psychoeducation with caregivers of older adults is an effective intervention for families affected by severe mental illness, acute physical illness, dementia, and chronic disease.

Learning Activities

Activity 5.1 My Life Course Perspective

1. Learn about applying the life course perspective to family assessment by first exploring your own life course in a Web-based activity. Paste the following Web tool into your Internet browser to explore your own life course: www.OurTimeLines.com.
2. Enter your birth year to see a comprehensive list of important historical events that have occurred during your lifetime.
3. Enter specific important events or transitions you have made. These might be choices you made related to when to get married, how long to remain employed, or at what age to become a parent. They might also be unexpected events like illness, death, winning the lottery, and so on.
4. Now enter specific events or transitions made by your significant others. How have you altered your time line to adjust to their choices?
5. How do your individual choices promote or constrain opportunities for your significant others?
6. How do large societal historical events, technological changes, disasters, and the like impact your time line?
7. What kinds of transitions caused the most disruption to your time line?

Activity 5.2 Tracing Normative and Nonnormative Life Events

The following questions are based on the Multigenerational Family Development Time Line: Normative and Unexpected Transitions, which follows these questions. Place your transition events directly on the time line.

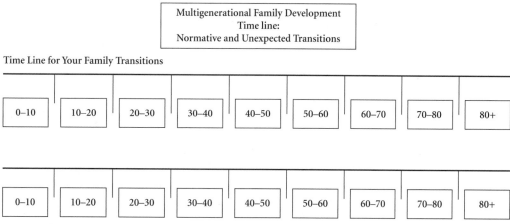

Multigenerational Family Development
Time line:
Normative and Unexpected Transitions

Time Line for Your Family Transitions

| 0–10 | 10–20 | 20–30 | 30–40 | 40–50 | 50–60 | 60–70 | 70–80 | 80+ |

| 0–10 | 10–20 | 20–30 | 30–40 | 40–50 | 50–60 | 60–70 | 70–80 | 80+ |

Time Line for Fernandez Transitions

1. On the first age line list up to five normative and five unexpected family transitions occurring in your own family.
2. On the second age line list up to five normative and five unexpected family transitions occurring in the Fernandez family (see Chapter 14).
3. Write a description addressing the normative and unexpected family transitions for your family. Now write a brief description addressing the normative and unexpected family transitions for the Fernandez family. Were these transitions welcomed?

Discouraged? Did they cause concern for family members? For whom? Were they difficult to manage?

4. How did various members of the family manage these transitions?
5. What were some family rituals and self-care techniques employed by you, the older adult, and the family as a whole to manage these transitions?
6. What interventions could have been used to support these transitions?

Activity 5.3 Case Study Activity: The Fernandez Family

1. Identify the current family life stage in the Fernandez family and describe the tasks of this stage. What is the primary task associated with this stage? (See Carter & McGoldrick, 1998.)
2. Have earlier stages been negotiated successfully? How will this affect the current stage?
3. Is it crucial for the practitioner to explore the cultural experience? If so, how might this process begin, and how will it assist the family?

▼▼▼

CHAPTER SIX

Family Assessment

Family assessment must reflect evidence-based practices, and these include interventions that are derived from sound research methodologies where the outcome findings consistently show that the interventions actually help clients change and improve (Drake, Goodman, Leff, Lehman, Dixon, Mueser, & Torry, 2003, as cited in Thomlison & Corcoran, in press). In general, you will search the empirical literature to locate assessment and treatment approaches—evidence-based treatment—based on the best available science (Gibbs, 2003). Within the context of this book, evidence of assessment practice effectiveness includes research-based and case-based information that an approach to working with families has a reasonable probability of effectiveness when applied to a problem or target client group (Gibbs, 2003). A comprehensive reference for learning to identify evidence-based information sources is *The Evidence-Based Social Work Skills Book* (Cournoyer, 2004), which directs students to specific and credible material rather than using a random approach to bibliographic databases.

Preparation for the Assessment

Family assessment is a process of collecting data about a family's functioning. It begins with the first contact. Data are collected from the family interview about family strengths, resources, and problems and needs; concerns are prioritized; and a decision is made about intervention. Assessment should profile a family's unique strengths, needs, and goals and result in tailored interventions for change. Assessment processes have several aims and outcomes: (1) to determine the family system functioning, (2) to assess family strengths, (3) to analyze areas for change, and (4) to collaborate in decision making with families regarding recommendations for intervention.

Change is sought in individual and family functioning in areas of family patterns (boundaries) and family functioning (roles, tasks, and communications) and often with interactions the family has with the community environment. The degree of change sought will depend on the family's needs and goals and the skill of the practitioner. It may be as simple as behavior change or as complex as a change in the whole family system. Preparing to interview a family requires reflection on the family as a system and knowledge of family issues prior to the first interview. Remember that not all presenting concerns require resolution.

Assessment will be guided by evidence-based practice effectiveness approaches, learned from scientific research. Finding research on particular populations, problems, and issues is not necessarily easy. In locating appropriate evidence-based information, consider not only the best available scientific studies but the relevance of that information for your client as well as you, the practitioner. Best practices are strategies, activities, or approaches that have been shown through research and evaluation to be effective at preventing or delaying problems. However, it is not easy for practitioners to engage in evidence-based practices when the evidence for effectiveness often comes from clients and settings different than community-based settings and from treatment manuals that seem inflexible. The findings may not be fully relevant to your client situation. Before you select a best practice, start by identifying the risk and protective factors for various problems that need to be addressed in the family you are working with. You need to learn about the risk and protective factors for common problems, such as substance abuse, Alzheimer's disease, depression, delinquency, mental disorders, child maltreatment, and other problems, before you determine the intervention strategies (Fraser, 2004; Roberts & Yaeger 2004; Thyer & Wodarski, 1998). Once you identify the general and specific risk and protective factors for a problem, your assessment interview will focus on the individual and family system factors that maintain the client problems. Specific procedures for assessing problems such as substance abuse will vary between programs and practitioners.

All family members should be invited to the first interview, and for a complete assessment, all should be present. Emphasizing that everyone should attend is a powerful restructuring and reframing move, indicating that the whole family is involved in the problem (Nichols & Schwartz, 2005) and that a family meeting is the first step in initiating change. Some practitioners feel so strongly about this that they refuse to see families if all members do not come to the meetings. However, it is advisable to see those who come and to encourage the missing members to participate. The disadvantage of missing members is that you do not have that person's perspective. If key family members fail to participate in the first meeting, their absence usually indicates a family structural problem (boundaries).

A decision to work with various subsystems may emerge after the initial meeting or if the practitioner believes there is good reason to do so, such as seeing the marital couple without children to discuss matters of their sexual relationship. Even while working with smaller units (spouse system, parent–child subsystem), however, the practitioner keeps a focus on family issues (Hepworth, Rooney, Dewberry-Rooney, Strom-Gottfried, & Larsen, 2006; Franklin & Jordan, 1999). For most family issues, the whole family is seen together. Sometimes others in the household, such as grandparents, are invited (see Chapter 5).

Having identified the context of the family issues and the strengths of the family through the first interview, the practitioner may decide not to invite all the members to the following interview. If this is the case, the practitioner must maintain the family system perspective throughout for the eventual return to family interviews. Successful joining with the family system is required for good family interviews. The terms *joining* and *accommodation* are used to describe how the practitioner attempts to put the family at ease and adjusts to accept their organization and style (Nichols & Schwartz, 2005).

Assessment Approaches

Assessment approaches and the types of tools employed during the meeting vary depending on where the practitioner looks for problems and what she or he sees. For example, looking at the whole family, looking at dyads or individuals, or focusing on the problems that maintain symptoms will determine the activities. For the first contact, interviews are generally the most accepted approach; structured evaluation procedures that are more empirically based can be introduced later. Whatever data gathering methods are employed, a thorough assessment of the family structure is the initial step.

Although interviews are the most common method for collecting data, they have one major drawback: They are the least systematic way to obtain information. Other assessment approaches, which involve formal tools and instruments, may be more efficient for collecting and organizing information, but they may seem less personal to the family at the first meeting. Practitioners need to select a method with which they and the family are comfortable.

In general, practitioners will use either direct or indirect approaches to gather data. Direct approaches involve interviews, using both standardized and nonstandardized formats, mapping and graphic approaches; and behavioral observations through experiential and task assignments that allow the practitioner to observe family interaction firsthand. Indirect approaches provide information from background information sheets, treatment or service records, questionnaires, self-report scales and measures, family logs, journals, and diaries (Jordan & Franklin, 2003). All assessment methods have strengths and limitations. Some require considerable competence for use; some provide greater accuracy than others. No method is adequate for all situations. One skill a practitioner will develop is learning which method is best in which circumstance.

Many family and parent–child problems are best examined through a combination of assessment approaches—using interviews supported with standardized measures. As a form of decision making, practitioners and organizations use interviews with the greatest frequency to obtain family assessment information. Standardized approaches to the assessment of problems in families provide more accurate data because these assessment tools are grounded in research. Standardized assessment measures provide information by formulating a score about an issue, feeling, perception, and attitude or severity of a problem. Combining information collected in interviews with standardized measures presents family information at a more reliable level. Choice of assessment measure ideally includes tools that are reliable and valid, easy to use, easy to interpret, and culturally sensitive and free of gender bias.

Tools for Collecting and Organizing Clinical Data

Four types of tools for collecting data are discussed in this section: (1) the family interview, (2) mapping and graphic tools, (3) self-report tools, and (4) teaching, observation, and role-play tools. Although each method of data collection can be used alone, family interviews with the addition of other tools provide the best source of information for a practitioner to become aware of the family's dynamics and events that make up their life. The use of tools is also the best way to monitor change.

Finding ways to organize interview data is a challenge for the beginning practitioner. Family assessment requires you to know the internal and external factors that impact the family and the risk and protective factors for a problem. A number of basic tools can assist you beyond the interview to focus on what changes will maximize and support the family resources while providing more adequate family organization. Tools that can help organize data from or during interviews are the genogram, ecomap, and social network map and grid. Each is simple to use and requires pencil and paper, a blackboard and chalk, or a flip chart and marker. Observational and teaching tools can help you provide interventions for families while teaching a behavior, labeling a feeling, coaching, or shaping behavior for improved communication and change in family alliances and coalitions.

The Family Interview
There are numerous good books and courses on interviewing, and it is not the intent here to teach the reader how to interview but rather to review basic guidelines. First, the basic interview guidelines are presented, followed by an overview of the interview process.

Preparing for an assessment requires that you are attentive to family dynamics and interview techniques. Family therapy assessment is focused on family dynamics and the strengths of the system. The primary task during the interview is to observe family interactions, which reveal family patterns along with the family system's strengths and negative patterns. Gathering information and identifying problems go hand-in-hand with paying attention to the dynamics and cues from family members. Interviewing alone will not discover some of the issues; however, asking the right questions and using a range of techniques can be useful. Underlying all successful interviews is the ability to communicate clearly and the ability to understand the communications of family members. A family interview is affected by several elements:

- Practitioner and family characteristics, such as physical, cognitive, and affective factors.
- Message components: language, nonverbal cues, and sensory cues.
- Interview environment or climate: physical, social, temporal, and psychological factors.

Your task is to control or manage as many of these factors as possible to obtain as much information as you can about family and member concerns. However, you cannot control all these factors; therefore you must consider how these factors contribute to and interweave within the interview process and affect your judgments about the information obtained. The following factors influence the interview (Jordan & Franklin, 2003; Sattler, 1998):

Environmental factors: *Be aware of the surroundings.*

- Interview the family in their home to see how they interact with the environment; when this is not possible, hold the family meeting in a private, quiet, comfortably sized room in the office with no disturbances.
- *Never* interview a child or victim of violence while the alleged offender is in the room or in the building.
- Conduct the interview in a safe and friendly environment and allow as much time as needed.

Listening: *Listening skills lead to informed impressions.*

- Do not become preoccupied with what you are going to say next or what questions to ask. This is distracting, and you will miss what the person is saying and how he or she is saying it.
- The ebb and flow of the interaction will continually modify the impressions both of you have.
- Impressions will emerge throughout, but do not allow them to bias your interview until you have a complete picture of all family information or without testing your initial hypotheses of the family problems.

Listening to yourself: *Learn about yourself from everything you do.*

- Become attuned to your thoughts, feelings, and actions, and learn how to deal with them appropriately during the family interview.
- Especially for beginning practitioners, and whenever possible, the family interviews should be videotaped or conducted under live supervision through a one-way mirror. This is an excellent method to see how your needs, values, belief system, and standards and skills emerge during the interview and how this may affect the family and their responses.

Body language: *Body language conveys meaning.*

- Be aware of your body language and what you do when talking or listening. You may unknowingly bite your nails, crack your knuckles, twirl your hair, tap your pen, rock in your chair, play with your hands, move your foot, or any other nervous habit that may distract or annoy family members in the interview.

- Supportive and accepting body language will put everyone at ease and convey a message of empathy and trust that allows the family to express themselves.
- Be cognizant of your body language and what it may convey to people of different backgrounds as you conduct the interview. You may have to alter your stance, posture, eye contact, or chair placement depending on what background or culture the family celebrates.

Observing family language and behavior: *Observe the words and behaviors of each family member throughout.*

- Notice if there are any differences in how the child behaves when he or she is with or without certain family members.
- Pay attention to facial expressions, postures, vocal behaviors, mannerisms, gestures, and motor behavior of each member. Videotaping the interview is helpful because practitioner and family behavior and subtle nuances may not be detected when you are first learning about family dynamics and may prove valuable to the successful outcome of family change.
- Pay attention to the logic of the communication. It is important to hear not just the words but the inflection, tone, and speed of the communication.

All interviews have stages: a preliminary planning stage and beginning, middle, and ending phases. Interviews with children and some adolescents are different and difficult. Experienced practitioners are best used for these situations. Of course, practicing interviews helps you improve, and good supervision is essential.

The First Interview   Planning for the first interview before the family meeting is critical. Some practice guidelines include the following:

1. The first interview is a planned event with the whole family. Book an appointment inviting the whole family to the meeting.
2. A family interview can take place anywhere—in the family home, in an office, in a room in a school, or some other place convenient for all. Advantages to the home visit include the possibility of seeing the complete family—infants, grandparents, the boarder, and any others who form part of the family's social environment. Seeing the home lets you see firsthand the physical environment and other interactions, which may not occur naturally in the office settings. For example, you might glimpse how parental competencies are carried out, the patterns of coming and going, and other social and interactional patterns that may be constrained in the office setting. Cultural and ethnic uniqueness can be observed more deeply in the home. Sleeping, cooking, and home management may be noted, as well as any other aspects that may contribute to family stressors.

   Seeing the family in the work setting does offer some advantages to the practitioner. There is more privacy than the family home, and control of the interview is possible without interruptions. Consultation and even live supervision may be available. However, many families find the office setting intimidating and inconvenient to reach. Some settings may reinforce the idea that one member is ill—for example, interviewing in a psychiatric setting may inadvertently foster the belief that mom is the sick one, an individual-based concern, and this belief may create difficulty in focusing on the family unit and the need for change in the whole family.
3. The purpose of the first interview is to obtain a broad picture of who the family is and the concerns, issues, and sources of stress. Various practice settings will require that you focus and collect information specific to the services. For example, a child and adolescent service will focus on the parent and parent–child issues, whereas a hospital asthma clinic may require you to focus more on the health aspects of the person with asthma, including a specific medical history.
4. Before meeting with the family, consider the purpose of the meeting. For example, are you trying to determine how well a family is coping with a member who has cancer, or are you assessing for family violence? The purpose determines how the meeting is conducted, and the flow of questions may be different.

5. Family therapists (Jordan & Franklin, 2003) suggest also that planning begins by designing hypotheses about the family relational patterns. There are no right or wrong explanations of what is happening. Hunches emerge that need to be tested. The hypotheses are designed to provide general direction for exploring the family's situation and to generate the most helpful explanations of the family's behavior—how a family is functioning. These hypotheses will guide the interview questions.

6. Invite the whole family to the interview at a designated time.

7. At the beginning of the interview set the foundation for participation and work by establishing the operating rules. Ask parents to handle the children in whatever way they usually do in the case of young children. Explain that participants will be expected to contribute. Make everyone feel comfortable. Minimize chaos and make the environment welcoming. This is necessary for joining the family.

8. There are four stages to family interviews—engagement, assessment, intervention, and termination. Every interview follows these stages, and the process follows these stages over the course of your contact with the family:

   a. *Engagement:* Establish and maintain a relational contact for therapeutic work to occur. Active listening, empathy, warmth, and respect are important qualities to demonstrate. Practitioners must not show alliances with any particular family members (Jordan & Franklin, 2003; Tomm, 1984).

   b. *Assessment:* Establish the concerns of the family. Here the focus is on identifying family resources; relationships between family members; and problems, issues, and concerns. Review the attempted solutions and explore what changes the family wants. This may take place over several family meetings. Do not engage in confrontation or interpretation of information too quickly because this may impede progress.

   c. *Intervention:* This provides the context for change. Family therapists (Franklin & Jordan, 1999; Nichols & Schwartz, 2005; Rothery & Enns, 2001) emphasize the need for assignments, tasks, and designing rituals and traditions (repeated patterns) to effect change. Beginning practitioners may need consultation with this task. Intervention can occur effectively over three sessions according to Epstein, Baldwin, and Bishop (1983) of the McMaster Model of Family Functioning; Gurman & Kniskern (1981); Corcoran (in press); and Thomlison (1984). Brief or short-term interventions are equally as effective as long-term treatment (Jordan & Franklin, 2003; Nichols & Schwartz, 2005; Roberts & Yeager, 2004). Change will occur in the individual system, the marital system, and the family as a whole.

   d. *Termination:* The family finishes with the practitioner and is encouraged to contact the practitioner if future concerns arise.

Table 6.1 (Questions for the First Family Interview) provides samples of the types of questions that should be asked in the first meeting with a family. Other questions to consider are circular questions about family functioning and impact, as well as cultural story questions such as those described in Chapter 3 in the section titled "Family Culture." An interview can last for various amounts of time, but it will not be less than one hour, and the length will depend largely on the setting. At the end of the interview, after summarizing the session, be sure to give the family a time for the next meeting.

Mapping and Graphic Tools

The genogram, ecomap, and social network map and grid are valuable mapping and graphic assessment tools. The genogram provides information about the family as a system as well as the internal and external structures of a family to help you understand family relations. Family of origin, culture, and attachment genograms are commonly used by practitioners (DeMaria Weeks, & Hof, 1999). The *genogram* is a pictorial chart of the people involved in a three-generational relationship system. The *ecomap* shows the interactions the family has outside the family environment. Ecomaps reveal the systems in the larger environment by pointing out connections beyond the immediate family. Identifying important relationships with friends, relatives, churches, schools, social groups, organizations, work, and other life settings gives the

Table 6.1 Questions for the First Family Interview

Who

Who is a member of this family?

Who is experiencing the concerns?

Who is most/least concerned about the problem?

Who is most affected/least affected by the concerns?

Who brought the family here?

What

What concern brings you here?

What meaning does the problem have for each of you?

What solutions have you attempted?

What perpetuates the concerns or problems?

What are the family beliefs about what maintains the problem?

What problems perpetuate the beliefs?

Why

Why is the family coming for assistance now?

Why is it important that the family change?

Where

Where did the information about the problem come from?

Where does the family view the problem as originating?

Where does the family go if there is no change?

When

When did the problem begin?

When does the problem occur?

When does the problem not occur?

How

How might the family look, behave, or feel without the problems or concerns?

How might the family relationships change without the concerns?

How does a change in the individual affect others?

How does the family maintain the concern or problem?

How will the family know when the concern or problem is not present?

How might this practitioner constrain or prevent the family from finding their own solution?

Source: Adapted and modified from Wright and Leahey (1994, p.149).

practitioner and family a sense of current environmental connections to other systems. The *social network map and grid* capture family behavior in the context of its social network and social support—emotional support, concrete support, and informational support. They allow a pictorial assessment of needed resources for the family.

The Family Genogram The intergenerational family genogram collects and organizes data along genealogical lines. Information depicting the family along intergenerational and historical lines is drawn using symbols. With these symbols, a practitioner can display various details of a family such as family history, current family membership, events such as births, deaths, miscarriages, adoptions, separations, divorces, education, illnesses, and other relevant information about the family that will be valuable in assessment.

Pictorial representation is used to show practical and comprehensive information in key areas of individual and family functioning, such as the family structures, boundaries, relationships, and composition within the context of family generations. Data are then added to help explain the family structure, history, and process and can reveal key intergenerational themes and patterns, relational patterns, and developmental issues in the family (DeMaria, Weeks, & Hof, 1999).

Genograms can illustrate many different aspects of the family patterns and relationships. A family genogram can be drawn to show intergenerational relationships, cultural identity, conflicts and supports, traditions and rituals; it can highlight issues such as obesity, alcoholism, corporal punishment, child abuse, adoptions, and other concerns about any family through the generations. Genograms provide a snapshot over time, and recreating them as an intervention strategy can be both revealing and productive of change.

Constructing the Genogram In using genograms, practitioners should be aware of several cautions concerning their interpretation. "Some studies suggest that there is actually very limited agreement among clinicians on using genogram symbols, and the symbols used do not describe the diversity of family interaction. The symbols focus primarily on closeness, distance, and conflict patterns in families" (DeMaria, Weeks, & Hof, 1999, p. 7). There are no standardized symbols for recording child abuse, addition patterns, or family violence. The practitioner should indicate through the use of a legend on the genogram what each symbol stands for. With a well-explained symbol system, genograms can help organize family information both qualitatively and quantitatively.

The usual practice is to draw three generations of the family, showing family composition, structure, relationships, and other information over time. Family members are placed on horizontal rows to signify a generation, such as a marriage or cohabitation. Children are represented by vertical lines and ordered from left to right beginning with the oldest child. Males are denoted by squares and females by circles. See the blank genogram in Figure 6.1 and the common genogram symbols in Figure 6.2.

Names and ages, and usually birth dates, appear in the squares or circles. Just outside the circles or boxes important information can be placed, such as an illness, problem, or reason for death. Other noteworthy comments can be used, such as mental health diagnoses. An example of the Joe Smith family genogram is shown in Figure 6.3, drawn with the markings and symbols from Figure 6.2.

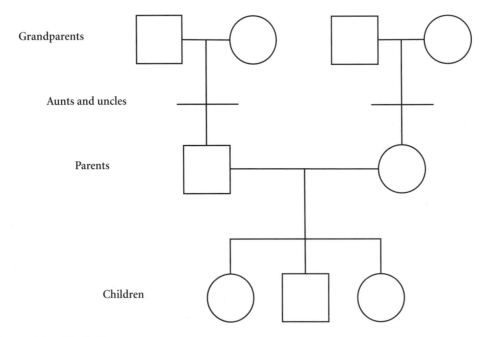

Figure 6.1 Blank Genogram

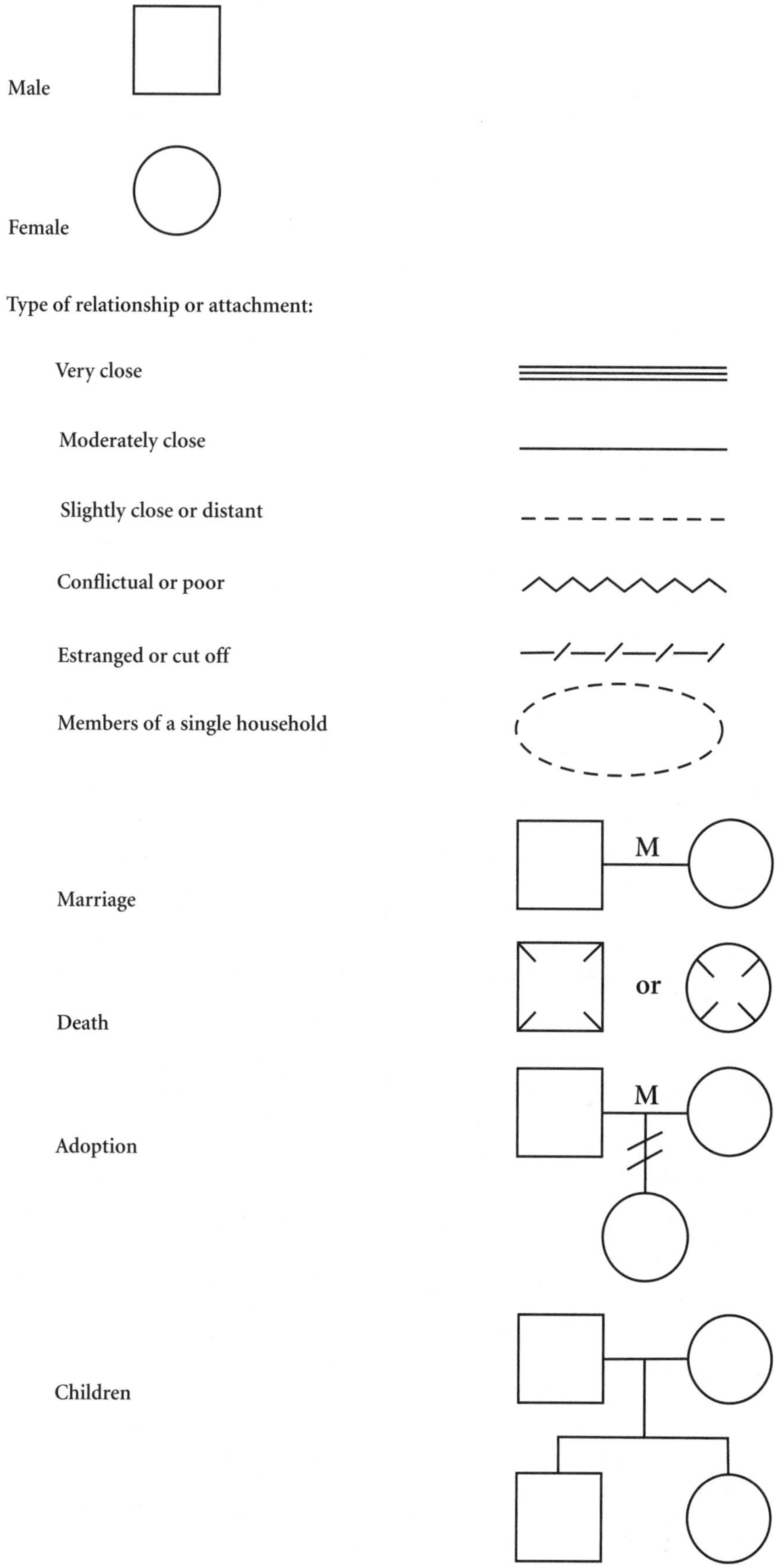

Male ☐

Female ◯

Type of relationship or attachment:

Very close ═══════

Moderately close ──────

Slightly close or distant − − − − −

Conflictual or poor ∿∿∿∿

Estranged or cut off —/—/—/—/

Members of a single household ⟨ − − − − ⟩

Marriage ☐—M—◯

Death ☒ or ⊗

Adoption ☐—M—◯

Children

Figure 6.2   Common Genogram Symbols

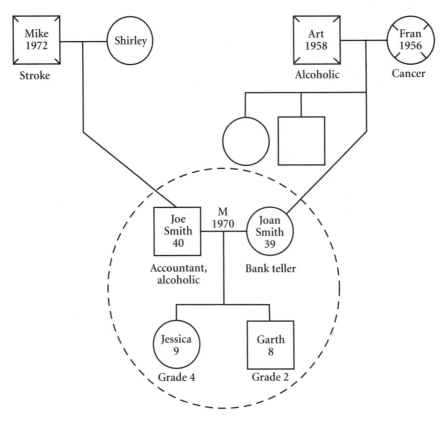

Figure 6.3 The Joe Smith Family Genogram

At the beginning of a family interview, tell the family you will be asking them questions about their background that are important for gaining a picture of the family and their situation. Using a large piece of paper, draw the genogram, allowing everyone to see what you are recording and explaining what the symbols mean as you draw. As you continue collecting information you may even ask family members to draw symbols and write comments on the genogram. Start by drawing a square and a circle with the family before you. Let the members know that you are interested in family composition and boundaries. It is often enlightening to everyone in the group to hear about family members in detail.

It is now possible to use a computer program to depict the family genogram, or to access Web sites such as GenoWare (http://www.genogram.org/) to draw a genogram. It takes a little practice to place the symbols using this tool, but the results are professional looking and impressive.

To help the family feel comfortable with information collection, you may find the following practice guidelines helpful:

1. Collect as much information as possible about the family's membership by drawing three generations.
2. Allow the family to go back at the end of the interview and comment on the genogram or add information that they did not at first include.
3. Remember that the individuals in the family are the experts on their family system.
4. The genogram may be referred to as a "family tree."
5. The family provides whatever information they are comfortable with and can decline to answer any question they do not have information about or do not wish to address. You can always return to the genogram—and probably should in later sessions. Update the information in later sessions, comparing the new entries to material in the original genogram.
6. Let the family members tell you, or draw for you, members of their family in the order that they choose.
7. Colored markers or crayons can be used to enhance the genogram in a way that makes it the family's interpretation.

8. Start with the least threatening questions about family structure, membership, and where family members live before asking about health, mental illnesses, and other matters requiring greater cooperation.

9. If the family is having difficulty remembering dates, help them by asking questions such as these: How old *might* you have been? Were you in high school? What season of the year was it?

10. Ask questions that help the family to think about themselves in relation to their family, such as these: Whom are you most like? Whom are you least like? Why? Whom would you call if you had a problem? Whom would you like to call if you had a problem?

11. Start with the immediate family members before going into the extended family. The amount of detail gathered about the extended family will depend on the family's difficulties, and this is a clinical judgment. It is usual to alternate between wife and husband when asking about each spouse's family of origin. This allows both to contribute to the session. Avoid getting sidetracked and overwhelmed with information.

12. Draw a circle around the members of the current household to distinguish them.

Most families are interested in viewing their family through the genogram. Indeed, it is likely this is the first time they seen their family information organized in this fashion. Therefore, it may be overwhelming, may trigger emotions that they had not expressed, or may initiate discussions about their own problems and family. Practitioners need to be aware of the range of reactions families can have to their genograms and therefore must be prepared to use the genograms both for collecting and organizing data and for helping families make connections to significant events and issues within their family systems. It has been suggested that the family genogram provides four times as much social, health, family history, and family structural and relational patterns as interviews (Wright & Leahey, 1994).

The Ecomap Another way to represent the family's interaction with various systems is by drawing an ecomap. Ecomaps depict systems the family interacts with and indicate where changes may be needed in the environmental systems to provide improved interactions and support for a family. Information about the family's social context is shown using squares or circles to represent social support. In these graphic pictures the practitioner can see where supportive relationships exist and where deficiencies and areas of conflict appear. Are there missing connections or interfaces that need to be changed? Is social isolation a problem? Ecomaps indicate the flow of resources between the family and other significant people, agencies, and organizations that may be supporting or stressing the family environment. Ecomaps help determine the resources and interventions necessary for resolution of many family stressors.

Constructing the Ecomap Start by explaining to the family that you wish to obtain a picture of their current situation. Place the family household in the center of the paper as a circle. Label the family within the circle. Around the family household, circles are drawn to indicate the family's environment such as work, child care, school, extended family, church, recreation, friends of family, friends of children, drinking buddies, and others as appropriate for the family. The circles can be drawn any size. Lines are drawn to show the quality of the relationships with the connections. Common depictions are (1) straight lines for strong connections—the wider the line, the stronger the connection; (2) dotted lines for tenuous relationships; (3) slashed lines for stressful relationships; and (4) arrows to indicate the flow of the relationships between the systems. These can be drawn in both directions or one way.

Ecomaps highlight the types of relationships families want inside their family structure and outside the immediate family. Ecomaps should be drawn at various times to indicate change. Drawing ecomaps at the beginning of family work and again after intervention provides a picture of the changing relationships in the family's environment. Ecomaps allow families to understand both the process and patterns that have developed with the family and its environment. Genograms and ecomaps can be used with all families. Three ecomaps are included here: Figure 6.4, which shows a blank ecomap; Figure 6.5, which shows the Smith family ecomap; and Figure 6.6, which shows a child's ecomap.

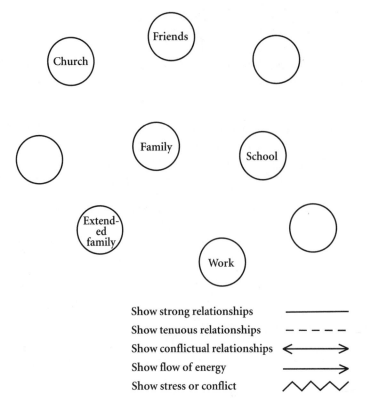

Show strong relationships   ———————

Show tenuous relationships   – – – – – – –

Show conflictual relationships   ⟵—————⟶

Show flow of energy   —————⟶

Show stress or conflict   ∿∿∿∿∿

Figure 6.4   Blank Ecomap

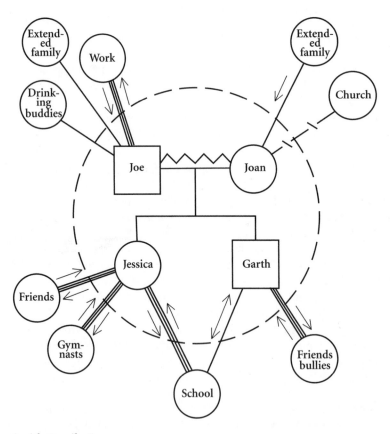

Figure 6.5   Smith Family Ecomap

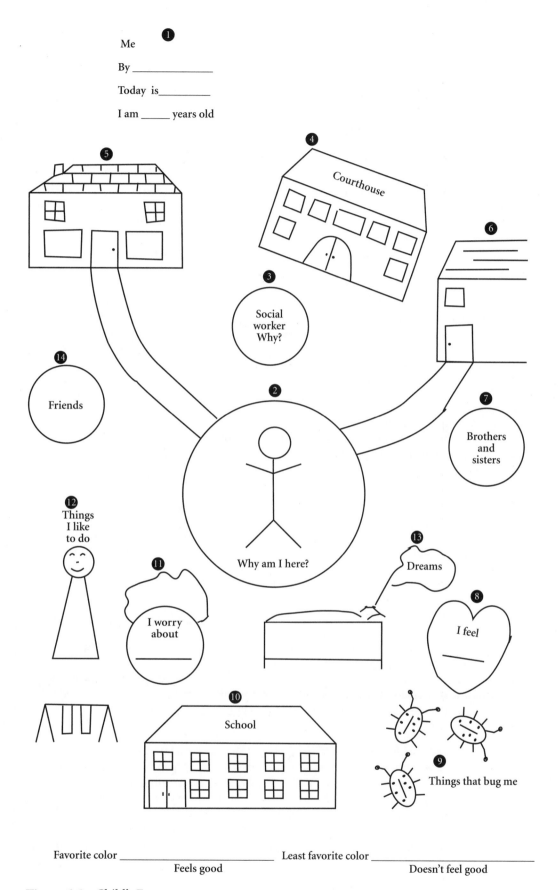

Figure 6.6 Child's Ecomap

Social Network Map and Grid   Social networks are patterns depicting the personal relationships that sustain each individual by helping him or her cope with the usual demands of daily living and the impact of serious stressful situations. Connections between people in a social network can be described as a set of relationships—represented as links in a chain—and can become quite complex. Social network maps help us identify the number of people available to support a family. A social network grid can document other aspects of a social network, such as the categories of informal social support provided, their frequency, and their reliability (Tracy & Whitaker, 1990).

One way to envision informal supports for families is to imagine a social network as a convoy—a group of people who travel alongside us protecting and escorting us through life. The size of our convoy, the kinds of people within it, and the degree to which people in it are close and available to help us during our lives will vary from person to person. Over a lifetime, members of your convoy change: Some people drop out, some relationships become closer, others more distant, and a few remain stable and consistent (Gammonley & Thomlison, 2000).

Families who have few close relationships in earlier years are less likely to have adequate informal supports as they age. There can be a number of contributing factors: recent immigration to the United States, personal disability for some or all of the adults' life, chronic mental illness or substance abuse, or the strains associated with caring for a child while struggling to cope with adult responsibilities. Families with fewer supports also may be less likely to have provided help to others. Whatever the reason, some families, when confronted with challenges and crisis, may have a much smaller and weaker informal social network available to assist them. Families who have adequate support networks are generally better able to get through crises and difficulties than are those who must confront their problems with no external help.

Support helps families by

- Reducing social isolation.
- Increasing knowledge of community resources.
- Offering an opportunity to learn and practice problem-solving skills.
- Allowing modeling and practice of family communication skills.
- Providing companionship.
- Providing emotional support during times of crisis.
- Enhancing self-esteem and coping.

Questions for exploring social support in the family include these:

- What is the family's history of providing informal social support to other people as well as its own members?
- What is the family's experience of receiving support from other people and family members?
- What is the current physical and mental health status of the family members and dependent children?
- What are the demands of the caregiving role that impact the range and number of persons in the social support network?
- Is the family receiving "negative" informal social support? "Negative" social support is assistance provided by friends, neighbors, and family members that is not wanted and has been demonstrated to actually harm the well-being of the family.

Constructing the Social Network Map and Grid   To construct a social network, draw a circle and divide it into seven sections. Label these sections work/school, organizations/church, friends, neighbors, formal services, household, and other family. To assess the presence of social support for a family, first ask the family members to identify all members of their network. List the name of each individual under one or more appropriate sections. The social network grid can help the practitioner assess the quality and amount of support provided by each named individual. For each person listed, the family member describes (1) the kind of support provide such as emotional, concrete, or informational; (2) the degree to which the individual is critical to the family member; (3) the direction of help provided to or by the family member; (4) the degree of closeness perceived by the family member; and (5) the frequency of contact and the

Social Network Map

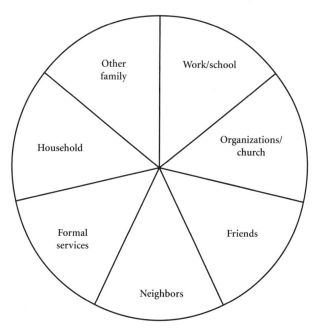

Instructions:
This version of the social network map is used to assess the presence of social support for the family.

Step 1: Sit with the family while completing this form. Ask the family members to name all individuals in their social network.

Step 2: List the names of each individual under the appropriate section.

Step 3: Use the social network grid to assess the quality and amount of support provided by each named individual.

Figure 6.7 Social Network Map

From: Tracy, E.M., & Whitaker, J.K. (1990, October). The social network map: Assessing social support in clinical practice. *Families in Society,* p. 463.

length of the relationship. Use the results to evaluate intervention and resource needs. See Figure 6.7 for an example of the social network map and Figure 6.8 for the social network grid.

Self-Report Tools

Incorporating standardized measures into the assessment and intervention process requires deciding what will be measured, when, and how. Chapter 7 discusses this matter in greater detail. Deciding what to measure is primarily grounded in what the family considers important and what you see as the problems. Essentially you are trying to measure an issue or problem and whether it changes over time. Standardized tools measure these types of change as follows:

- Change in *circumstances,* such as decreased conflict.
- Change in *attitude,* such as increased self-respect and family identity.
- Change in *skills,* such as increased parenting skills.
- Change in *behavior,* such as increased contact with a parent or increased positive sibling contact.

Two general methods or approaches to self-report measures are identified in the literature: the use of standardized tools and the use of pragmatic indicators. *Standardized self-report tools* include tests, questionnaires, rating scales, checklists, inventories, or any instrument that is systematically used between the family and practitioner. These measures will have uniform administration and scoring procedures, increasing assurance that you are measuring what you think you are measuring.

Pragmatic self-report indicators rely largely on family self-statements. These tools, such as journals, logs, and self-anchored scales, are considered less efficient and more prone to bias than standardized instruments, but they can elicit important qualitative information about family functioning. Family members record their thoughts, feelings, and behaviors with these tools. For example, you may ask a wife to record the number of times she has thought about wanting to leave the marriage, or the number of disagreements between the husband and wife on weekends about how they should spend their time together. These statements create a baseline

Social Network Grid

Name	Areas of Life 1. Household 2. Other family 3. Work/school 4. Organizations 5. Other friends 6. Neighbors 7. Professionals 8. Other	Concrete Support 1. Hardly ever 2. Sometimes 3. Almost always	Emotional Support 1. Hardly ever 2. Sometimes 3. Almost always	Information/ Advice 1. Hardly ever 2. Sometimes 3. Almost always	Critical of Your Activities? 1. Hardly ever 2. Sometimes 3. Almost always	Direction of Help Provided? 1. Goes both ways 2. You to them 3. They to you	Closeness 1. Not very close 2. Sort of close 3. Very close	How Often Do You See Them? 0. Does not see 1. Few times per year 2. Monthly 3. Weekly 4. Daily	How Long Have You Known Them? 1. Less than 1 year 2. 1–5 years 3. >5 years

Instructions: Use the first column of the grid to record the name of each person listed on the social network map. For each person listed, ask the family member to describe the kind of support provided (concrete, emotional, information/advice), the degree to which an individual is critical of the family member, the direction of help provided to and/or provided by the family member, the degree of closeness perceived by the family member, and the frequency of contact and length of the relationship.

Figure 6.8   Social Network Grid

From: Tracy, E.M., & Whitaker, J.K. (1990, October). The social network map: Assessing social support in clinical practice. *Families in Society,* p. 466.

Instructions: Circle the number that applies every morning.

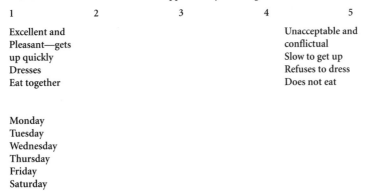

1	2	3	4	5
Excellent and Pleasant—gets up quickly Dresses Eat together				Unacceptable and conflictual Slow to get up Refuses to dress Does not eat

Monday
Tuesday
Wednesday
Thursday
Friday
Saturday

Figure 6.9   Self-Anchored Rating Scale for Family Wakeup Communication

for how frequently a situation, occurs by measuring the thoughts, feelings, or behaviors of family members. This is done by collecting information from them through the use of a chart, journal, or log-recording technique. Self-recording has both practical and clinical relevance in family work and is compatible with interviewing, mapping, and other graphic depictions, as well as standardized forms of measurement.

Self-Anchored and Rating Scales   To measure a problem using a self-anchored or rating scale, the family and practitioner construct a scale that is specific to the family situation. Descriptors are developed to measure or rate the problem or concern. For example, a scale may be constructed to measure family morning communication skills, as depicted in Figure 6.9.

The numbers represent measures of improvement and are used to monitor progress and change. Families like these measures because they are simple to understand and use, and they can help develop the anchors.

Rating lists can be constructed for specific problems such as communication skills: talking for self, listening to others, asking questions, asking questions without interrupting, or summarizing messages. Scales can be developed to rate each skill on a scale from 1 (very clear) to 5 (not clear at all). Self-anchored and rating scales provide ways to quantify practice problems that are meaningful to the family situation. These are not rigorous measures because they have not been scientifically developed. They are meaningful, however, to both the practitioner and family; sometimes they are the best available tool for a particular problem situation.

Teaching and Role-Play Tools

Observing behavior is one of the most common ways of collecting information about individual and family behaviors. It is time-consuming and often impractical, but behavior occurring in the meeting can certainly be observed, as can behavior in the family home environment when the family and practitioner meet there. These times provide opportunities for change in the moment as the practitioner teaches or shows the family how to behave differently through coaching, role-playing, and feedback about behavior. This typically involves asking the family to perform a task or procedure while a person external to the family evaluates the interaction. Tasks and procedures can be rated systematically or by informal observation. Behavior is rated by its frequency and duration or both—for example, the number of times you observe that father does not answer mother's questions and turns his head away. The practitioner or family member can record the frequency of a behavior or time its duration.

Role-plays help family members practice and experience behaviors and feelings in non-threatening situations. Essentially the people have an opportunity to rehearse behavior and responses. Repeated practice opportunities with feedback from family members and the practitioner can often result in the newly learned responses being integrated into daily functioning behaviors and patterns. Practicing communication skills, job interviewing skills, parent–child requests, and other behaviors over time can help family members improve these skills. Improvements can be documented through self-monitoring methods, such as logs and journals, or through videotape. Learning occurs with repetition, and the role-play can be used for both assessment and measurement of changes in behavior.

Issues of Concern

The main objective in collecting data and assessing the family system is to gain an accurate picture of family strengths and problems to create appropriate matches between a family's needs and the services offered to them. Moreover, because of the demands for service, it is important to attend to families with the most immediate needs with an acceptable level of service intensity. Families with lower need levels can receive less intensive service and less restrictive, less intrusive levels of service delivery. Finally, structured family assessment instruments can assist with practitioner consistency. As practitioners face more complex social, clinical, and administrative conditions, the application of a multidimensional family assessment measure can promote consistency in interpretation of problems and decision making in similar types of cases.

Culturally Sensitive Assessment

American families are culturally and racially diverse. The richness of family culture will become evident as you explore such factors as varying expectations and attitudes resulting from ethnic, religious, cultural, racial, and gender differences. These factors may shape your ability to form a trusting relationship with families. You will want to be aware of your own expectations, communication patterns, and responses to power and authority. Failure to address your sense of being different may cause unwillingness among the family members to be open with you, and thus interferes with the establishment of a helping relationship. Such factors will differ in families depending on culture and your ease in exploring these through your relationship; but in some families these may be subjects that are controversial, taboo, or simply provocative.

Many families will view you, the helper, with caution—particularly if you are from the dominant culture. In many situations it is best to match worker and family culturally. If you are a member of a minority group working with families from your own culture, you may be able to understand their difficulties from a culturally competent perspective.

The complexity of these differences creates challenges. The challenge for the practitioner is to discern, validate, and simplify the complexity. For practitioners to work successfully with culturally diverse families, McGill (1992, p. 339) believes that they need to:

1. Have knowledge of the particular content of many different cultures.
2. Be able to make the presence of differences within the family, between the family and the practitioner, and between the family and the larger societal system an opportunity rather than a problem.
3. Hear the complexity of the family's story within the context of society's stories in a way that simplifies the story for ordinary daily family life.

Selecting Dimensions for Assessment

As a fact-finding method that gathers pertinent information about a family system, assessment should include a quantitative measure. The purposes of measuring family problems and resources are the following:

- *Quantifying family problems:* Practitioners can focus on the most critical areas of child, family, and environmental functioning. When the severity of problems or factors facing family members is determined, interventions can be allocated so that more time and resources are spent on family concerns that are most problematic.

- *Supporting and improving clinical judgment:* Measuring family behavior guides practitioners in developing case plans that specifically address the most pressing concerns. Measurement adds to the quality of information on which practitioners base their clinical decisions.
- *Providing a common and consistent perspective to problems:* Through documentation of information provided by a qualitative measure of assessment, family problems can be reassessed during service. All measures should be given at the beginning (pretest) and at the end of the intervention (posttest). Follow-up is also desirable. This permits monitoring and evaluation of change and family functioning. Reassessing the same factors makes it possible to determine the progress a family has made in reducing problems. From these data, relevant and timely plans can be made for a family.
- *Determining the appropriate level of service:* Using a quantitative measure with clinical interviewing, practitioners can identify the key factors that must be addressed through intervention. By developing baseline indicators of family functioning, practitioners can base decisions on objective criteria and recognize family strengths in culturally appropriate ways.

The use of family measures can be adversely affected by the following issues: practitioner or system misuse of instruments; inadequate practitioner knowledge and skill; poor reliability and validity of the instrument; use of an inappropriate instrument; and use of an instrument in an inappropriate context (not all cases are amenable to quantification).

A combination of tools for collecting information and evaluating family change is desirable. In determining which tools to use, consider the following:

- Start with this question: What information is needed?
- Choose a measure that is simple, practical, and meaningful to the family.
- Measure one or two things well.
- Involve the family in defining the outcomes to measure.
- Review the measure with the family who will be using it.
- Build on what the family is prepared to document. Do not overwhelm the family.
- Collect multiple and repeated measures.

Remember that using family measures is not an end in itself but an important way in which you and the family can gain clarity about the focus of change, and a way for both of you to know when change has occurred. The success or failure of measurement depends on how you present the measurement task to the family.

Fischer and Corcoran (2000) have compiled a list of measures for adults, children, and couples related to a number of psychological, behavioral, and interpersonal difficulties. The measures have been reproduced in their books, and you can examine them to find one suitable for the family's concerns.

Summary

Key practice principles in the use of measurement tools for family assessment include the following (Thomlison & Bradshaw, 1999, p. 174):

- Approach assessment from the perspective of applying evidence-based practice to guide a particular intervention with a unique client.
- Assessment is the guide to selecting the appropriate diagnosis, practice guideline, and intervention.
- Use information from empirical literature and case-based research as a guide for determining the most appropriate intervention.

- Practice guidelines are only guides; they do not replace sound clinical judgment, interpersonal skills, and communication for professional practice.
- Be familiar with how a measurement works. Try the task yourself first and practice on friends or colleagues. Know how it works and how long it will take to complete.
- Assure the family of the importance, purpose, and use of the information obtained from the measure. One of the most important messages a practitioner can convey to a family is confidence in the value or importance of obtaining the family's responses.
- Reassure the family that there are no right or wrong answers. Always stress accuracy and honesty.
- Review the entire measurement task with the family before they need to complete it on their own. Be sensitive to the educational, social, and cultural background of the family, such as reading and language difficulties. Remember that the objective of measurement is to obtain information that will assist you and the family in evaluating progress toward goal achievement.
- Review the results with the family. Explain the significance of the results and how you will use them. This shows respect for the family and decreases the "expert mystique" of the practitioner.
- Use the individual items or details provided by the measurement task to discuss strengths as well as areas for further development. Do not just use the total score or gross outcome. Remember, all measurement needs to be simple, practical, unobtrusive, culturally appropriate, and of importance to both the family and the practitioner.

Learning Activities

Activity 6.1 Role-Play the First Interview (30 minutes)

1. Students should prepare for this role-play interview by reading the Jacques family case (Chapter 15).
2. The task is to role-play the first interview with the Jacques family to develop an assessment and treatment plan. To identify the first steps, the person role-playing the practitioner should get only an overall picture of what is occurring in the family by (a) obtaining descriptive data through interview; (b) obtaining a global view of the family in its environment; and (c) developing a genogram and ecomap depicting overall client functioning. Determine the strategies the family has used to resolve their problems. The task is to introduce yourself, meet the family members, and orient the family to the room and to the session—who you are, what will happen, how long you will need, paperwork, confidentiality, and the purpose of the family meeting. Use Table 6.1 to guide the questions for the first family interview with the Jacques family for the role play.
3. After the role-play, discuss the skill used in gathering the data and what could be done to improve the quantity and quality of the information collected.
4. Using the case example, each student should design a treatment plan. Then have the class discuss various treatment plans. What problem(s) should the family focus on first? Why?
5. Here are suggestions for ongoing role-plays to assess strengths and resources:
   a. Begin the role-play by asking what other challenges the family has faced and how they resolved these issues. *Hint:* If you don't balance between seeking information about difficulties and strengths, the problems may feel overwhelming to the family.
   b. When finished, identify the hypothesis, strengths, and issues in the family. With classmates and role-players, discuss the hypothesis and how well you conducted the first interview. Is the assessment accurate? What other suggestions for questions or techniques may have generated more family information?

Activity 6.2 My Family Journal: Assessing the Impact of Culture

The task is to draw a three-generation cultural genogram of your own family and summarize the impact of your culture in several pages. The purpose is to understand and assess the role of uniqueness and culture in your family system. Use any of the symbols suggested in the chapter or devise your own to illustrate cultural aspects of your family system. Use colors, pictures, stickers, or any other symbols to designate unique aspects of your family system culture. Then write a summary addressing the following points: (1) how these influences have impacted you, your behavior, your attitudes, and your belief system; (2) how your cultural influences and experiences might be a barrier or strength in working with a family.

Activity 6.3 Case Study: Sources of Support

Select either the McCoy family or the Del Sol family case and assess the sources of social support for that family using a social network map and grid. Based on one area of support—for example, concrete, emotional, or informational support—what thoughts or conclusions can you draw from this assessment tool? Using the information in this chapter to guide your assessment, determine three interventions to help this family based on the social support information.

▼▼▼

CHAPTER SEVEN

Evidence-Based
Family Interventions

How do we know what the best evidence-based practice is to use with a family? It depends on how much is known about a problem area and what the quality of the available research evidence is about that intervention. What do we mean by *evidence* in *evidence-based practice*? Evidence-based practices are interventions derived from sound research methodologies where the outcome findings consistently show that the interventions actually help clients change and improve (Drake, Goodman, Leff, Lehman, Dixon, Mueser, & Torry, 2003, cited in Thomlison & Corcoran, in press). It is the best available science about an intervention or treatment (McNeece & Thyer, 2004). The goal of evidence-based practice is to select the most accurate information derived from the best available research methods and to apply the information with fidelity. By *accurate* we simply mean the valid interventions (Corcoran, in press). There are different levels of quality or acceptable scientific evidence. It is not the intention of this book to review the research criteria (see Chambless & Hollon, 1998; McNeece & Thyer, 2004) needed, but rather to emphasize that the research should have used rigorous methods to test, support, or refute the approach, whether it was a case study or randomized controlled trials. As a clinician you will be interested in not only the research rigor used, but whether the best intervention available is the most useful for your client's circumstances (Corcoran & Vandiver, 2004; Gibbs, 2003).

The point to be emphasized here is that your treatment plans should select an intervention from the best available information to reflect your client's values and your practice preferences. Identifying evidence-based interventions requires that you first know what you want before you begin a search of the current literature to identify the best practice. You may find this information in a textbook, but the Internet now gives you access to many research sites and articles identifying best and promising interventions for specific problems experienced by families such as obsessive-compulsive disorders; parent–child behavior problems such as conduct disorder in a child; alcoholism and substance abuse; Alzheimer's or other chronic illness; delinquency; or child maltreatment. Within the context of this book, use of evidence-based family intervention means the following: a specific set of activities and accompanying skills developed to prevent a problem or promote, improve, or sustain functioning and the factors that contribute to it (Corcoran, 1992).

Effective family interventions are based on knowledge of the literature about what strategies are helpful for the assessed difficulties in the family system. Matching the interventions with the types of family issues and concerns is important. In general, data suggest that family-centered strategies are effective in modifying family and child relational functioning. The focus of family interventions is directed on three areas: cognitive, affective, and behavioral changes in families (Thornton, Craft, Dahlberg, Lynch, & Baer, 2000). Interventions need to examine or change problems and strengths in families. Addressing risk factors and providing protection from these factors are more likely to have powerful change effects.

Think about what goes on during daily family life within the presenting problem framework; you will see that problems can be addressed through strategies conceptualized as parenting (caregiving), teaching, supporting, providing, and relating. Understanding the behavioral and contextual factors of families, including the external and social factors of resources and supports, helps in planning the most appropriate resources. The goal of assessment is to plan the most appropriate intervention.

Developing an Intervention Plan

The family system is organized for stability; when its structure is threatened, the family's sense of stability is threatened. Any change from outside or inside the family system has the potential to disrupt the family system. Change can be both positive and negative, and families learn to cope with the stress of change by minimizing disruption and adapting. Problem-solving patterns emerge, and families find solutions to their stressors, for the most part. Thus habitual patterns arise through which issues and problems can be addressed as a matter of fact.

Sometimes families adhere to their patterns too rigidly and lack the flexibility to adapt when new problems arise. When families are "stuck" in these patterns, seeking help is a solution. Both the practitioner and the family need to understand the nature of this change process and what prevents the system from adapting to stressors.

Families are constantly confronted with the stability–change dilemma. Family practitioners differ in their opinions of how change occurs, but they know that change is ongoing in all families. Change does not always come from internal family sources; interactions with various systems outside the family can be change factors. As someone external to the family, the practitioner can serve as a catalyst for change.

Change can occur within individuals in the family and within the family structure itself. Change in family members is often called *first order* change. First order change is quantitative, gradual, and continuous and does not exceed the rules of the family. These changes are temporary and superficial in the family system because they leave the basic family structure and functioning unchanged. Second order changes are longer lasting (Nichols & Schwartz, 2005).

As a beginning practitioner, you should probably work on first order changes developing family members' inner strengths and beliefs that they can improve their situations—even if the change is modest at first. Small changes can positively affect future family functioning that will extend beyond the direct support of the practitioner and other social systems. It will move you toward the ultimate family goal: greater self-sufficiency and fewer total treatment needs (Thornton, Craft, Dahlberg, Lynch, & Baer, 2000).

All family interventions will fall into one of three areas: cognitive, affective, and behavioral domains. Interventions can be targeted at any one or all three domains. Many theorists (Alexander & Parsons, 1982; Franklin, 1999; Henggeler et al., 1998; Rothery & Enns, 2001 in press; Thyer, 1989; Whittaker, Schinke, & Gilchrist, 1986) agree that the most profound and sustained change will occur through changes in the family's belief system (cognitive). How a family thinks will determine how a family functions or behaves. In turn, these changes can affect the way family members relate to and feel about one another. The following situations are indications for family intervention:

- The family is experiencing suffering as a result of an emotional, physical or situational crisis.
- The family is experiencing stress due to a developmental milestone.
- The family defines a challenging behavior or problem.
- A child or adolescent is identified as having a challenging behavior or problem for the family.
- The family is experiencing communication and relationship issues.
- A family member is in need of mental health care.
- The family is experiencing stress due to intergenerational issues.

Selecting Realistic Goals

One of the most common practitioner errors is to establish unrealistic goals in an unrealistic time frame for families. Often practitioners set too many goals, and families find it impossible to reach them. Realistic expectations of what can be achieved need to be agreed on early in the relationship and spelled out in a contract with the family. Contracts can be written or verbal, but their goals must be explicit and never left only in the mind of the practitioner. Vague goals are unachievable goals. Together with the family, establish the goals for treatment based on the problems the family is most concerned with, the resources of the family, and the changes they would like to see. When families are involved in setting goals, they are more likely to achieve them.

The contract should describe both the practitioner's role and the family's role in the intervention. Expected gains, benefits, and other outcomes that may occur are also clearly explained, along with costs and time involved.

Focusing on Solutions

When practitioners focus on trying to understand *why* the family system is the way it is, little change will occur. Using *why* questions conveys a judgmental attitude, and the *why* question does not focus on solutions. These are called *lineal questions,* and they assume linear cause and effect (Tomm, 1988), focusing on identifying a problem in the family and producing less information about causality, interconnectedness, and recurrent patterns in the family relationships. Minimizing the use of questions that ask "*Why* did you . . . " serves the therapeutic change. Instead you should look at the here and now. Consider questions as a type of intervention: They should ask *what* is maintaining the problem, *what* is needed to make a change, *what* would it look like in the family if the problem was not here, and most important, *what* can be done to effect a change. These types of questions help initiate change in the family system by placing emphasis on family strengths, focusing on solutions, and avoid blaming someone or some event for the troubles. Focusing on solutions rather than causes is ultimately more useful.

Change is initiated when you ask questions that highlight *difference* in the family situation between the way it is now and the way it can be. The family seeks solutions, and self-direction is an important attribute to change. For example, what would be different if Carlos were not asthmatic? What would be different if mom did not work? What would you do differently if dad were to attend your soccer games? Benefits of these questions include a shift in family cognitive, affective, and behavioral functioning as they look differently, think differently, and begin to feel differently about the family and their circumstances.

Focusing on Family Strengths

Families have assets, strengths, energy sources, and other resources that can help them resolve their problems. Helping the family evaluate their strengths permits them to review their resources for solving their own dilemmas. Twelve family strengths have been identified, and this checklist helps practitioners build interventions for family change (Wright & Leahey, 1994):

1. Ability to address the physical, emotional, and spiritual needs of family members.
2. Ability to be sensitive to family members.
3. Ability to communicate through thoughts and feelings.
4. Ability to provide security, support, and encouragement.
5. Ability to initiate and maintain growth-producing relationships and experiences within and without the family.
6. Capacity to maintain and create constructive and responsible community relationships.
7. Ability to perform family roles flexibly.
8. Ability for self-help and to accept help when appropriate.
9. Capacity for mutual respect for the individuality of family members.
10. Ability to use a crisis experience as a means of growth—a challenge.
11. Concern for family unity, loyalty, and interfamily cooperation.
12. Ability to grow with and through children.

Changing Cognitions

Good intervention questions generate new ideas, opinions, or information about problem solving or behavior change. When you focus on what family members are thinking, you gather more data on the interactive family patterns. What does dad think when mom withdraws to the bedroom behind a closed door? Such questions focus on the connections between the ways families think, feel, and act about problem solving. The intent is to change a family's perceptions and beliefs about a problem or behavior. You can help families change the way they process information by changing the kinds of questions you ask. You can guide them toward thinking about their circumstances and solutions in a new light. These questions enhance family engagement in the process as families are asked what they think, feel, or do. Productive intervention questions may include these (Wright & Leahey, 1994, p.103):

- *Survival questions:* How have you managed to survive?
- *Support questions:* What people have given you special understanding? How did you find them?
- *Exception questions:* When things were going well in life, what was different?
- *Possibility questions:* What are your hopes, visions, and aspirations?
- *Esteem questions:* What are people likely to say about your good qualities? What about your life gives you real pride? How do you know when things are going well in your life?

When families think about your questions, they can see that they have attained accomplishments, and their past coping is a form of strength that includes relevant competencies to build on. As they change their view of themselves, frequently they can see solutions to their difficulties. Two techniques that can help with this are reframing and teaching.

Reframing   Turning problems into strengths requires practitioners to reframe family problems into abilities, a technique frequently used in family practice. This is accomplished by keeping the focus on individual and family strengths rather than problems and pathology. Reframing an issue or problem by relabeling a family's description of a behavior can change their conceptual or informational view of the situation and change the meaning and thinking associated with a situation or behavior. The new meaning may be a more acceptable one—for example, describing mother as loving rather than nosey; describing an adolescent as depressed rather than lazy; describing a young child as energetic and motivated rather than bad.

Teaching   Often both children and adults in families can benefit from education or information about a problem or way of handling a problem. Families develop myths about illness or behavior; parent skills, child development information, or health education can teach families how new information and information processing affects their behavior. Changing behavior changes beliefs. Families learn strategies for recognizing and regulating feelings, and through modeling and coaching practice, they learn to apply new skills. Many times education and information are not sufficient, and in these situations coaching, mentoring, and parent–child management in the form of parent training are necessary. These interventions are effective if applied in the early stages of most child problems and when parents are engaged in parent-training activities for a prolonged period. Parents in the most need and with the most difficult child problems, such as early signs of aggression, are more difficult to retain in these approaches, but parent–child management programs are effective (Corcoran, 2000; Mulvey, Arthur, & Reppucci, 2000). To effect change with these families, practitioners must be persistent and patient.

Changing Affective Factors

The emotional state of families influences their abilities to deal with problems. Although many factors contribute to the way family members feel and the affect they display in certain situations, their reactions are often related to their lives, and they frequently reflect the stress and disorder of poverty, past experiences of trauma, or other contextual and structural factors that are discouraging and overwhelming. There may be specific psychological diagnoses among one or more family members, such as conduct disorders, anxiety disorders, depression, schizophrenia, or substance abuse. Some family members may have deeply ingrained but unproductive ways of responding to conflict, such a being quick to withdraw, shout, become angry, or leave the room. Emotional states play an important role in how people process information, and this affects their problem solving. Family members need to recognize that what they feel and what they say and do or don't do affects others. Help individuals shift their focus through role-playing with family members with whom they have emotional or interpersonal difficulties: this can help them see the issue from the other people's perspectives, as well as how they feel.

Practitioners can help families see the connections between feelings and behaviors. A wife may feel isolated because her husband does not involve her in family decision making. Her sense that she is undervalued may express itself as anger toward her husband on many levels. The practitioner can help her identify her feelings when she is left out of family decisions and clarify what is needed to effect change. The practitioner must also help the husband realize that listening to others' concerns and feelings develops support and competencies throughout the family unit. Developing support in families is important to changing emotional and affectional states and developing positive relations.

Changing Behavioral Factors

Most problems in families concern behaviors. Behavior is regulated through both cognitive and behavioral processes. This is important information for practitioners because it has direct implications for practice. Behavior and affect problems are the result of faulty or distorted thinking or belief systems, which contribute to inappropriate behaviors. That is, family problems are translated into behaviors. Behaviors are observable, measurable, and changeable. Change is accomplished through altering what happens before and after the specified behavior occurs. There are many reinforcing and aversive events in any family situation, and identifying current and alternative triggers is the first step in changing them.

Initially you must determine who has the problem (for example, father and son), what the difficulty is or what needs to be changed (father never spends time with son), and when the problem occurs (after dinner). The family system involved in the interaction must acknowledge the difficulty, confirm the context in which it occurs, and then agree on aspects of the relationship that need change. Information or cues from father to son may be misinterpreted as "I don't want to spend time with you." This is in part based on their prior experiences and characteristics. If the father has a history of always going to sleep on the couch after dinner and becoming angry if someone wakes him, then the son is likely to avoid his father, act rejected and angry, and interpret his father's behavior as negative toward him. You will need to help the family imagine a number of possible solutions or behavioral responses to the presenting interaction, a process called *generating alternatives*. From these, father and son can choose a solution or alternative to the situation. Then the parent and son will need to practice or rehearse the interaction to learn how to modify their existing behavior. Both may need assistance in expressing appropriate and effective responses. After the role-play interaction, the father and son should analyze their behavior and reformulate other responses, if necessary. Role-play, rehearsal, and coaching are techniques to address behavior change. Be sure to critique both the content of what is said or performed and the way it is presented (actions).

Devising rituals can help families develop new behaviors. Daily rituals such as bedtime reading with father, yearly rituals such as celebrating each family member's successes, and cultural rituals such as eating an ethnic meal dressed in traditional clothes can all improve the family environment. Rituals do not always need to have a celebratory purpose; sometimes they can be created to provide clarity in a family system or to break the family's conflict patterns (DeMaria, Weeks, & Hof, 1999). Suppose stepparents cannot agree on parenting practices and often give conflicting messages to their children. Confusion is the message received by children, and this may exacerbate any problem behaviors they are exhibiting. Introducing a ritual of odd-day and even-day parenting may reduce the chaos. Mother may assume care of children on odd-numbered days, with father taking care of them on even-numbered days. On Sundays both parents could share the responsibility and not comment on the other's parenting. This ritual can help the family develop a routine and understand the impact of their behavior (Wright & Leahey, 1994).

Creating Opportunities

Regardless of how family problems manifest themselves, complex problems are embedded in psychosocial systems—primarily the family and community. These multisystemic influences shape the family, and change efforts will be affected by these interactions. Be aware of systems in the community such as schools, hospitals, and other agencies with which the family is involved. Each of these systems operates within a practice and policy context, and their larger context can produce information that may be conflicting and confusing to the family; their services may replace the family's own resources (Henggeler et al., 1998; Imber Coppersmith, 1983; Rothery & Enns, 2001), leaving the family feeling inadequate. Practitioners should also examine carefully the environments of the family—its cultural milieu, biculturalism, ethnic status, language, acculturation stress, social class, customs, history, and sexual orientation. Creating opportunities for supporting the family in these social systems can help return resources and stability to the family system.

Practitioners must understand that both positive and negative family behaviors influence and are influenced by multiple systems, internally and externally. Understanding and comparing the values and attitudes of the multiple systems interacting with the family system are critical and necessary practitioner tasks. To serve families, the practitioner and the systems interacting with families must be free of personal, policy, and practice biases that tend to force families into unproductive patterns (Henggeler et al., 1998). These multiple systems can undermine, thwart, or even inhibit change within a family if they are not working together. Creative use of the families' own resources cannot emerge if barriers impede the family members' opportunities for growth and change.

Choosing interventions in multiple systems requires consideration of the following information:

- What are the systems the family is involved with?
- What are the relationships between the family and the systems?
- Is the family blamed for their problems by any of the systems they are involved with?
- What is the perception of the problem from each system's view?
- How do the family and the systems define the problems? (Imber Coppersmith, 1983)

When the nature of the family's relationships with other systems has been determined, interventions can be directed at the appropriate systems to address the external elements that must be involved in family change. Within the system relationship, the interventions are based on having the family take responsibility for viewing their resources as an asset and the community services as a support. The family and its members begin to build skills and knowledge that will help them to be independent of the practitioner and self-sufficient.

The information imparted to families contributes to changing their perceptions and beliefs about their problems, needs, and resources. Therefore, one way to shift how families perceive their reality and way of interacting is to focus on the cognitive, affective, and behavioral constructs of the family system.

Selecting Interventions

A search for evidence-based interventions will likely provide several interventions to select and adapt to your client. You will find that your client is not exactly the same as noted in the literature or the description by experts, and you will have to carefully consider the credibility of the evidence and your client's unique characteristics to guide the procedures (Corcoran, in press). On the other hand, interventions do not start some time after the relationship is under way; they begin with the first contact the family has with you, continuing through interviewing and on to termination. With so many types of interventions available, how do you choose? Start by reviewing the characteristics of the family and their referred concerns and issues. Also, consider the most appropriate settings the intervention is to be used in, based on research about the identified problems of the family. Then review the family goals and objectives. The intervention you choose should satisfy all of the requirements identified. It should also be culturally appropriate. The family must participate in the choice of intervention.

The goal is to ensure that the most effective services available are provided to families. However, what does this mean, exactly, for the practitioner and family? Corcoran and Videka-Sherman (1992, p. 25) offer this: "You need to fit your practice to the client problem . . . the client must be prepared for the intervention, and . . . you must specify the purpose of the intervention and provide as much prescriptive, time-limited structure as possible . . . defining [everything] as clearly and concisely as possible in order to replicate the components that facilitate client change." Clearly, families should have the intervention that has been shown to be the most effective in solving their type of difficulty. Vandiver (2002) notes that more successful work has been done on developing evidence-based interventions than has occurred in distributing guidelines and protocols or seeing that they are easily available for routine or real-world practice (Thomlison & Corcoran, in press). The burden of this task, then, falls to you. This is much facilitated if you can find interventions that are manualized, such as family psychoeducation for mental illness (Botsford & Rule, 2004; Goodman, 2004; Toseland, McCallion, Smith, & Banks, 2004) that are structured in a step-by-step format, for example, obsessive compulsive disorder (Steketee, 1999); or contain treatment protocols, such as the best practice guidelines for assessment of domestic violence in health care settings developed by the Domestic Violence Prevention Fund (see http://www.guideline.gov/summary/summary.aspx?view_id=1&doc_id=5529), which provide practical steps and procedures for facilitating client change. Most likely you will need to structure the intervention into a workable treatment plan, which means the session-by-session planning is critical for the particular client condition (Thomlison & Corcoran, in press).

Usually no single intervention can address all issues in a family; problem behaviors are generally maintained by multiple factors. Therefore, it is best to consider several interventions or strategies that are coordinated and will complement one another. For example, social skills training for aggressive young children to develop competence in peer play may be complemented with a home visit strategy focused on parent training (LeCroy, 1994; Thomlison & Craig, 2005). These are both evidence-supported interventions to improve social and emotional competence and skills in young children and their families (Thornton et al., 2000). Families have a right to receive the intervention strategy that is noted to be effective, even though it is argued that not all clients are "guaranteed to benefit from" the intervention (Thyer & Wodarski, 1998, p. 13). Carefully consider the interventions based on resources, level of acceptance for the family, and your experience.

Ideally, best practices are based on rigorous evaluations of interventions for specific problems and then reported in peer-reviewed literature. However, a number of factors complicate this. First, for some problem areas research is not well developed and contains few longitudinal and randomized control studies. Second, when studies have evaluated the outcome of interventions, the effectiveness for various populations usually requires more research and support. Finally, it is not the intention of this book to provide in-depth information about interventions, but rather to suggest strategies based on the empirically tested principles and experience of the application of multisystemic family work for certain common family problems, particularly for settings where time-limited constraints exist. Practitioners have a responsibility to keep abreast of the literature so they will be aware of the most current and effective treatments for various problems and populations. Those who systematically plan and evaluate their own work will greatly improve the accuracy of their clinical judgment in assessment and in monitoring change during intervention (Roberts & Yeager, 2004; Thyer, 1994; Thomlison, 1984; Tutty, 1990; Vandiver, 1992). The following practice guidelines have evolved from research on intervention outcome:

- *Planned*, systematic efforts at facilitating change lead to more effective outcomes than *unplanned*, informal help for families.
- Intervention of a structured, directed, and time-limited nature is effective.
- Some interventions are better than no interventions.

Parent and Family-Based Strategies

Parent and family-based interventions are strategies that combine parenting skills and education about child development with skills for improving communication and reducing conflict in families. These strategies improve family relationships. Interventions should be introduced at the first signs of risk factors so that they may have a substantial effect in reducing problems, particularly in children with early aggression, which can be identified at age 3 (Tremblay, 2000).

Using parent training or parent education strategies with a behavioral focus for families of children with conduct problems has substantial empirical support (Corcoran, 2000). Home-based family strategies are highly recommended as the treatment of choice because they allow practitioners to observe and address parenting practices that need modification in the actual setting and time that they occur. Parenting practices and family environment play an important role in the development of conduct difficulties among preschool children (Dishion & Kavanagh, 2003). Coercive parenting practices and poor supervision account for about 50% of the conduct problems displayed in fifth grade children from all reports.

Common parenting and family protective factors used by effective parents include:

- Nonviolent methods of teaching and discipline with children.
- High levels of warmth and acceptance and low levels of criticism.
- Low levels of stress and aggression in the family.
- High levels of monitoring and supervision of children.
- A positive and supportive parent–child relationship.
- The presence of a supportive spouse or partner.
- Socioeconomic stability and success at work and school.
- Sufficient social supports and positive adult role models in their lives (Dishion & Kavanagh, 2003; Thomlison & Craig, 2005; Thomlison, 2004).

Poor parenting practices significantly increase the risk of children's psychosocial problems, mental disorders, and adverse outcomes, whereas effective parenting during infancy and early childhood is a protective pathway for health, well-being, and competence of children and adolescents (Ehrensaft, Wasserman, Verdelli, Greenwald, Miller, & Davies, 2003).

Parent training programs are an effective evidence-based intervention to teach parents of difficult children how to discipline more effectively and manage disruptive behaviors and conduct disorders. These programs have four components: assessment of parenting issues; teaching parents new skills; helping parents apply the new techniques, through homework or out-of-session practice, with their children; and facilitator feedback (Taylor & Biglan, 1998). Parenting problems rest on the following assumptions:

- Conduct problems in young children are formed and maintained by the family environment.
- Parents unknowingly reinforce noncompliant child behaviors or fail to reinforce the behaviors they wish to see more often in the child.

- Coercive parent–child cycles develop when parents use harsh parenting practices (such as corporal punishment) to deal with disruptive or noncompliant behavior in their children.
- Parents can be taught to have greater positive influence on their children's behaviors.
- Parents can be taught to implement and reinforce prosocial conduct in their children's behaviors.
- Positive parent–child interaction is critical for attachment to develop.

Changing Boundaries

Many child–parent problems involve family system boundaries—that is, the limits between subsystems. The invisible boundaries of family systems can be thought of as barriers holding outsiders out and holding insiders in and setting limits on the kinds of communication that will occur between the subsystems. In an effort to remain stable and respond to various stressors, families can make their boundaries too rigid and unyielding or can develop boundaries that are so permeable they fail to define the subsystem sufficiently. Either too rigid or overly flexible boundaries can be maladaptive. For example, the boundaries between parents and children should allow parental direction and control and no confusion. When the boundaries are too permeable, then children are in control and authority is removed from the parent role. To change the boundary separating parent and child, consider the following:

- What needs to be strengthened? This may mean providing information and education for reinforcing positive ideas about parenting and supporting strategies for renegotiating new boundaries.
- Whom must I support to promote the change? A parent who fears loss of power, or a parent who fears losing what little control he or she has, needs support. Adding a boundary is necessary when the parent treats all children the same, failing to recognize they are in different developmental stages. Recognizing that differences exist between the children, the parents must define a boundary by implementing a new practice in the family—such as different bedtimes, more responsibility for the older child, or some other way of acknowledging the oldest child. Removing a boundary may also be necessary. An example might be an excessively rigid boundary between the parent subsystem. Marital difficulties may emerge, spilling into the parent–child subsystem. Breaking triangles and forming or rearranging alliances will be necessary.
- What change is necessary? When changing boundaries, people can make them more rigid or loose, adding or removing them. This is done by methods called "joining with the family" (accepting or accommodating to families to win their confidence and circumvent resistance), suggesting change, and coaching parents through the process. No matter what you do, regarding boundaries, you will be ineffective unless you have joined appropriately with all those who will be influenced by the changes you initiate.

Changing the emotional climate is necessary. The mood of a family needing help will vary from anger to depression to frustration to discouragement. Your task is to identify the mood by acknowledging each member's right to feel this way under the circumstances and then to lighten the load by providing a clear message of hope that something can be done. Regardless of the severity of the difficulties, family systems and their individual members need opportunities to grow, learn, and develop. Asking the family for an inventory of their preferred solutions, action steps, previous attempts at intervention, and barriers to success keeps the focus on the family system strengths.

Evidence-Based Family Interventions

Literature evaluating the benefits of interventions and program outcomes to support family problems and parent–child problems can be found in the empirical literature and evidence-based practice Web site directly applicable to practice with specific problems (McNeece & Thyer, 2004).

Here are some useful databases and organizational resources for beginning practitioners to access for common family problems:

- For substance abuse treatment and family therapy, see SAMHSA; there are several treatment improvement protocols (TIP 39): http://alcoholism.about.com/od/fam/a/blsam041004.htm.
- For families with juvenile offenders, multisystemic family treatment can be explored at http://www.dsgonline.com/Model_Programs_Guide/Web/mpg_index_flash.htm.
- Brief strategic family therapy to prevent and treat child and adolescent behavior problems is discussed at http://www.dsgonline.com/mpg_non_flash/WebForm4_Demo_Supplemental_Detail.aspx?id=305.
- Functional family therapy for complex adolescent problems, high-risk youth, and their families is examined at http://www.dsgonline.com/mpg_non_flash/WebForm4_Demo_Supplemental_Detail.aspx?id=29.
- Multidimensional family therapy is for youth with behavior and substance abuse problems and their families is discussed at http://www.dsgonline.com/mpg_non_flash/WebForm4_Demo_Supplemental_Detail.aspx?id=361.
- Multisystemic family therapy to reduce system barriers for youth with substance abuse and conduct problems and their families is explored at http://www.dsgonline.com/mpg_non_flash/WebForm4_Demo_Supplemental_Detail.aspx?id=363.

The Family Assessment Report

Practitioners may be asked to write up the information from a family assessment in one of several different ways; each agency and supervisor will have a preferred way of recording data gathered from a family. Regardless of the headings used, the information should be organized to indicate system problems and strengths in an integrated fashion. The assessment for each of these areas is summarized and the goal for change is recorded. The intervention plan flows from the data and from what you know about the effectiveness of treatment protocols. When you do not have complete data, it is also wise to record "practitioner impressions" until more information is available to substantiate or change the impressions. Hypotheses can also be recorded and verified later. The following headings are suggested.

Assessment of _____ Family

1. Identify specific problems, issues, and concerns.
2. Referred by_____.
3. Date(s) and location(s) of family assessment.

Family Structure and Development

1. Composition, including members of extended family (genogram data).
2. Descriptive data such as ages, marriages, employment.
3. Culture, religion.

Family Functioning (Attachment and Relational Systems of Family)

1. Roles
2. Communication
3. Problem solving
4. Beliefs
5. Alliances/coalitions
6. Concrete supports
7. Emotional supports
8. Instrumental supports

Family Strengths and Problems (Structural, Developmental, and Functional)

Individual Strengths and Problems (Physical, Psychological, and Social)
Marital subsystem, parent–child subsystem, sibling subsystem, individual subsystem.

Assessment Measures Used

Summary/Hypothesis

Goals

Intervention Plan

Plan for Update and Review
Remember that the report is a summary and will not contain all of the information gleaned from the family meetings. It represents an integration of theory and practice, and it must be written in a professional style. Interventions are based on the level of family functioning, the practitioner's expertise, and the context of service. Always keep progress notes and record information as it changes.

Summary

- Intervention planning follows logically from the assessment and must address the problems (risk factors) or strengths (protective factors) targeted for change.
- Assessment is ongoing, multifaceted, and focused on understanding the ways in which behavioral problems function with family relationship systems. Interventions in the same way are ongoing, multipronged, and focused on change in cognitions, affect, and behavior.
- Understand the fact that you, the practitioner, are an active part of the family system and the construction of change.
- What you perceive about a family's situation is obtained by the information you have from the family, your experiences, and the literature.
- Documenting the assessment information is the plan of action.
- Evidence-based interventions and practices are informed by research.
- When thoughtfully applied, evidence-based practice will likely strengthen a treatment plan, and in turn will increase the likelihood of client change and the goal of the intervention.
- Assessment is the guide to selecting the appropriate diagnosis, practice guideline, and intervention.
- Use information from all evidence-based sources (systematic reviews, expert consensus, and practice guidelines) as a guide for determining the most appropriate intervention (Vandiver, 2002).

Learning Activities

Activity 7.1 Exploring Resources

Write your answers to the following questions, and then discuss your response with your classmates.
1. How similar or dissimilar are the interventions and resources needed among individuals?
   a. In exploring your current situation, what might you do to enhance your situation so you have sufficient psychological, emotional, physical, spiritual, and social resources to succeed in school?

b. Based on your current level of self-awareness and self-understanding, what one issue would you want to explore with a social worker? What can be done differently to change your problem?

2. After thinking about your situation with respect to the above questions, what resources do you think families are most likely to require for success?

3. Locate a Web site with evidence-based information about whether social support is an effective intervention. Check out the empirically based literature. Identify the problem area that social support is best matched to.

Activity 7.2 Case Study

1. Choose either the McCoy family or the LaTorre family. Use circular questioning to change cognitive thinking as both an assessment and an intervention technique.

2. Using the same case, apply these questions to changing cognitive thinking:
   a. Write a question that highlights differences in relationship.
   b. Write a question that highlights differences in time.
   c. Construct a working hypothesis about what is happening.
   d. Write a question that indicates survival of their circumstances.
   e. Write a question that illustrates exceptions to their difficulties.
   f. What would the possibility question be for the family?

3. Identify an evidence-based intervention for the case to introduce to the family. Using role-play, have a student therapist and members of the family present to introduce the intervention during a family meeting.

▼▼▼

CHAPTER EIGHT

Linking Assessment and Intervention

Tools for collecting and organizing data were discussed in Chapter 6, but along with organizing family data you will need to know whether improvement has taken place. Information about change helps the family to maintain or increase their motivation and involvement in the process of change. It helps you understand whether specific intervention strategies need to be maintained, adjusted, changed, or stopped and whether goals have been met. This monitoring allows you to determine the effectiveness of the intervention. There are various ways to measure the changes, and regardless of which one you use, the important point is for you to assess the family's progress. It is best to obtain information about family functioning by gathering data from several perspectives.

Selecting Measures to Use

Two primary concerns for evaluation of practice are deciding what measure to use and deciding where and when to obtain the measurements. Data from multiple perspectives help determine *what* types of information you will need to evaluate progress on. You must still decide *how* you will collect information in a systematic way. Corcoran and Gingerich (1992) identify two ways to obtain this information: by individualized and standardized measures of family functioning. They recommend that both be used in practice evaluation.

Individualized Measures
Individualized measures are designed specifically for the family's unique problem or situation of concern. Individualized measures are tailored and developed for the personal concerns of the family. They are usually suitable for obtaining daily feedback on the targeted behavior, which can be stated in behavioral terms for ease of observation (Corcoran & Gingerich, 1992, p. 35). Individualized measures were discussed in Chapter 6 under mapping, graphic, and self-report tools. These individualized tools are not standardized measures, but they show change,

are meaningful to the family and practitioner, and are easy to use because family members are involved in their development.

Standardized Measures

Standardized self-report measures or questionnaires provide information based on constructs from various theoretical models of family functioning. These measures provide information about family functioning in comparison to other families on specific areas or problems. Standardized measures help us verify the findings obtained from the individualized measures. These measures are scales and questionnaires that have known reliability and validity and often have been developed or normed for specific populations with clinical problems. It is usual to administer such measures only a few times during treatment, such as before and after the intervention and at some follow-up period. You need to be sure that the measure is administered in a standardized way so you can be certain that you are measuring the same thing each time you use it (Corcoran & Gingerich, 1992, p. 35).

The type of measure most commonly used is often referred to as *rapid assessment instruments (RAI)*. A rapid assessment instrument may be referred to as an *index, checklist, scale,* or *inventory*. *Rapid* refers to the ease with which such instruments can be completed due to their clear, simple language, uncomplicated instructions, and brevity. RAIs are completed by the family, the practitioner, or significant others and are used to assess the degree, intensity, or magnitude of the problem being measured. Twenty or fewer items are considered short, but measures will vary in length and in the amount of time needed by a family or individual to complete them. Scoring is also uncomplicated and takes little time. The results are easily interpreted using the guidelines provided with the instrument.

Using a rapid assessment instrument can help evaluate the accuracy of the family assessment, determine the appropriateness of the intervention plan, and indicate the degree of success of the interventions used. Clinical judgments can be enhanced through systematic measurement using a standardized measure. These measures do not require adherence to a particular theoretical stance or specific intervention strategies. Flexibility in thinking is possible. The scores collected by measuring the same problem or concern at various points can easily be plotted on a graph and provide a visual representation of change because the score obtained at one time can be compared to another. Visual accounts are powerful feedback mechanisms of change.

Rapid assessment instruments have many advantages, but it is important that you do not rely fully on these tools for a complete picture of the family or its problems. Remember that the information you receive from these measures is only an estimate—a one-time picture of the problem as measured by the instrument. These measures rely on a small set of domains of a given problem and as such do not provide information about all dimensions of the situation. Family functioning is complex. For example, a depression scale may ask about withdrawing from friends but not tap similar behavior with family or the fact that the person has few social contacts to begin with. After comparing the psychometric and practical considerations of six commonly used family functioning scales, Tutty (1995) has suggested that practitioners approach measures with caution. She recommends three measures of family functioning—Family Assessment Device (FAD), Index of Family Relations (IFR), and Self-Report Family Inventory (SFI) (Tutty, 1995). More specific tools are discussed in later sections of this chapter.

Guidelines for Using Measurement Tools

Measurement is not an end in itself. It is a means by which you and family members can gain clarity about the focus of change and how you will know when change has occurred. The success or failure of measuring progress may well depend on how you present the measurement tasks to the family. The following guidelines adapted from Thomlison and Bradshaw (2002) will help you present the measure in the best possible light to the family:

1. *Be familiar with the measure:* Gain some firsthand experience by completing the measure yourself. This way you will know how it works and how long it will take to complete.

You will also become familiar with the language used in the measure. Families often ask the meaning of words or the intent of questions that we might take for granted. Do it yourself first!

2. *Discuss with the family the importance and purpose of the measure:* Let them know what they will gain from the experience and what information they will and will not receive from it. An open discussion is essential; it alleviates anxieties and generates cooperation.

3. *Address the family with accuracy and honesty about the purpose and focus of the measure:* They may need to be convinced that an accurate snapshot is more beneficial than a flattering one. This will be more possible if you have developed trust within the engagement phase of the helping relationship.

4. *Make sure the measure is culturally sensitive and gender bias free:* Review the measure with the family before you ask them to complete it on their own. Be sensitive to a number of family factors, including literacy and social and cultural issues that may influence the family's ability to complete the measure. You may need to make some adaptations for the administration of the measure, such as reading it to the family, making a tape recording of the measure, or substituting more appropriate language.

5. *Give feedback:* Give the family specific feedback from the measure. This means giving them more than just the total score. You can use individual items or details from the measure to discuss strengths as well as areas for further intervention and change. Measures are a form of clinical intervention, and families want to know how their problem is viewed and how it is changing. This is a form of feedback and motivation.

Remember that all measurement should be simple, practical, unobtrusive, and culturally appropriate and should provide valuable information for you and the family.

Measuring Common Family Problems

Many varied standardized measures in the literature can be used as part of assessing change and goal attainment of the family system or members of the family. An overview of a few of these measures is provided here. For a comprehensive review of the RAI literature you may want to refer to Corcoran and Fischer (2000).

Rapid assessment instruments that can be useful in the assessment of families include both multidimensional and specific problem indexes. These problem-oriented rapid assessment measures are helpful for tracking progress. Even though the measures focus on problems, you can use details from the instrument to highlight family strengths. While you focus on these problem areas, keep in mind the impact of other environmental systems on the functioning of the family and family members. Rapid assessment instruments developed by social worker W. W. Hudson (1982, 1990a, 1990b, 1992a) are presented as relevant to family and individual functioning and meeting the criteria discussed earlier.

Many families who come to see you have multiple problem areas of concern. A multiproblem assessment instrument may be the best way to obtain an overall picture of family functioning during assessment. An excellent example of this type of assessment instrument is the *Multi-Problem Screening Inventory* (MPSI) (Hudson, 1990b). This instrument assesses 27 common areas of family and individual functioning, such as family relationship problems, alcohol and drug abuse, personal stress, and partner or child problems. With some families the MPSI may be given in its entirety to focus attention toward specific problem areas. These specific areas may then be explored in more depth with problem-specific standardized measures. With other families one or several parts of the MPSI may be of specific relevance, and only these parts may need to be administered.

Measures that contribute to the assessment of families with multiple problems cluster around issues such as child problems, parent and/or marital problems, and family stress. A review of some rapid assessment instruments will be organized using these broad categories. The reader is referred to Corcoran and Fischer (2000) for greater detail and information about obtaining the measures to follow.

Family Functioning

Measures for overall family functioning, with children age 12 or above, include the following inventories:

- The *Family Assessment Device* (FAD) (Epstein, Baldwin, & Bishop, 1983) contains 60 items on a 4-point Likert-type scale measuring family problem solving, communication, roles, affective responsiveness, affective involvement, and behavior control. There is also a 12-item General Functioning Scale that can be used as a global measure of family health/pathology (Tutty, 1995).
- The *Index of Family Relations* (IFR) (Hudson, 1990a) is a 25-item measure on a 5-point Likert-type scale requiring 10 minutes to administer. This unidimensional scale measures the severity and extent of problems experienced by family members (overall family stress—how well family members get along).
- The *Self-Report Family Inventory* (SFI) (Beavers & Hampson, 1990) is a 36-item measure on 5-point Likert-type scale requiring 15 minutes to administer. This scale is associated with a model of health family functioning (Tutty, 1995) and may be useful for diverse ethnic and socioeconomic family structures.

Child Problems

Hard-to-manage child behaviors may result in many different forms of parent–child conflict. The following measures focus on the parent–child relationship or subsystem. They measure the impact of both child and parent behaviors on the quality of this relationship. Assessing specifics of child behaviors can be done with other standardized assessment instruments, such as the *Behavior Rating Index for Children* (Stiffman et al., 1984) or the *Eyberg Child Behavior Inventory* (Burns & Patterson, 1990).

- The *Multi-Problem Screening Inventory* (Hudson, 1990b) contains 13 items about the parents' perception of their relationship with the child, while other scales assess areas of functioning such as school problems and family problems. The *Index of Family Relations* and the *Index of Brother and Sister Relations* (Hudson, 1992) measure the extent to which family members have problems in their relationships with one another.
- The *Child's Attitude Toward Father and Mother Scales* (Hudson, 1992) uses 25 items to assess some problems children have with their parents.
- The *Parent–Child Relationship Survey* (Fine & Schwebel, 1983) has 24 items that are designed to assess the quality of the parent–child relationship from the parent's point of view.

Parent and Marital Problems

Parenting skills and parent characteristics such as depression, marital conflict, or substance abuse have a profound effect on the negative feedback loop between parent and child that often develops into negative event chains within the family. A number of rapid assessment instruments measure the degree or intensity of such parent problems.

Parenting Skills   Poor parenting skills often influence the child problems that bring families to seek help.

- The *Adult–Adolescent Parenting Inventory* (Bavolek, 1984) is a 32-item measure that assesses the parenting and child-rearing domains of expectations, empathy to child needs, discipline practices, and parent–child roles of both the adolescent and the parents.

- The *Parental Nurturance Scale* (Buri, Misukanis, & Mueller, 1989) assesses the level of parental nurturance and care from the child's perspective.
- The *Parental Locus of Control Scale* (Campis, Lyman, & Prentice-Dunn, 1986) is designed to assess child versus parent power in child-rearing situations.
- The *Parental Bonding Instrument* (Parker, Tupling, & Brown, 1979) offers an assessment of the parental attitudes and behaviors from the child's viewpoint.

Marital Conflict   Marital conflict can lead to significant repercussions within the family, such as family dissolution and divided loyalty.

- The *Multi-Problem Screening Inventory* (Hudson, 1990a contains sections on sexual discord and partner problems. The *Index of Marital Satisfaction* (Hudson, 1992) measures the presence and magnitude of problems in the couple relationship.
- The *Kansas Marital Conflict Scale* (Eggeman, Moxley, & Schumm, 1985) assesses the stages of marital conflict and the responses of both parties.
- The *Beier–Sternberg Discord Questionnaire* (Beier & Sternberg, 1977) assesses two domains of the couple relationship: the degree of agreement/disagreement on key couple issues and the level of unhappiness associated with any marital relationship.

Family Violence   Family problems can be related to partner abuse. This abuse may take many forms: emotional, financial, physical, and/or sexual abuse. The abuse may be limited to the adult partner or may also involve the children directly. Either way, any form of within-family abuse will impact the family as a whole and each member.

- The *Multi-Problem Screening Inventory* (Hudson, 1990a contains 13 questions about the parents' perception of their relationship with the child and possible child maltreatment. The *Partner Abuse Scale (non-physical and physical)* (Hudson, 1992) as well as the *Non-Physical Abuse of Partner Scale* and *Physical Abuse of Partner Scale* (Garner & Hudson, 1992) assesses the physical and nonphysical abuse that families disclose having inflicted on their partners or having been inflicted by their partners. The scales measure three types of nonphysical abuse: emotional, sexual, and financial abuse.
- The *Conflict Tactics Scales* (Straus & Gelles, 1990) attempts to measure three factors related to violence in the family: reasoning, verbal aggression, and physical violence.

Child Maltreatment   Risk assessment for child maltreatment forms an important part of some family assessments. These measures attempt to predict the harm potential for the children *within* the family setting. These instruments generally consider multiple dimensions, including child, caretaker, and family characteristics as well as environmental and parent–child interaction factors. Evaluating the likelihood of future harm to children remaining in the family is a daunting task even with the assistance of risk assessment scales. Risk assessment is related to but not identical to safety assessment. The safety assessment focuses on immediate risk of severe harm in order that decisions can be made about remaining with a caretaker. Risk assessment however is concerned with maltreatment over the long term or in the future. Limitations of these measures have been noted by Gambrill and Shlonsky (2000; 2001) and Rycus and Hughes (2003), but many child protection agencies use these measures as well as others to assess family potential for re-abuse. Some characteristics measured by these multidimensional measures include child characteristics, family characteristics, environmental factors, access to the child by the perpetrator, caretaker characteristics, maltreatment characteristics, and parent–child interaction (Jordan & Franklin, 2003, p. 255). Three examples of risk assessment scales follow:

- The *Child Well-Being Scales* (Magura & Moses, 1986) measure a child's well-being in terms of the degree to which physical, social, and emotional needs are met. These scales are used to document the severity of various forms of maltreatment in behavior-specific terms. Forty-three separate factors measure four categories: parenting role performance, familial capacities, child role performance, and child capacities, from adequate to increasing degrees of inadequate.

- The *Family Risk Scales* (Magura, Moses, & Jones, 1987) measure parent characteristics and family conditions using individual rating scales on 26 dimensions of child and caretaker characteristics. This measure looks specifically at the need for out-of-home placement and the need for and effectiveness of preventive services (Baird & Wagner, 2000; Rycus & Hughes, 2001).
- The *Illinois CANTS* (Illinois Division of Child Protection) (Lyons, Doueck & Wodarski, 1996) measure identifies 13 risk factors grouped into the categories of child factors and family caretaker factors and assesses risk of both abuse and neglect. Priority assignment of cases, risk of harm to a child, and resolution of eight investigative decisions are included.

Substance Abuse   Substance abuse may be an important factor in family problem development and maintenance.

- The *Multi-Problem Screening Inventory* (Hudson, 1990a, 1992) contains two sections related to substance abuse: alcohol abuse and drug abuse. The statements explore the extent of the problem and the impact on family members.
- The *Index of Alcohol Involvement* (Hudson & Garner, 1992) measures the degree of problems related to the use of alcohol by a family member.

Family and Environmental Stress   Stress strongly influences family problems. At times of stress, family members are often not able to access usual areas of strengths. Stress may be chronic or more situational. The sources of stress may be related to child or family development events, marital stress, extended family situations, and community factors.

- The *Multi-Problem Screening Inventory* (Hudson, 1990b) contains a section on personal stress. The *Index of Clinical Stress* (Hudson, 1992) measures the family's level of stress as they perceive it.
- The *Impact of Events Scale* (Horowitz, Wilner, & Alvarez, 1979) can be used to assess the level of stress associated with traumatic events.
- The *Adolescent–Family Inventory of Life Events and Changes* (McCubbin, Patterson, Bauman, & Harris, 1991) is designed to measure changes within the family through assessing changes in the level of family stress as perceived by adolescent family members.
- The *Family Coping Inventory* (McCubbin, Boss, Wilson & Dahl, 1991) is a 70-item measure of partner responses to family stress.
- The *Family Hardiness Index* (McCubbin, McCubbin, & Thompson, 1991) is designed to assess family hardiness using 20 statements that indicate the amount of control that family members perceive they have over outcomes of life events.

Evaluating Family Change

Although you are probably observing positive results during the treatment of the family, the best results are those that are maintained over time or continue long after you have terminated services. But remember, the goals you set with the family in the beginning provide a basis for the evaluation of the intervention plan. You had a set of goals that you established in some priority order. You defined the goals clearly and with specific objectives so you would know if you were progressing toward the goals. This is the evaluation process. Evaluation is a systematic set of activities designed to measure either the effectiveness of the change process or the outcomes of the change efforts. Monitoring helps keep track of changes and considers how well these goals are being achieved. Is there progress toward the resolution of the target problem behaviors?

Monitoring   Monitoring involves ongoing data collection to obtain new information and/or evaluate the need for a change of interventions. This is usually done to provide continuous output information about the family's problems. Data are collected about family characteristics, problems, and services provided, as well as changes during treatment, at termination, and even after discharge. Thus continuous evaluation functions as a feedback system for both the family and the practitioner in order to modify and improve intervention activities. By tracking efforts toward family goal achievement, a continuous identification of intervention activities or strategies can be facilitated (Thomlison & Bradshaw, 2000).

Evaluation   A number of factors may go into your decision about how to evaluate progress. Various reasons for using practice evaluation strategies include these:

- Evaluation assists the practitioner and the family in identifying and assessing the impact of problem areas on family functioning.
- Evaluation provides evidence of improvement to the family and the practitioner, as well as others, such as a child's school. Regular feedback can be instrumental in helping everyone maintain an effective motivation level and commitment to the change process.
- Ongoing evaluation gives the practitioner objective information to report at case conferences.
- Agency services can be enhanced through commitment to outcome evaluation.
- Consistent use of evaluation strategies promotes a more objective, systematic approach to the provision of services to families (Thomlison & Bradshaw, 1999).

Evaluation of practice parallels the clinical problem-solving process as follows: (1) deciding what to measure and specifying the goal; (2) determining the method of evaluation; (3) collecting and analyzing the data; and (4) sharing the knowledge gained with the family. The chosen measurements are repeated at specified points throughout the assessment, intervention, and follow-up periods. The results are recorded in such a way as to facilitate change comparisons.

Zastrow (1995) summarizes seven steps in evaluation:

1. *Specify the goal:* Goals need to be formulated in specific, concrete, and measurable terms. A specific goal should reflect the presence of, rather than the absence of, something. Well-formulated goals concretely state what will be different when treatment has been completed. A concrete goal is measurable and usually involves a change in *behavior* (thoughts, actions, feelings, or attitudes), a change in the *quantity and/or quality of relationships,* or a change in some aspect of the *environment,* such as a change in living arrangements or school situation.
2. *Select suitable measures:* One of the most challenging issues is determining how you will measure change. Selecting a suitable measurement tool for the goals involves considering how you can quantify the desired outcomes. For example, has change occurred? A yes or no answer would represent the most basic means of evaluating change. However, most evaluations include various levels or degrees of change. There are a number of evaluation or measurement tools, as discussed earlier. The strengths, needs, and diversity of the family system, as well as your agency requirements, must be taken into account in selecting appropriate ways of measuring. Whenever possible choose measurement instruments with reported reliability and validity. Examples for each of these types of measures for practitioners are readily available in social work texts (for example, see Corcoran & Fischer, 2000; Hudson, 1982; Tripodi, 1994; Zastrow, 1995).
3. *Record baseline data:* The baseline establishes the level, stability, and trend of the family's functioning before a specific intervention. During the assessment period, this usually requires a minimum of three data points, or until a stable data pattern is obtained. This becomes the standard against which any changes accompanying intervention can be evaluated. If the family system is in crisis or danger, immediate intervention is essential. In such circumstances the social worker would proceed with intervention and repeatedly measure the family's progress during treatment.
4. *Implement intervention and continue monitoring:* At specified intervals, such as every month or every week, the same measurement tool would be given as the baseline. This shows whether progress is being made and can be valuable information for deciding if revision of change strategies or objectives needs to be made.

5. *Assess change:* Creating a chart or graph from the data collected facilitates a visual analysis of your measurements. This visual representation of change can provide important information to both you and the family about whether change is occurring in the desired direction.

6. *Infer effectiveness:* Making an inference about whether your intervention was responsible for family outcomes involves determining if there could be other explanations for the change. Possible sources of change besides your interventions include history (events that occurred during treatment but were not related to treatment); maturation (the effects of time); multiple treatment interference (more than one treatment received); and statistical regression (high and low scores on measures tend to move toward the mean or average score during retesting) (Zastrow, 1995). These factors make it difficult to be certain whether the change is the result of the intervention.

7. *Follow up:* It is important to assess the maintenance and generalization of change by contacting the family three months and six months after termination. "The purposes of follow-up are to determine whether the positive changes during intervention persist on removal of the intervention, the problem recurs or relapses, new problems appear, and/or the social worker should reinstitute intervention (Tripodi, 1994, p. 86)." If maintenance of the change is an issue, activities can include stabilizing success, firming up social supports, and transitioning to the future (Ivanoff & Stern, 1992; Zastrow, 1995).

Achievements need to be integrated into the daily functioning of families for maximum stabilization of success. This is best accomplished throughout the treatment process by emphasizing practice of learned skills and behaviors. This type of behavior change will promote family self-confidence. Reviewing successes and strengths helps families feel more confident in approaching related issues in the future. Support networks outside that of formal social services are important for maintaining changes accomplished during intervention.

Incorporating evaluation into the intervention process requires deciding who will measure what, when, and how the information will be shared. Deciding what to measure is primarily grounded in what the family considers important; for example,

- Change in circumstances, such as separation or move of a child from home.
- Change in attitude, such as increased self-respect and family identity.
- Change in skills, such as increased parenting skills.
- Change in behavior, such as increased time spent with parents or increased life satisfaction.

Remember that measurement is not an end in itself but an important way in which you and the family can gain clarity about the focus of change and how both of you will know when change has occurred. The success or failure of measurement depends on how you present the measurement task to the family.

Summary

- Social workers and practitioners use a combination of practical and empirical strategies for evaluating family change. Corcoran and Fischer (2000) have compiled a list of measures for adults, children, and couples related to a number of psychological, behavioral, and interpersonal difficulties. The measures have been reproduced, and you can examine them to find one suitable for clinical practice.
- Standardized self-report measures or questionnaires provide information based on constructs from various theoretical models of family functioning. These measures provide information about family functioning in comparison to other families on specific areas or problems.
- There are several guidelines that you should follow before using any type of measurement method in your practice. Remember, all measurement needs to be simple, practical, unobtrusive, culturally appropriate, and of importance to client and social worker.

In summary assessment is linked to intervention planning and to outcomes. In order to determine whether the intervention is changing the issue or problem it must be measured. The guidelines for linking assessment to intervention are as follows:

- Start by asking what information is needed.
- Choose goals (outcomes) that are simple, practical, and meaningful to the family.
- Measure one or two things well.
- Involve the family in defining the outcomes to measure.
- Review and revise the measure with the family who will be using it.
- Build on what the family is prepared to document.
- Measure often.

Learning Activities

Activity 8.1 Evaluate Yourself

Look for a standardized assessment instrument (Corcoran & Fischer 2000) and complete an assessment of yourself.

1. Write an assessment and treatment plan based on the results of that one test.
2. Are the scores you obtained similar to your professional judgment about the most relevant problems you face?
3. If you were providing services to a family, what would be your initial point of focus in the introduction of an assessment measure?
4. What were your experiences in conducting an assessment on yourself? Were you uncomfortable? How would you address these feelings in families?
5. Now administer the same measure or a different one to a colleague. Practice introducing the measure and scoring and interpreting the results. Give the results orally to your colleague.

▼▼▼

CHAPTER NINE

The Del Sol Family: Marital Conflict and Parenting Concerns

T he case study of the Del Sol family provides opportunities for you to practice and discuss family assessment in a case with environmental stress and parenting history of abuse. Study questions and exercises may be done independently as a form of self-study and course assignment or in peer group learning situations. Identifying evidence-based practice approaches to the case will strengthen a treatment plan and will in turn increase the likelihood of client change and goal attainment. Carefully consider the credibility of the evidence that will guide the procedures (Corcoran & Vandiver, 2004).

Case Study Activities

Activity 1: Writing an Assessment Report

Your instructor will assign the relevant question(s) for you to complete. Not all items will apply to the case directly, but all are included here to stimulate your thinking about identifying and applying evidence-based family assessment and intervention.

1. *Analyze the family system:* Determine family interaction patterns, roles and power, and parenting issues.
   a. *Boundaries:* Describe the boundaries, interaction patterns, roles and power, and parenting issues in the case.
   b. *Attachments:* Describe the situation in the family regarding the following:
      i.   Emotional connections
      ii. Resources within the family
      iii. Concrete, instrumental support
      iv. Information, knowledge, and skills

  v. Emotional supports

  vi. Identification and affiliational supports

2. Identify an evidence-based assessment procedure for use with this family. Be sure to include the relevant articles from the literature.

3. *Assessing the family:* Write an assessment report and include information about the family unit in the following areas:

  a. Identify the various family systems.

  b. What functions are performed by which family systems and how well do the systems function?

  c. What boundaries need to be changed? Describe how you will help the family do this.

  d. What are the family system strengths and problems?

  e. What are the risk factors for the problems in this case?

  f. What are the protective factors for developing strengths in this case?

  g. Family behaviors are best understood from a circular causality rather than linear causality. Using an example from this case, where might you use a circular question to make a cognitive change, affective change, or behavioral change?

4. What stage of development is the family in?

  a. What tasks are associated with this stage of development?

  b. What stressors are associated with these tasks?

  c. How have the stressors impacted family development?

  d. What events have impacted the family structure and family membership at this stage?

5. *Culture:* Draw a cultural genogram of the Del Sol family; then write a cultural assessment and include responses to at least the following:

  a. Where did the family come from?

  b. When did they come to this country?

  c. What circumstances brought them to this country?

  d. What is important to this family?

  e. Who are the current members of this family?

  f. What kind of people would they describe themselves as?

  g. How do family members describe themselves racially?

  h. What good and bad things have happened to them over time?

  i. What were or are the family's experiences with oppression?

  j. What lessons have they learned from their experiences?

  k. What are the ways in which pride and shame issues are shown in this family?

  l. Identify the family beliefs in the case.

  m. Use the social network map to assess family external connections. Write a summary of the strengths and limitations of social support for this family.

  n. Design a family ritual to change existing unproductive patterns for this family and to reinforce internal and external connections.

6. Identify an evidence-based intervention for use with the primary family issue. Be sure to include copies of relevant articles from the literature.

Activity 2: Family Interview — Role-Play for Assessment and Planning

The goal of this activity is to role-play the Del Sol family attending a family interview. One week prior to class presentation, students should read the Del Sol family case. Assign a group of students to role-play the family; include an interviewer, and have the rest of the class take observation notes for feedback and discussion after the role-play. If the class is large enough, different interviewers can focus on each of the issues identified next. Allow 45 minutes to complete the role-play, and have handy a flip chart to document or illustrate the genogram and mapping tools during the interview.

  Choose one focus for the interview from the following: (1) identify the family strengths and resources, including the subsystems, boundaries, and roles and power in the family;

(2) engage in a cultural assessment; (3) develop a family genogram; or (4) complete a social support network map or social network grid tool to identify the types and range of existing support networks.

- Students should assume the roles of the Del Sol family members (Rosa, mother; Miguel, father; Christopher, stepson age 9) and an interviewer. Other classmates are the observers and provide feedback to the role-players regarding the techniques demonstrated and the areas needed for improvement.
- The focus of the family meeting is on obtaining information related to the family's culture and history. Use questions 1–6 from the first activity to guide the chosen interview focus.
- During the interview, the interviewer should be completing the pictorial or mapping representation and using this to engage the family fully in problem solving. The genogram should illustrate how the family's culture and history play a role in shaping their personal and family values in their current situation.
- If the interviewer uses the social network map for the family social support resources, this evaluation can help the family assess family structure and functioning of a support network.
- After this role-play, students should write a critical appraisal of the interview noting the strengths and limitations and suggesting how it might be improved. Use the following headings to critically appraise the role-play:

  Presenting issues: Appraise the accuracy of these in one or two sentences.

  Family membership: How well was the genogram developed? What family members and information may be missing that could have improved the genogram?

  Family culture: What information about cultural bonding is a strength among the family members? How might this be used in an intervention?

  Developmental history: Provide pertinent information concerning family of origin and significant personal, social, vocational, and medical events that informed assessment and intervention.

  Strengths and problems: What three family strengths and issues or problems contribute to the family structure, developmentally and functionally? Comment on either the marital system strengths and problems or parent–child system strengths and problems.

  Summarize: Write a summative statement of the family situation, the issues, the strengths, and the resources in the family.

  Goals and plans for intervention: Describe the goals for the family and its members and the intervention plan, based on best practices. What might the family's reaction to this be?

Activity 3: The Del Sol Family

The designated assessment activities to be completed by students in this case can be used for class discussion and intervention planning.

Referral Route

Rosa Del Sol was self-referred to the North Beach Neighborhood Outreach Center by Christopher's teacher. At the time of intake, Rosa's presenting concerns were marital conflict and parenting concerns, especially how to manage her 9-year-old son, Christopher.

Family Composition

The Del Sol family consists of Rosa, age 35, and Miguel, age 37, as well as three children—Christopher, age 9; Teresa, age 3; and Tina, 18 months of age. Rosa and Miguel have been married for four years. Christopher is Rosa's son from a previous common-law relationship. Christopher's biological father, Jim, age 36, has not been involved in his life since he was 2 years old, and Rosa does not know Jim's whereabouts. Rosa states Jim was a heavy drinker and became physically abusive during the pregnancy, and they separated shortly before Christopher's second birthday.

Rosa is the only child of Maria and Juan Valdez, ages 55 and 60 respectively. Juan was verbally and physically abusive toward Maria, and they separated when Rosa was 12 years old. Rosa has had no contact with her biological father since that time. Maria continued to parent Rosa on her own and has not remarried.

Miguel is the oldest son of Sophia and Thomas Del Sol, ages 62 and 66 respectively. Miguel's younger brother, Juan, age 34, is not married and according to Miguel has a "drinking problem." Miguel's father "abandoned" the family when Miguel was 7 years old. Miguel remembers the loud arguing and fighting between his parents. His mother was remarried, when Miguel was 10 years old, to Ken Wheeler.

The Del Sol Family Genogram

Each student will complete an intergenerational family genogram of the Del Sol family. Students should share these with classmates and compare them for accuracy and family patterns to assist in the family assessment and intervention planning.

The Family System

Rosa was in tears for most of the initial session, claiming she "just can't take it anymore." Miguel is constantly putting her down, insulting her in front of other people (even in the grocery store), and yelling at the children. Rosa feels that no matter what she does she cannot seem to do anything right (according to Miguel). Rosa is beginning to realize that she is being verbally abused as her father abused her mother. She is also uncomfortable with her reactions because she has been yelling back at Miguel and feels like the "war is on." Rosa feels the situation is "out of control." Sometimes her own anger and Miguel's intensity of anger have frightened her. Physical abuse has not occurred up to this point, according to Rosa. She states that Miguel knows if he ever touches her that would end the relationship. She is determined not to raise her children in an "abusive home" like the home of her own childhood. Rosa says she cries frequently and has had little energy to deal with the conflicts. Christopher has been having difficulty at school as well as the daily "battles" with Miguel.

Miguel feels the problems between Rosa and him can be "solved on their own." Miguel admits that he yells a lot at Rosa and calls her names. However, he points out that he always tells Rosa he is sorry. Miguel is of average height and slim build; he appears agitated and tense. He admits to experiencing a number of physical symptoms of stress, including a pounding heart, frequent headaches, and constant feelings of edginess and restlessness. Miguel describes himself as a loner with no close friends. Miguel agrees with Rosa that he is moody but says, "A guy can't be in a good mood all of the time." Miguel's posture and manner appear defensive, and he indicates he is only here because Rosa had threatened to leave him if they didn't get help. His family is important to him, and he realizes now that despite not wanting to repeat the actions of his stepfather, he can see that he is doing the same to his children.

Christopher attends North Beach Elementary and Middle School and is in grade 3. He is in a regular class after having repeated grade 1. Christopher was diagnosed with attention deficit disorder (ADD) six months ago. He is currently on a trial of Ritalin. In the past month the school has complained to Rosa that Christopher has become increasingly aggressive with his peers. Christopher's teacher reports that he has made no friends in his class and has become socially isolated, either withdrawing or acting out angrily. The teacher notes that Christopher has poor social skills but is quite good in sport activities such as soccer and football. Christopher' favorite sport is soccer, and in the summer he loves to swim, play football, and ride his bike.

Three-year-old Teresa is a talkative girl who is generally good-natured. Tina, 18 months, tends to be quiet and allows Teresa to do all the talking for her. Both girls have been achieving their respective developmental milestones. Rosa has no concerns in this area. However, Rosa has noticed in the past three weeks that both girls have not been sleeping through the night.

They have been whining and crying a lot more than usual. Teresa complains of a stomachache frequently. Rosa became upset when she told about Miguel coming home from work and marching into the bedroom in silence and Teresa asking, "Is Daddy mad again?"

Family Background Information

Rosa completed grade 12 and then worked in a bank as a teller until the birth of Teresa. Her mother helped her raise Christopher when he was an infant and openly stated her disapproval of Rosa's relationship with Jim. Maria lives nearby and, despite what Rosa describes as a "conflictual" relationship, is a source of support for Rosa. Maria often babysits the girls, although Maria now refuses to look after Christopher because "he is too difficult—just like his father." Rosa describes the relationship between her mother and Miguel as "unfriendly"; "they tolerate one another" as each tends to put the other down. Rosa feels stuck in the middle of a "no-win" situation.

Miguel never got along with his stepfather, Ken. Ken frequently became "drunk" on the weekends with Sophia, leaving the boys to fend for themselves. Ken was not physically abusive, but when he was drinking "you stayed out of his way so he wouldn't yell at you." Miguel says his mother Sophia is an alcoholic, and he has chosen not to have contact with her or his stepfather. Miguel quit school and left home at age 15. He worked at odd jobs to support himself. Miguel admits to "being in the wrong crowd" and heavily involved with drugs and alcohol as a teenager. Miguel feels proud that he is no longer involved "in that scene," having quit on his own "without anyone's help."

Family Strengths and Challenges

Stress or Demand Factors

Family System   All family members appear to be suffering symptoms of stress both physically and emotionally and have experienced a number of changes recently. The purchase of their own home and the resulting high payments have left little money to cover remaining bills and groceries. The lack of money and high debt load have become a daily stressor. Rosa and Miguel agree that financial issues regularly precipitate most of their arguments.

Christopher's recent diagnosis of ADD is confusing to Miguel and Rosa. They have little information on this disorder or how to best deal with Christopher in managing his behaviors appropriately. Medication is expensive, and they do not have health insurance.

Marital/Parental Subsystem   Miguel has completed grade 6 school education and has always worked and is employed full-time at a small auto repair shop. He also works a second job in an auto parts store in the evenings and weekends to make ends meet. Miguel complains about his coworkers stating he has nothing in common with them and doesn't want to waste his time with them. Miguel feels his boss is always pressuring him to do more, and they often have loud disagreements. Miguel aspires to be a manager of his own shop and not have people telling him what to do.

Miguel and Rosa purchased their home four months ago. It is located about 45 minutes by car from their old neighborhood, where Rosa was well connected to the church and a number of friends. The couple enjoy owning their own home, but the mortgage payments are high. This leaves little money for other expenses and has been a source of daily conflict.

Rosa and Miguel had decided that Rosa would stay home to care for the girls while they were young. Lately, however, Rosa has been suggesting that she work part-time at a gardening shop to help out financially and to be out of the house. Miguel then could cut down on his hours of work and spend time with the family. Miguel reacted angrily to this issue and stated that he was "sick and tired of everyone hassling him about working and can't a guy just make a living." Miguel works hard at his two jobs and is very committed to doing the best for his family. However, all his energies have been devoted to making a living with little time for any outside interests. Rosa disagrees with Miguel about the importance of money and prefers that Miguel spend time with her and the children as a family. Miguel admits he is getting physically tired and irritable and finds he is less able to handle life's minor annoyances. He would like to be able to spend time with the children and get back into playing recreational soccer.

Parent–Child Subsystem (*To be completed by the student.*) Describe the parent–child subsystems.

Sibling Subsystems (*To be completed by the student.*) Describe the sibling subsystems.

Resource Factors Rosa describes herself as an outgoing, social person with a sense of humor, but lately she has been feeling alone and "down." The family has one car that Miguel uses to travel to work, and Rosa feels isolated and "stuck in the house."

The family has few outside supports. Rosa, due to the move and transportation limitations, is isolated from her previous support network, which included neighborhood friends and the church community. Miguel has few friends and relies on Rosa to be his constant cheerleader to make him feel good. Rosa has said it feels at times that she has four children, not three. The girls don't have friends in the new neighborhood because the children living nearby are much older. The girls are becoming quite bored and cranky with Rosa, adding to the tension in the home. Christopher has made a couple of new friends; however, his poor social skills and short attention span have made this a challenge for him.

Competence and Coping Factors Rosa grew up in an abusive home and is determined to not raise her children in that environment. She is very motivated to make changes in her life and has attempted over the last year to involve Miguel in activities to strengthen their family; he has refused to attend any couple enrichment weekends or courses that were available at no cost through the church. Rosa attended the sessions on her own, including a weekend retreat for families.

Rosa has a wonderful sense of humor that has helped her cope with a number of adverse conditions. Rosa feels she has no support from Miguel in raising the children due to his drive to make money and his discomfort in being with the children. Rosa is a good mother to her children and is determined to continue to learn about positive parenting approaches.

Miguel is a hard worker, and any job he takes on he feels he must do the very best. High expectations create added pressure and stress. Miguel has been reluctant to tackle areas in which he feels incompetent. These include parenting, so he tends to avoid it when he can, often choosing work over time with the family.

Miguel grew up in an abusive, alcoholic family and exhibits some of the symptoms common to this environment such as poor self-image, a need for constant approval, and anger. He believes strongly that the husband's role is to provide for his family. Miguel has difficulty recognizing that his family has other needs from a husband and father than just money. This pattern was established in his family of origin. His strong desire to raise his children differently and to keep his family together will help him in achieving his goals.

Intervention Planning

Miguel and Rosa have decided on the following goals:

1. To develop appropriate strategies for managing anger.
2. To learn effective, respectful communication.
3. To learn more appropriate parent–child discipline strategies.
4. To expand the current support network of their family.
5. To increase their understanding of attention deficit disorder and parenting techniques.

Assessment Tools

(*To be completed by the student.*) Students should go to the literature and determine the evidence-based information for the following questions and discuss the expected outcomes that will enhance individual and family functioning and problem resolution.

Summarize the best practices and write an intervention plan selected from the best available information, appropriate to the values and preferences of the family.

1. What intervention strategies are effective in managing anger?
2. What family therapy models are effective in improving communication problems?
3. What are the differences between parent training, parent education, and parent support programs? Which approach is best for this family?
4. Identify parent training programs that are the most successful in reducing negative or coercive parenting practices.
5. What social support interventions reduce family isolation?
6. What treatments are effective in managing attention deficit disorder in children?
7. What, if any, cultural adaptations are needed to introduce any of the interventions?

Contract

(To be completed by the student.) The student should complete a contract for services based on the research in this chapter.

▼▼▼

CHAPTER TEN

The McCoy Family Coping with a Mother's Death and Role Change

The case study of the McCoy family provides opportunities for you to practice and discuss family assessment in a case with loss and grief issues related to a mother's death and the subsequent family system changes in roles, boundaries, power, and alliances. Study questions and exercises may be done independently as a form of self-study and course assignment or in peer group learning situations. Identifying evidence-based practice approaches to the case will strengthen a treatment plan and will in turn increase the likelihood of client change and goal attainment. Carefully consider the credibility of the evidence that will guide the procedures (Corcoran & Vandiver, 2004).

Case Study Activities

Activity 1: Family Assessment Report

Write a family assessment report of this family. Include a genogram and social network map. Also include the goals and treatment invention plan.

Activity 2: Family Interview — Role-Play

1. Use the questions for a first family assessment interview to role-play a meeting with the McCoy family members. Identify this family's strengths and resources.
2. Draw a social network map for the McCoy family, including a social network grid. As a class, divide into small groups with four to six participants in each group. Each group should identify a recorder and a reporter to complete this exercise.
3. Describe the structure and functioning of this family's informal social support network. Use the social network map and social network grid tools to identify the types, range, and reliability of informal support provided to the McCoy family. Consider

how suitable the existing informal support network is for supporting this family based on the five factors contributing to the structure and functioning of a support network.

4. Have each group share their responses with the rest of the class. Conclude the exercise by having the class brainstorm ideas for ways to enhance informal social supports to assist the McCoy family with their care-giving roles.

Activity 3: Family Needs

Students should work in small groups to discuss the following family needs and then share their responses with the class for a broader perspective:

1. What are the family and individual needs for
   a. Concrete, instrumental support?
   b. Information, knowledge, and skills?
   c. Emotional supports?
   d. Affiliational supports?
2. What needs to be done in the family system to improve
   a. Emotional connections?
   b. Resources within the family?
3. What functions are performed by which family systems, and how well do the systems function?
4. Do any boundaries need to be changed? What needs to be done? Describe how you will do this.
5. Give an example from this case of where you might use circular questions as an intervention to make a cognitive change, affective change, or behavioral change.
6. What stage of development is the family in?
   a. What tasks are associated with this stage of development?
   b. What stressors are associated with the tasks?
   c. How have the stressors impacted family development?
   d. Design a family ritual to mark passage of change for this family to help negotiate a change, and to help the family restructure how its members perceive events and belief systems.

Case Study: The McCoy Family

Referral Route
Ed McCoy was referred to the Children's Hospital for counseling by the family doctor following the death of his wife. The problem Ed identified, at the time of intake, was his need for assistance in adjusting to parenting without his partner.

Family Composition
The McCoy family consists of Ed, age 36, and his three children: Tamara, age 10; Kayla, age 8; and Kyle, age 4. Ed's wife, Tina McCoy, died approximately three months ago from a connective tissue disorder. Tina was the younger of two children born to Grace and John Redding. John died at the age of 50 from heart disease 20 years ago. Grace, age 68, retired two years ago from teaching. She was recently diagnosed with cancer. Grace lives in the same city and has always been involved with her grandchildren. She frequently babysits the three children. It is unknown how her involvement with the children will be affected because of the change in her health status.

Tina had one older sister with whom she shared a close relationship. Rhonda, age 38, is married and living in the same city as the McCoys. Rhonda has a daughter, age 12, and a son, age 11. Rhonda works full-time in a professional position that frequently requires long hours. Rhonda has also been quite involved in the children's lives and has offered to raise the McCoy children with Ed. Ed describes his relationship with his sister-in-law as conflictual.

Ed McCoy, age 36, is the oldest of two children born to Edwin and Katherine McCoy. Edwin died from heart disease at the age of 58. He was a university professor. Katherine, age 60, is described as healthy and active. Because she lives in another state, she does not visit often, and she has a distant relationship with her son and grandchildren.

Ed's younger sister, Patricia, age 30, is recently married and lives close to her mother. She also has a somewhat distant relationship with her brother and his family.

The McCoy Family Genogram

Students should complete the extended family genogram.

The Family System

The entire McCoy family was identified as the client system. This includes Ed, Tamara, Kayla, and Kyle.

Ed is a tall, slim, attractive man. He appears somewhat unkempt and frequently seems distracted. Ed has a college diploma and has been steadily employed for the last 16 years. Currently he is employed full-time as a computer technician in a large manufacturing company. He has some degree of flexibility in his work, but he has established the pattern of working long hours and occasional weekends.

Tamara, age 10, is presently in grade 5 at Woodview Elementary School. She has long brown hair, is a straight "A" student, and appears to be a quiet and compliant girl. She seems to have shouldered a great deal of additional responsibility during her mother's illness and since her death. During the initial interviews with the McCoy family, Ed applauded Tamara for being a "good little mother" when she took charge of her younger brother after he became restless in the family session.

Kayla, age 8, is in grade 3 at Woodview Elementary School. She has short dark hair and an engaging grin. She is tall and quite thin and could be described as loose-limbed. She apparently looks most like her mother, and Ed fears she may have some of the characteristics that would indicate a possible connective tissue disorder. The genetics department at the Children's Hospital will be investigating this possibility. Ed indicates that Kayla is the child whom he finds most challenging. She is quite active, questions decisions openly, and frequently does not comply with her father's wishes. Ed feels that his wife was better able to manage Kayla and that she was the child closest to her mother. Kayla, who has always been an average student, has also experienced some difficulties at school since her mother's death. She has not been completing her homework, has had difficulty focusing, and has been in the center of several conflicts with peers. Ed is feeling overwhelmed since the death of his wife and has asked the school to manage her behavior as much as possible.

Kyle, age 4, is enrolled in a community preschool program three mornings per week. He is a charming, engaging boy who appears content. He looks to his sisters for comfort and support. Kyle's grandmother, Grace, has been looking after him during the day since the death of his mother. Grace also frequently keeps him overnight when his father works overtime.

Family Background Information

Ed McCoy describes his upbringing as highly structured. His parents had high expectations for his academic achievements, which he did not fulfill. Ed indicates that his parents were not openly affectionate with each other or with the children. Discipline for misbehavior usually meant being confined to the home for short periods. Ed feels that he parents in a style similar to that of his parents. He is not sure if this style of parenting will be beneficial to his children as they mourn the loss of their mother.

Ed's father died suddenly, two years ago, as a result of heart disease. Ed did not have an opportunity to see his father before he died. Because the relationship had been distant for some time, it had been approximately eight years since his last contact with his father.

Developmental History of the Family

Students should complete an assessment of family patterns or attempts to cope with past significant events, as well as identifying current strengths, supports, and stressors.

Family Strengths and Challenges

Stress or Demand Factors

The Family System   Tina died approximately six weeks ago from an inherited connective tissue disorder. This disorder was diagnosed one year ago when Tina began experiencing health difficulties. Because of complications from the disorder, Tina's health deteriorated quickly over the last year, ending in heart failure. She was hospitalized much of the last year, and because her condition deteriorated more quickly than anticipated, Ed feels that neither he nor his wife were able to assist the children in coping with the period of illness.

Ed feels somewhat distant from his children and has been relying heavily on outside resources to assist him in his parenting responsibilities. With support, it is anticipated that he will be able to provide adequately for his children both emotionally and functionally. There appears to be some role confusion for both the children and Ed. Tamara is taking on some of the household and nurturing tasks while Ed appears to be relinquishing his parent role to others outside the home. Even the school is attempting to help by not involving Ed in some potentially serious difficulties that Kayla is experiencing. The risk for Ed is that if he doesn't take charge of his family and feel some degree of confidence in his ability to provide for them, he will, by default, lose any position of authority in the family.

Another factor impacting the family is how both Grace and her daughter Rhonda are dealing with the loss of their daughter and sister. In their attempts to cope they are undermining Ed's role. However, potentially both grandmother and aunt could be a tremendous support for the McCoy family.

Marital/Parental Subsystem   Prior to Tina's illness and her subsequent death, Ed indicated that there had been a great deal of conflict in the relationship. Tina had expressed a desire to return to work and had requested that Ed share some of the child care responsibilities to enable her to do this. Ed had argued that his role was that of the "breadwinner" and that all other responsibilities had fallen to his wife. Ed expresses sadness and a sense of loss at the death of his partner.

Ed appears to have come from a disengaged family system, where boundaries and family ties were not always clear. His own father was not actively involved in the parenting role, and there was a likely issue outstanding between father and son at the time of Ed's father's death. Ed McCoy's attitude toward parenting is much the same as his father's, but he is now being forced to take a more active role.

Parent–Child Subsystem   Students should describe the current parent–child subsystem and assess the current functioning in terms of generational roles and boundaries within the family system and external to the family system.

Sibling Subsystem   Students should describe the current sibling relationships. What issues or problems is the sibling subsystem facing?

Resource Factors   The McCoys are a loving family who have suffered the loss of their wife and mother. A number of supports exist within the family system. Grace, the maternal grandmother, and Rhonda, Tina's sister, are both involved and supportive of the children. Ed also indicates that several neighbors and parents of his children's friends have been supportive and have offered to help—particularly with the two girls. Staff at the school the girls attend have also extended an offer to assist in whatever way possible. They have already demonstrated their willingness to help by not contacting Ed with continuing concerns regarding Kayla and attempting to deal with the issues without Ed's input.

Ed enjoys stable employment with some degree of flexibility. He is bright, caring, and open to input on how best to assist his children in coping with the loss of their mother. Ed has been managing household tasks by hiring help. He indicates that this is not a good long-term solution because of the cost, but he feels that in the short term it is worth the additional financial burden.

While having support from Tina's family has been a real advantage for Ed, he has found that Grace and Rhonda have been making more of the decisions regarding the children and that he feels less and less important in his own children's lives as time goes by. Rhonda's offer to parent the children appears to have been threatening to Ed because it raised doubts in him about his competence as a parent.

Competence and Coping Factors   The family system demonstrates a number of strengths: their caring and affection for each other, Ed's ability to reach out to the community for assistance, his stable employment, and the support of extended family and the community in general.

Assessment and Plan for Family

Students should complete the recommendations for family system work by writing a plan for intervention addressing the following family issues:

- Grief and loss issues for the children and father.
- Family roles.
- Communication and interaction patterns.
- The differential developmentally appropriate levels at which the children are expressing the loss of their mother,
- How Ed will deal with his issues about the death of his wife.
- Belief systems affecting the McCoy family functioning.

Planning for Services

Ed McCoy has identified the following goals:

- To assist the family in mourning the death of Tina.
- To get assistance with the responsibilities of single parenthood.

Assessment and evaluation tools used included the Generalized Contentment Scale and the Index of Family Relations (Hudson Scales). These measures were completed by Ed, Tamara, and Kayla. Kyle drew a picture of his family while the others completed these measures. The Adult–Adolescent Parenting Inventory (AAPI) was used to assess a baseline for Ed's attitudes regarding parenting.

Intervention Choices   Students should locate evidence-based interventions for the following identified issues. What does the empirical literature suggest?

1. To reinforce generational boundaries, Ed will learn about parenting roles and his responsibilities. What is the best parenting intervention for the single-parent household?
2. Is there a relationship between school behaviors and the loss of the mother? What intervention should be identified to address Kayla's problem school behaviors?

CHAPTER ELEVEN

The Yellowbird Family Foster Care, Delinquency, and Transition to Independent Living

The case study of the Yellowbird family provides opportunities for you to practice and discuss family assessment in a case with multiple issues including foster care, delinquency, family reunification, and transition to independent living. Study questions and exercises may be done independently as a form of self-study and course assignment or in peer group learning situations. Identifying evidence-based practice approaches to this case will strengthen a treatment plan and will in turn increase the likelihood of client change and goal attainment. Carefully consider the credibility of the evidence that will guide the procedures (Corcoran & Vandiver, 2004).

Case Study Activities

Activity 1: Discuss the Case

Read the Yellowbird case and discuss the following issues:

1. What risk factors are present in the family of origin and in the treatment foster care family in this case?
2. How do the background knowledge and sense of family life of the parents' childhood and adolescence contribute to their current sense of parenting and family life with Jason?
3. What are examples of the strength factors in this case?
4. What stage of development is the family in? What tasks are associated with this stage of development? What stressors are associated with the tasks? How have the stressors impacted family development?
5. Assume the family heritage is native indigenous (this term is preferred to American Indian). Discuss cultural identity issues for the child and family. How does growing up

with foster parents and others who are not culturally and ethnically similar to Jason affect his identity and sense of belonging and permanency? How does living between different cultures affect children, family members, and families? How may this problem of acculturation impact belief systems, behavior, and attitudes?

6. How are pride and shame issues shown in this family?

7. Identify the family beliefs in the case. What are your beliefs about how the family functions?

8. Design a family ritual or tradition this family can use to reinforce connections.

Activity 2: Role-Play

This wraparound service case collaboration activity requires advance one-week preparation.

1. Read the case summary of the Yellowbird family. Students should select roles from the case to role-play a wraparound service case planning conference for transition to adulthood. All individuals shall attend the planning meetings as indicated in wraparound service planning. Roles include Jason and his parents, social worker, foster parents, teacher, housing worker, vocational teacher, physician, and others needed to plan and support Jason's transition to adulthood. Based on an understanding of the assessment of Jason's needs, students role-play the providers of service. The case describes the child's developmental and placement history, current foster family, biological family, and issues Jason will face as he transitions from the child welfare system to independent living. Your instructor can help decide who will be involved in the wraparound service case planning conference for Jason Yellowbird. You can prepare for the role-play by assessing Jason and his strengths and problems, as well as reading about wraparound services and the role you will assume at the case planning conference. Students should come to the role-play after preparing independently for the conference and play their roles as realistically as possible.

2. *Evidence-based source of information:*

    a. The following book chapter is available from the instructor (on Instructor Resources): Hiebert, B., & Thomlison, B. (1996). Facilitating transitions to adulthood: Research and policy implications. In B. Galaway & J. Hudson (Eds.), *Youth in transition: Perspectives on research and policy.* Toronto: Thompson Educational Publishing.

    b. Go the following Web site for recent evidence-based research (promising practices) on transition to adulthood issues and concerns of youth: National Center for Youth in Transition (NCYT) Web site: http://ntacyt.fmhi.usf.edu/promisepractice/index.cfm. Based on this Web site, assess the needs of Jason Yellowbird in each domain presented for successful development and adulthood.

3. It is helpful to videotape the role-play so you can replay it and discuss the content and the process. The videotape can be reviewed so you can analyze the case planning process and further assess the collaborative practice skills derived from this learning experience.

4. The case planning conference should be approximately 45 minutes to 1 hour. In advance, a chairperson for the case conference will be determined. The case conference chair will explain the purpose, expectations, and expected outcome of the collaboration; ask for introductions; and ensure that everyone contributes to the plan. Each person will then describe her or his connection to the meeting and suggest plans for Jason based on preparation for the role.

5. At the completion of the role-play the class will review the videotape; consider the evidence-based research and readings; and discuss what was learned about (a) the skills, knowledge, and expertise of the interview subject; (b) your own values, attitudes, biases, and feeling about working with other professionals, parents, and youths in issues associated with transition to adulthood; (c) the ways in which you might help or hinder

parent, professional, and interprofessional collaboration in transition to adulthood; and (d) strategies for successful collaborative wraparound case planning conferences.

6. Conclude by brainstorming ideas for ways to enhance informal social supports to assist families with their care-giving roles at all developmental points in the lives of children and youths.

Case Study: The Yellowbird Family

Referral Source

Issues of abuse and neglect prompted the referral of Jason Yellowbird, age 8, and his family for child protective services. The Child Welfare Placement, Assessment, and Review Committee (PARC) recommended that Jason be placed into treatment foster care following a 6-month placement at the W. H. Hatton Center for emotionally disturbed children. By age 9, the Valleyview Treatment Foster Family Care program was serving Jason. Following a short-term placement in treatment foster care, Jason was reunited with his mother and stepfather even though the parents were initially hostile to this idea. Eventually Jason entered the juvenile justice system, and a second period of treatment foster care was recommended. Now 13 years old, Jason has begun to live with Sue and Brian Lasting, treatment foster care parents with the Valleyview program. Jason remains in contact with his mother Carol and stepfather Jeff. The goal of the second placement in treatment foster family care was to prepare Jason for return to his parents.

Family Composition

Jason Yellowbird, age 13, is the son of Carol and Stone Yellowbird. Carol, age 31 at the time of Jason's second treatment foster care placement, divorced Stone when Jason was 4 years old. Carol and Stone had married when she was 17 years old and pregnant with Jason. Jason has had only intermittent contact with his biological father.

No other information is known about this family.

The Yellowbird Family Genogram Students should complete a genogram for this family.

Family Background Information

Carol didn't much like the idea of Jason being in the W. H. Hatton Center because she had spent her teenage years in an institution herself. However, after a childhood with an alcoholic father and a rejecting mother, and after an early and disastrous first marriage to Jason's father, having Jason in out-of-home care was the only peace she had ever had.

With Jason in out-of-home care, Jeff, too, was enjoying his first taste of a stable lifestyle. His own mother had died when he was a child, and he had lived with his grandparents until his father remarried. He had then returned to his father, but his stepmother had made it clear that she didn't want Jeff, which was why Jeff, as a stepfather, had done his best for Jason.

Placement Information

Jason Yellowbird, at the age of 8, was mean and tough. He boasted, he argued, and he broke things—his own and other people's. He lied, stole, cheated, and bullied his schoolmates. He hit his mother and sometimes his mother's husband. He knew that people thought he was a bad boy. His mother's husband did not like him much. No one liked him much. Moreover, he was not allowed to say that he felt lonely and confused sometimes. Carol didn't like him to say how he felt. Jeff liked him to do as he was told.

Jason's teacher had put him in a short-term observation program at school, which didn't help. Jason continued his life as a tough guy, occasionally becoming a baby. During his times as a baby, he clung to adults and demanded their attention and sometimes soiled his pants.

He could read, though, and he could count, and he liked to write. For a kid in grade 4, as far as his schoolwork went, Jason was doing all right.

Carol approached a center she knew about that took children like Jason. The children lived together in cottages and were disciplined and cared for. It would be good for Jason, Carol thought, and it might keep her marriage together. Jeff, her second husband, didn't hit her and Jason, as her first husband had. In fact, Jeff had adopted Jason to make her happy, but enough was enough. Jeff and Carol were tired of Jason and were fighting daily over him. Jason had to go; he was out of control. In summarizing their thoughts about 8-year-old Jason, his mother and stepfather concluded, "This kid is crazy!"

Jason was one of 68 residents at the center for emotionally disturbed children. He was accepted into the residential treatment center under custody by agreement order. The voluntary placement agreement said that he would go home in six months; but in six months, his parents did not want him back. His mother and Jeff were doing all right without Jason. At the end of the six-month period, Jason was nearly 9 and nothing had changed. In fact, Jason's behavior had deteriorated rapidly. He did not get along with the boys in the residential treatment center; he did not get along with anyone well. He still lied, stole, and bullied. He still broke things and argued and hit people, and he didn't do as he was told. The consulting psychiatrist had prescribed a program of medication but discontinued the drugs after observing no appreciable changes in Jason's behavior.

Jason's case went before the Child Welfare Placement, Assessment, and Review Committee (PARC) in December, and this was the first of many reviews to come. His social worker from the Child Welfare Department was there, but Jason wasn't and neither were his mother or Jeff. The conclusion of the PARC, which included Jason's social worker, a psychologist, consulting psychiatrist, teachers, and supervisors, was unanimous. Although moving Jason would most likely compound his problems, Jason could no longer stay at the institution. His social worker advocated a less restrictive placement, but the response from others who knew Jason was that Jason's problems were too severe for a regular foster home. The only alternative was to put him into a treatment foster home as soon as a bed became available. Meanwhile, he was placed in a group receiving and assessment home. His child welfare status changed to temporary guardianship.

Once a treatment foster family placement was found for Jason at the beginning of February, contacts with Jason and his family were initiated. Jason had several overnight visits with the foster family. Carol and Jeff met a few times with the treatment foster parents at their home. Meanwhile, Jason's case records from the institution and child welfare had been sent to the treatment foster care program. Meetings took place between the treatment foster care staff, the institution staff, and Jason's child welfare worker to discuss what Jason would need from treatment foster care services. On the basis of these discussions and the treatment foster parents' observations of Jason, the treatment foster care staff decided to formulate tentative goals that were discussed with Jason before being entered into the case plan.

Within a month, Jason moved into the treatment foster care placement. His treatment foster parents, Diane and Lee Barker, had taken one other foster child since the program began, and this child was still with them. When Jason arrived, there were already three children living in the home: Lee and Diane's own two children, a boy of 12 and a girl of 7, and one foster child, a boy of 10.

One of the first things Lee and Diane did was contact Jason's school to talk to his teachers about his new situation. Jason had been lucky enough to stay at the same school despite his changes in living environments, so his teachers were familiar with his history. However, his behavior had been troublesome, and his teachers had not related well to his mother. Much work needed to be done to establish the necessary cooperation between school and home. It was decided that Jason would have a homework book that would list the day's assignments. A school card would be stapled to the book on which the teacher would check off Jason's daily observed behaviors. How many times did he obey or fail to obey instructions? Did he hit another child? Did he make any self-praising statements or act supportively toward another student? How did he react when he was criticized or praised? Diane and Lee would look at this book every evening and focus their work with Jason on the areas that seemed to need improvement. They also kept a daily log for the other foster child, for whom they noted progress toward individual goals, the child's general emotional state, and any major incidents.

Jason went home to visit twice in April, and his parents visited him three times in the placement. His mother had spoken to his teacher, and this interview went much better than previous interviews because Jason's behavior at school had improved, his teacher felt involved in his improvement, and Jason's mother was more relaxed. There was a bake sale at school in April for which Jason's mother made cookies. There was an operetta the following month with Jason on stage and his mother and grandmother clapping in the audience. Jason made five visits home in May, three of them overnight stays, and these visits went well. Nevertheless, when the end of May came, Jeff did not want Jason to return home, and Jason's mother was uneasy about it because of Jeff's attitude.

After discussion among all the parties involved, it was decided that Jason should go home, but with a lot of in-home support from the treatment foster parents and staff. A staff member would visit Jason's home as often and for as long as required, staying overnight for a week at a time if necessary. Between these visits, Jason's parents or Jason himself could phone the treatment parents or staff for help with any problem. The return home worked better than Jeff had expected. Jason was now doing well at school; relations between the school and his parents were good; and Carol had learned from Diane and Lee how to improve Jason's self-esteem, how to handle his aggression, and how to communicate with him. Her expectations of Jason had been reduced to expectations reasonable for a child of his age.

When Jason was 11, he transferred to the local junior high school. His reputation for being a "bad kid" still lingered, and incidents were related with relish by schoolmates who remembered that Jason had hit the teacher and refused to do as he was told. Older boys who wanted to use his locker "to store some things" approached Jason. Jason agreed. He knew that the things being stored included drugs and stolen goods, but by now he was one of the "in" crowd. He began to carry a knife as the others did. He experimented with drugs. He started to take an interest in the gun that Jeff had at home. Meanwhile, he was skipping classes, his grades were going down, and he was becoming increasingly aggressive toward his mother and Jeff. Jeff and Carol argued about him, Jeff saying that it had been a mistake to ever have him home, and his mother pleading on his behalf, saying that it was puberty, a phase he would get over. She suggested phoning the treatment foster care staff for help, but Jeff didn't want help. He didn't want a social worker present in his home. Essentially, he didn't want Jason.

One night, Jason took the gun to show to his friends at their regular meeting place. It impressed them, it raised Jason's status in the group, and he began to take it on other occasions. A few months later, the gun went off accidentally. No one was hurt, but Jason was charged with careless use of firearms and received 10 days in juvenile detention with one year's probation. His parents refused to have him home when the 10 days were up, and he was sent to a group receiving and assessment placement.

After two weeks in the group receiving and assessment placement, Jason ran away and stole a motorcycle. He and his friends had engaged in a good deal of theft over the past year, and Jason thought that he could manage a motorcycle without being caught. However, he was caught. He was charged with theft and spent another two days in a youth detention center, where he threatened a staff member with a knife and brought on the attentions of more professionals.

Despite the strong arguments of professionals who worked with Jason, his social worker believed that treatment foster care was not only the best choice for Jason, but offered the only chance for this 13-year-old to learn to live an everyday life in an everyday community. Jason's record showed that he had once been involved with treatment foster care, and the treatment had seemed effective, at least until he entered junior high school. The treatment foster care staff made a point of asking that children who had once been with them be referred back to them if they subsequently got into trouble. Accordingly, the referral was made, and Jason was once more involved in the treatment foster care program.

Jason Yellowbird was now 13. He had acquired skills in theft and was familiar with alcohol, drugs, and the use of weapons, and his school record and relationship with his parents were both abysmal. He was described as sneaky and as having an oppositional disorder. Jason had become particularly aggressive when he was physically restrained for his own and others' safety.

When restrained, he often lashed out at staff with obscenities. Other behaviors that made Jason difficult to care for included enuresis, nightmares, terrible hygiene and table manners, and personal property destruction, including the belongings of his peers as well as the furnishings in the room.

He was not able to live with Diane and Lee because their home was already full, but another treatment foster care family was available. Because mutual support between treatment foster parents was a large component of the program and treatment parents met with each other regularly to exchange ideas about their children, Lee and Diane were able to help with the "getting acquainted" period between Jason and his new treatment foster parents. Jason met once more with Lee and Diane's own children and the foster child he had lived with before, who was still with them. The people around him were therefore not entirely strange, and he was already familiar with the procedures that would be adopted.

Jason Yellowbird's Placement Sequence

Jason first entered out-of-home care and was placed in a residential treatment center at the age of 9. He was 10 years old when he was first placed in treatment foster family care, and 13 years old at the time of his second intake to treatment foster family care. If the first residential treatment setting had been avoided and the child and family services had been directed to the goal of surrounding this family with services in the least restrictive and most normalized environment possible, these events may have influenced Jason's subsequent behavior and adaptation at home.

Here is the history of Jason's placement locations:

- Home of natural parents.
- Residential treatment center.
- Group emergency home.
- Foster family–based treatment.
- Home of natural parents.
- Youth correctional center.
- Group emergency home.
- Run away.
- Youth correctional center.
- Foster family–based treatment.

Since first entering out-of-home care, Jason had experienced 10 placement changes or living environments, one from which he had run away, and five placements more restrictive than treatment foster families. He had lived in group emergency homes (shelters) on two occasions. Jason's placement history provides a useful review of the frequency and types of out-of-home care provided for him. Ideally, Jason's out-of-home placements should reduce restrictiveness of his environment and care over time. The degree of restrictiveness of each setting varied.

Goals for Future Living Arrangements   The aim will be for Jason to live with his biological mother and stepfather, in semi-independent living, or independent living. General goals include increasing Jason's social competency skills, as well as drug counseling and treatment focused on increasing positive behaviors and self-esteem.

Planning for Services   Planning for Jason was undertaken on the basis of all his records to date, observations made by his treatment foster parents, and the assessment of his social worker.

Evidence-based practices are needed to address transition to semi-independent or independent living status for Jason. Include information about best practices for this population and discuss (1) housing, (2) connections with family and other supports, (3) health and well-being, (4) culture and identity supports, (5) work and vocational plans, (6) recreation, and (7) other skills and competencies as needed for self-sufficiency. The best practice service model used with Jason and his family should be based on the concept of "wrapping" services around the child in the family and community setting with the goal of transition to adulthood. What policies need to be in place to support youths like Jason?

▼▼▼

CHAPTER TWELVE

The Foxx Family: Physical Abuse, Aggression, and Parent–Child Management

The case study of the Foxx family provides opportunities for you to learn about assessing a family as well as to practice discussing family assessment. Study questions and exercises may be done independently as a form of self-study or in peer group learning situations. Some exercises are more relevant than others to the work of particular individuals and groups. Remember that different and creative responses are acceptable as your planned interventions, but ensure that you are following evidence-based practices for your client. Child welfare cases are extremely complex, and identifying the best option for John may be less than perfect given the lengthy problem history and damage from excessive placement breakdown.

Study Activities

Activity 1: Consider the Case

1. What do you consider to be the biggest challenge this case presents in terms of family reunification? What family subsystems need to be changed, and what changes are necessary? Who is the family?
2. How have the negative stressful events in childhood and adolescence affected John's developmental process? How can social support help?
3. Families of origin provide instrumental and emotional social support through childhood and long into adulthood. Discuss the supports that need to be created or reinforced for John.
4. What would you need from the other community service providers to reach case goals? What are (or could be) obstacles to meeting case goals?

Activity 2: Web Site Exploration

1. Examine interventions for treatment of physical abuse and neglect, such as family preservation and shared family care. Shared family ca[...] which host caregivers and the parent(s) care for the ch[...]

2. Parenting programs are important, and the Child W[...] research at the research to practice site. After reviewin[...] intervention do you recommend for the Foxx famil[...] programs/r2p/biblioparenting.pdf.

3. Promising practices research interventions can be [...] express Web site. Check out the co-occurrence of dom[...] ment: http://cbexpress.acf.hhs.gov/articles.cfm?sectio[...] examine promising practices to strengthen tribal families: http://cbexpress.acf.hhs.gov/articles.cfm?issue_id=2005-02&article_id=911.

4. A well-known review of the empirical literature examines the cycle of abuse by Cathy Widom. What characteristics are present in this case for the continuing cycle of abuse? http://www.aic.gov.au/publications/aust-violence-2/widom.pdf. Identify the individual, family, and system risk factors present in this case.

5. Retrieve and read the following articles and discuss which parenting program is suitable for the Foxx family. What cultural adaptations would you suggest?

   a. Thomlison, B. (2003). Characteristics of evidence-based child maltreatment interventions. *Child Welfare: Special Issue on Building Evidence to Improve Outcomes for Children, Youth, and Families, 82,* 541–569.

   b. Thomlison, B. (2004). Child maltreatment. In L. Rapp-Paglicci, C. Dulmus, & J. Wodarski (Eds.), *Handbook of preventive interventions for children and adolescents* (pp. 381–414). New York: John Wiley & Sons.

   c. Thomlison B., & Craig, S. (2005). Ineffective parenting. In C. Dulmus & L. Rapp-Paglicci (Eds.), *Handbook of preventive interventions for adults* (pp. 327–359). New York: John Wiley & Sons.

   d. Additional information on evidence-based parenting can be downloaded from Child Welfare League of America, Research to Practice Initiative Web site: http://www.cwla.org/programs/r2p/biblioparenting.pdf. What parenting program do you think is the best fit for the Foxx Family? Why?

Case Study: John Foxx

Identifying Information

- *Parents:* Jennifer Smith, age 35, now living in Colorado; Samuel Foxx, age 38, now living in Niagara Falls.
- *Children:* John, age 16.
- *Race:* Native American.
- *Religion:* Roman Catholic.
- *Languages:* Member of the Blood Tribe.
- *Parents' occupation:* unknown
- *Referral source:* Child Protective Services (CPS).

Presenting Problem

John Foxx, now age 16, was born when Jennifer Smith was age 19 and Samuel Foxx was age 22. His mother recalls both her pregnancy and the delivery of John as difficult. She feels that there were likely some complications at the time of birth. Jennifer describes her relationship with Samuel as physically abusive. She was battered both during and after her pregnancy. When

John was approximately seven months old, she left Samuel and moved to Denver, Colorado, where she presently resides. Samuel did not remain involved in John's life, although he made sure John was registered at his birth with the Sioux Tribe, Samuel's homeland (reservation).

John's first contact with Child Protective Services was at the age of 3, when he was found wandering in his neighborhood. He had apparently unlocked his babysitter's door and left while his mother was working. After he was found wandering a second time, his mother was given information on choosing appropriate child care and referred for observation in a special child interdisciplinary developmental center and to her family medical doctor.

At the age of 6, in first grade, John was the subject of a police report sent to Child Protective Services (CPS) for information only, regarding John's theft of a bicycle. The police had caught John, returned the bicycle, and at the request of his mother, spoken to John sternly about the theft. Approximately one week after the police report was sent, in October, John's school principal contacted Child Protective Services (CPS) reporting that John was threatening other children on the school grounds with a knife. When these concerns were investigated, Jennifer indicated that although John had always been a challenge to manage, his behavior had worsened approximately four months earlier, in June, when he had been severely battered by the spouse of his babysitter. A police complaint had been made after the incident and a warrant issued for the arrest of the abuser, who had already left the state. There were concerns about possible neurological damage as a result of the abuse. Jennifer was described as appropriate in her parenting and in developing more effective strategies for managing her son's behavior. The file was closed in December, three months after the report was initially taken.

The school again contacted CPS in February, two months after the closure of the file. Jennifer was contacted, but no services were offered. Five months after the file was reopened, CPS was contacted by Jennifer and her therapist, requesting services due to physical and emotional abuse of Jennifer and John by Jennifer's common-law partner. Jennifer and the school had moved John to a specialized school program for children with severe management problems. The abuse was disclosed to the therapist working with the family. John was age 7 at this time.

Two months following the disclosure of the physical abuse, a supervision order was requested in family court. A two-month adjournment was granted to serve court documents to the common-law partner. On the return to court, a four-month supervision order was granted. At the end of the supervision order, Jennifer agreed to a voluntary support supervision agreement. The school contacted Child Protective Services again in June, shortly after John's eighth birthday, indicating that John was exposing himself to other children at school. During this period Jennifer gave birth to a healthy baby boy.

The family was reportedly doing well when they moved in September with the common-law partner to his homeland. Jennifer was working full-time at a seasonal position and was commuting to the homeland on weekends. Her common-law husband was looking after the children. The file was transferred to the social services department on the reserve and was closed in February.

In the same month the file was closed, Jennifer left her partner and returned to the city. Jennifer contacted Child Protective Services with concerns about John and requesting a residential treatment program. John's behaviors included stealing, lying, hurting small animals, running away from home, and managing his anger poorly. Also according to the file, John either was not wiping himself well after bowel movements or was soiling his pants.

Child Protective Services was able to place John in a receiving and assessment home immediately and to reconnect Jennifer and John with the therapist who had been involved when John was 7. In March, a school report assessed John as failing in school, using avoidance techniques (such as talk avoidance and no eye contact), being afraid of making mistakes, having difficulty with peers, and behaving aggressively with peers and adults.

A neurological assessment was requested and scheduled based on Jennifer's information about John's battering by his former babysitter's spouse. There was no evidence of follow-through. Questions were also raised regarding a possible conduct disorder. The pediatrician involved did not recommend an assessment.

At age 9, John was returned home to the care of his mother and her common-law partner, who had reconciled with Jennifer. Jennifer had completed an intensive parenting program, and her partner had been referred to a program for men who batter. Jennifer was again employed seasonally, and the partner was looking after the children.

In August John was again placed in a foster home and concerns were raised regarding his behavior and treatment of animals. John was returned home, and in September an emergency placement was located in a treatment facility.

Two years later, in October, John was again placed back into out-of-home care. Three months later, in January, a termination of parental rights order was granted. Since John has come into the foster care system he has experienced approximately 51 placements. The high number may be partly because of John's tendency to run away and partly because of the inability of foster parents to manage his behavior. The majority of John's placements have been in group care. John has been in and out of juvenile offenders' facilities since the age of 13. He was sexually abused at the age of 12 while in care and is believed to be a sexual offender himself, although there is nothing written to support this belief.

John continues to have contact with his mother and his three half-siblings. She is not included in the planning for John because she no longer has parental rights. John initiates the majority of the contacts. John's biological father was located when John was 12 because John had requested contact with his father. Nothing resulted from this contact.

John is presently 17 years of age, has approximately a grade 7 education and no job or life skills, and continues to present the same behaviors that brought him into care. John is described as angry and aggressive. He lies and steals. His primary coping strategies are abusing drugs and alcohol, running away, and sleeping. He is likely depressed but unlikely to take medication regularly. Although he is of Native American descent on his father's side, he does not identify with his father's tribe. He is presently in a youth detention center for auto theft. It is possible that his sentence will extend to at least his 18th birthday, at which time his child welfare status will end.

Assessment Plan for John Foxx

It appears likely that John has some neurological damage. This could be from difficulties experienced during his mother's pregnancy and delivery, from the severe battering he received from a babysitter's spouse when he was 6, or from factors unknown when he was in foster care or detention placements.

John experienced severe abuse from his mother's common-law partner. When John was 12, a peer reportedly sexually assaulted him while they in a treatment facility. It is possible that John has experienced other abuse that we are not aware of.

The result is that John has difficulty problem solving, needs constant repetition to learn new information, and must have short-term concrete goals to learn new behavior. John appears to function most effectively in a highly structured environment; however, he resists structure when he is not in a restrictive setting. John has typically not done well in group living situations such as group homes. John's strengths include his desire to visit with his father and to learn to live independently. He has volunteered to work in the kitchen twice per day while in the Colorado Youth Offenders' Center, to learn new skills, and to become productive. John is able to identify his deficits and areas for growth. He has also shown a desire to remain connected to his family and has taken responsibility for maintaining his relationship with his mother.

Several recommendations that might positively influence John's future are presently being pursued for him:

1. John needs to be allowed to develop the skills necessary to experience some success as an independent adult. This would include actively pursuing a supported independent living situation, as John has requested. John should also be helped to find a vocational assessment and placement that would address his specific learning needs. The Taking Care of Families Program believes that John's child welfare status should be extended while pursuing a vocational skill, with John's consent, to allow for this.
2. John needs an opportunity to visit his family in Michigan with supervision and support for both John and his family.

3. John should be provided the opportunity and support to explore his culture and heritage, including traditional spiritual healing. A Native mentor has consented to see John while he is incarcerated to allow him to explore traditional Native spirituality. John would benefit from exposure to traditional activities while visiting with family in Michigan.

John has difficulty developing and maintaining relationships and appears to use distancing tactics, such as running away, to avoid allowing others to become close to him. John anticipates that he will let people down, and he may deliberately sabotage relationships that are important to him. Like most adolescents with John's history, he has learned survival skills such as not letting others know about weaknesses and not trusting others quickly. John has shut down his feelings for such an extended time that he appears to have limited ability to express or identify his feelings. This may be why his predominant emotion, particularly under stress, is displayed as anger. John's primary coping strategies are running away, drugs and alcohol, reacting with anger, and sleeping. John shows symptoms of depression including his sleeping pattern, his slow movement, and a similar history, which would all be risk factors for depression. John's history notwithstanding, he typically presents to people as a young man who has great potential that has been given little opportunity to flourish. He can demonstrate caring for others.

▼▼▼

CHAPTER THIRTEEN

The Sherman Family: Applying for Adoption

T his case example is an assessment of the Sherman family and highlights adoption issues. Students can complete three activities.

Study Activities

Activity 1: Assessment

1. Develop a three-generation genogram, noting patterns and themes in the family. What additional information can you learn from this genogram?
2. Complete a social network map and grid. Write a brief assessment of the resources this family has for problem solving.

Activity 2: Discuss Attitudes, Beliefs, and Values

Discuss with your classmates whether there are special problems in this family, if this were a gay or lesbian family seeking adoption. Do you anticipate any special problems in this family during early childhood, during adolescence, or in later life? What are these issues affecting the family? How might this experience affect the child, if at all?

Activity 3: Design an Adoption Support Group

Psychoeducation groups are models of best practice. Do you think this approach is suitable for postadoption family groups? Design a psychoeducation group program for families using an evidence-based approach. Locate one empirically based study supporting adoptive families using family groups.

The Sherman Family: Home Assessment Report for Private Adoption

Part 1: Identifying Information and Personal History

Robert and Angela Sherman are a Caucasian American couple who hope to adopt a child. The couple met in 1984 shortly after Angela was divorced from her first husband, and they married in 1988. The following assessment information is the result of interviews at their home. Figure 13.1 is a guide for collecting the pre-adoption assessment data.

Robert Sherman

Identifying Information   Robert Sherman, age 32 years, is 6 feet tall, weighs 160 pounds, and is of medium build. He has blue eyes, brown hair, and a dark complexion. Robert was born and raised in Cleveland, Ohio.

Family Background/History   Robert is Caucasian of German descent. He is the younger of two children born to Sue and Sonny Sherman. In 1976 Sue died at the age of 38 from complications of an ulcer. Robert was 8 years old at the time. Sonny Sherman died of cancer in July of 1988 at the age of 73. He had been a successful small businessman while raising his children. Robert and his father were close. Robert has one older brother, Bill, who lives in Cleveland with his wife and two children. They maintain weekly contact and share a close relationship. Bill is an electrician and holds a supervisory position in a service company.

Robert describes his childhood as both difficult and rewarding. Following his mother's death, he began to take on increasing amounts of responsibility for himself and household tasks. His older brother was in his adolescence and so was not as actively involved in daily tasks as was Robert. Their father worked long hours, and Robert became responsible for cooking, cleaning, grocery shopping, and looking after the family pet. In some ways it was like a partnership with his father. As a result of this shared family responsibility, Robert and his father became very good friends, as well as close as a father and son. They spent a great deal of their free time in mutual interests like restoring antique boats. These mutual interests and shared time continued until his father's death.

From his father Robert learned to value independence, hard work, and the importance of family. Robert has worked hard for everything he has achieved in his life and feels that this is an important part of what children should learn in families. He values education and places importance on open communication in relationships. Robert does not recall that he was ever spanked as a child. Rather, his father would spend time with him discussing the inappropriate behavior and more appropriate alternatives.

Robert would like to raise his children in the same manner that he was raised. A major difference would be that his children would not need to take on the same degree of responsibility that he did at such an early age. Robert was raised a Roman Catholic and attended Catholic schools while growing up. He continues to see religion as an important part of his life and would raise a child as a Christian. However, because he and his wife are of different faiths they have not yet made a final decision on what faith the child would be raised in or if the child would have a dual religious upbringing. Robert's brother is aware of and supportive of Robert's desire to adopt a child.

Education and Employment   Robert graduated from high school in Cleveland in 1986. He attended the Ohio Institute of Technology from 1986 to 1991, completing his training as an electrician. Following graduation he worked for Sharpe & Sharpe from 1991 to 1998. The last four years he worked for Sharpe & Sharpe were in Cleveland, Ohio, where he had moved in 1998. In 2000 Robert moved to his present position with Trans-Cleveland Electricians as a senior electrician. Robert indicates that he enjoys his present position and finds it both challenging and stimulating. His career goals include obtaining a managerial position, and he

Adoptive applicants:
Address:
Telephone:
Others in the home:

    Date/place of marriage:
    Religion:

Dates of assessment interviews:
Dates of reference interviews:
Date of report:
Report completed for:
Report completed by:
Name of adoptive father:

    Birth date and place:

Name of adoptive mother:

    Birth date and place:

Address:

    Residence:
    Work (wife):
    Work (husband):

Collateral checks:

    Vital statistics documentation:
    Police records:
    Child welfare records:
    Marriage certificate:
    Cleveland Police Service:
    Other documentation:

References:

    Name:
    Address:
    Telephone:
    Occupation:
    Relationship/length:

Ohio family and social services:
Divorce documentation:

Figure 13.1   Example of Assessment Outline for Private Adoption

continues to pursue this objective. Robert works long hours but enjoys his time off for family and personal interests.

Health and Lifestyle   Robert reports that he is in excellent health. He experienced all the usual childhood ailments. He was hospitalized for removal of a kidney stone in 1996. He has never had any mental health concerns and presents as an emotionally stable individual.

Robert maintains a healthful lifestyle through regular exercise, not smoking, and drinking only on occasion. The use of nonprescription drugs has never been part of his lifestyle. Robert has no criminal record, and physical violence is unacceptable to him.

Personal Qualities   Robert presents as a mature, intelligent, and dependable man with a charming sense of humor. He describes himself as friendly and caring and feels his best qualities are his ability to get along with anyone and his intelligence. His spouse describes him as loving, witty, artistic, compassionate, fun to be with, sensitive, and a good friend. She appreciates most his encouraging and supportive manner. Robert identifies work as being stressful to some degree, but he copes with stress by relying on the support systems he has established— for example his spouse, family, and friends—and by leaving work problems at work. He finds that he needs time away from work to maximize his ability to manage the ongoing stress of his job.

Robert also has a wide range of interests and activities that he enjoys in his leisure time, including restoring antique autos, bike riding, watching movies, and spending time with his dog.

Angela Sherman

Identifying Information   Angela Sherman, age 33 years, is 5 feet 6 inches tall and weighs 159 pounds. She has blue eyes, dark red hair, and a fair complexion. Angela was born in Charlotte, North Carolina. She moved to Cincinnati, Ohio, when she was 9 years old, and approximately three years later her family moved to Cleveland, Ohio.

Family Background/History   Angela is of German and Irish descent. She is the second of three children born to Sid and Margaret Porter. Sid, age 67 years, is a retired manager for a large oil company. Margaret, age 67, was an executive before becoming a homemaker. She continues to be active in volunteer work. The Porters have been married approximately 43 years. Angela describes her parents' marriage as strong. Her parents continue to be active in their church and their community, and they are enjoying extensive traveling. Because her parents now live in North Carolina, Angela does not see them as much as she would like. She does, however, visit with them approximately three times per year. Between visits she talks with them by telephone every other week.

Angela's older brother, George, age 37, is married with two children and living in North Carolina. He is employed as a manager. Angela's younger sister, Judy, age 29, lives in North Carolina with her husband and two small children. She is employed part-time as a technician. Angela indicates that she is close to her siblings and sees them when she goes home to visit with her parents.

Angela describes her family as loving and affectionate. They focused on shared activities, and she recalls time spent on family vacations and camping trips, playing games and putting puzzles together. She does not recall that she was ever physically punished as a child. Rather her parents talked to their children about expectations regarding behavior, and if there was a problem, time was spent problem solving. Angela indicates that her family experienced no major difficulties as she was growing up.

Angela's family was active in the Baptist Church. Angela was involved in church youth groups, and she continues to attend church services. Because Robert is of a different religion, they alternate between attending his and her religious services. Both feel strongly about the importance of raising a child with Christian beliefs, and they do not anticipate difficulty in deciding on the child's Christian education.

From her family, Angela learned to value her religious beliefs, her family, and education. She would like to raise her children as she was raised. She would also encourage more open communication with her children because she feels that with all the difficulties facing children and adolescents in today's society, good communication is more essential than ever.

Angela's family is aware of and supports her desire to adopt. Angela indicates that six of her cousins are adopted and that within her extended family, adoption is viewed as a natural and loving way of forming your family.

Education and Employment   Angela graduated from high school in 1983. She attended the university from 1983 to 1987 and obtained her bachelor of education degree with a major in early childhood services. Angela paid for her education by working. On graduation, she had accumulated a great deal of experience in the area and found employment with another great company. She enjoys her work and finds it challenging. Because her work is important to her, she is unsure exactly what she will do following an adoption. She feels it is likely that after a maternity leave she will continue at least part-time in some type of work. No plans have been made as to the exact type of child care the family would use, although options such as day care, day homes, and a nanny have been discussed.

Health and Lifestyle   Angela reports that she is in excellent health. She had all the usual childhood diseases. Angela's commitment to good health is reflected in her lifestyle. She is a nonsmoker and occasional drinker. The use of nonprescription drugs has never been part of her lifestyle. Angela has never been in trouble with the law, and physical violence is unacceptable to her.

Personal Qualities   Angela presents as a friendly, competent, and caring individual. She describes herself as enthusiastic, loving, compassionate, and sympathetic. She feels one of her strongest points is her caring for others. Her spouse describes her as sensitive and fun. He feels she is his best friend. Angela has found her infertility to be a source of stress in the last several years. She copes with this stress by talking to her husband, her family, and her wide circle of friends. She finds that talking about her concerns is an important part of how she deals with difficulties in her life. She also has a variety of interests including sewing, all types of crafts, golfing, art, home decorating, traveling, walking, and bike riding.

Part 2: Family Dynamics and Community Relationships

Previous Marital Relationship   Angela was married before her present relationship. She knew her first husband for two years prior to marrying him in 1982. She did not feel that the relationship was bad or unhealthy in any way and was surprised when, without notice, her husband left the marriage. They were separated in 1984 and received their final divorce decree in the same year. In retrospect, Angela suspects that her husband might have been having an extramarital affair because he married a coworker shortly after the divorce was final. Having had one unsuccessful marriage, Angela feels it is important, in a relationship, to have open communication about both thoughts and feelings. She indicates that she has been able to adequately resolve her feelings about the failure of her first marriage but that resolution would have been easier had she been aware of the reasons for her husband's leaving the marriage.

Present Marital Relationship   The Shermans met at a company party in 1984. Two weeks after they met, Robert was transferred to Cleveland Shores. Robert and Angela dated long distance for four years before Robert was able to find employment in Cleveland and move back in 1988. They both knew early in the relationship that it was serious, and this motivated their almost weekly visits with each other. After Robert moved back to Cleveland in June, the couple was married in October of the same year.

The Shermans describe their marriage as a loving and supportive relationship. They feel that they are similar in that they are careful, thoughtful, and analytical people. This similarity has helped them when they are attempting to work through a problem situation because they can be objective in looking at all possible problems and solutions. They make their choices based on all the information available to them at the time. When dealing with conflict in their relationship, the

Shermans attempt to acknowledge differences, communicate how they feel about the issue, and make a choice in which the individual needs of both are taken into consideration. Angela indicates that Robert is not always forthcoming with his feelings, and she attempts to give him an opportunity to think through what is bothering him while trying to offer him opportunities to communicate his worries to her. Thus far, this approach has met with some success, and they continue to work on strengthening and improving their already strong commitment to each other.

The Shermans also share beliefs on child rearing. They would like their children to develop respect for themselves and others, to have Christian morals and values, to have their parents' value of family, and to understand the importance of striving to achieve their goals. Neither Robert nor Angela believes that physical punishment is really necessary to discipline a child. They cannot anticipate exactly how they might react as parents but believe that nonpunitive methods of discipline would be more likely options for them.

The Shermans have a wide and varied support network. Because they are close to Angela's family and Robert's brother, they maintain regular contact with them.

They have a wide circle of friends, and Angela also has a number of work-related friendships on which she relies for support. The Shermans believe that traditions and rituals have a role in the family and invite their family and friends to join them in their traditions. Christmas is an especially important time for this couple, and they look forward to sharing it with children.

The Shermans foster a child in a third-world country through the Global Foster Parents Network. They believe it is important to assist others who have not been as fortunate as they have. They see themselves as becoming more active in their local community when they have children who become involved. They believe that it may be helpful to seek the support of other adoptive parents at some time to help them deal effectively with issues common to adopted children and adoptive parents. They see the Adoptive Parents Association as an appropriate agency for these types of issues. They feel comfortable seeking professional assistance with problems that they are unable to resolve on their own.

Part 3: Home and Neighborhood

Robert and Angela moved into their new home in December 1988. It is a 2,254 square foot, two-story home. There are three bedrooms upstairs and a den on the main floor; they are completing a large recreational area in the basement. The Shermans' home is warm, welcoming, and beautifully decorated. Schools, parks, and recreational facilities are all in close proximity.

Part 4: Income

This couple is confident in their ability to meet the financial needs of a child and to provide a financially secure home for their family. Robert's gross annual income is $63,648.00 and his net monthly income is $3,400.00. Angela's gross annual income is $61,620.00 and her net monthly income is $3,492.00. They both have benefits packages through their work.

This couple's assets include $37,000.00 in savings, a $250,000.00 home, $75,000.00 in automobiles, $40,000.00 in real estate equity, and $44,000.00 in retirement savings plans.

Their monthly expenses are estimated at $1,898.00 including food, clothing, utilities, property taxes, transportation, and entertainment costs. Although they own their home, they also have investment property on which they have a mortgage of $154,500.00. The monthly payment of $1,758.00 is covered by a renter.

Financial decision making and responsibility are shared by Robert and Angela. They share similar goals and values in this area of their lives and feel able to more than adequately meet the financial responsibilities of children.

Part 5: Understanding of Adoption and Motivation

Angela became aware that she might have fertility difficulties during her first marriage. In 1983 she was referred to a specialist for an introductory consultation. Because her marriage ended shortly after that, she did not pursue the matter. The Shermans were referred to an infertility clinic in March 1989. In August 1989 a laparoscopy was done on Angela, and it was determined that she had no apparent problems except for endometriosis, which does not necessarily result in infertility. In January 1991 Angela had surgery for the endometriosis. Both she and her husband hope that the surgery may result in a pregnancy. However, they consider adoption an acceptable way of building their family if they continue to be unable to conceive. As a result of this ongoing uncertainty, the Shermans have not completely resolved their infertility issues. If they continue to be unable to conceive following the surgery, they feel that they will need to deal with and accept their infertility. They are very motivated to become parents, and if they are unable to do so through pregnancy, would like to adopt a child into their home.

Robert and Angela first began discussing adoption in 1988. They registered with an adoption agency in November 1990. Because Angela has so many adopted cousins, she is comfortable with the idea of adoption. The Shermans feel that adoption should be an open issue and that children should be told from the time they are small that they are adopted. They feel sure that adoptees will go through periods of wondering about their birth parents and that adoptive parents can help by being honest and giving them any age-appropriate information they want.

Robert and Angela express great empathy for the birth mother and the difficult decision she has to make for her child. They would be comfortable with meeting the birth parents prior to placement and would accept letters, photographs, and gifts from the birth parents of their child. The Shermans would not be comfortable with ongoing contact following placement.

Robert and Angela attended a workshop for adoptive couples in November 1990 and show a good understanding of the issues specific to parenting an adopted child. They both feel strongly that is important to treat children with love and respect and to deal with any issues about adoption with openness and honesty. They feel that the challenges associated with parenting an adopted child would be worth undertaking, considering the rewards of parenting.

Part 6: Child Desired

The Shermans would like to adopt a healthy, Caucasian infant of either sex. They would consider a child of up to six months of age and would be open to twins. They are not open to a child conceived by rape or incest. They would prefer to have information about the background of both birth parents. They would have concerns if there was a history of mental illness, learning disabilities, developmental difficulties, a criminal history, history of drug use, prostitution, or smoking and drinking in the background of either birth parent. They would consider a child born with a minor repairable birth defect but would not be willing to accept a child with an obvious physical defect or handicap.

Part 7: References

All references were interviewed, and support was given to the Shermans' application to adopt a child. This couple was described as honest, hardworking, and loving, and they were seen to value family relationships highly. They have a desire to parent and the ability to manage the challenge of parenting an adopted child. The references felt that the Shermans share a relationship based on mutual respect, caring, and shared interests and values. All of the references stated that they would be comfortable leaving their children in the care of Robert and Angela, knowing they would be well cared for. Overall, the couple were seen as being highly motivated to parent and well able to meet, and to share together, the social, emotional, physical, and intellectual needs of a child placed in their care.

Part 8: Overview of Assessment Process

The Shermans were interviewed in their home on December 1 and December 2, 1999. Prior to their home assessment, the couple had given the issue of adding to their family through adoption considerable thought and had discussed their hopes of adopting with others in their support network. In November 1990 they registered with a private adoption agency and attended a pre-adoption workshop for adoptive parents.

Robert and Angela present as a mature couple whose marriage is marked by caring, support, and respect. This couple is sincere in their desire to parent and if unable to conceive would like to build their family through adoption. They have given the issues of adoption serious consideration. They display comfort with the process of open adoption, and it is believed they will manage the challenges of adoption with success. The Shermans are realistic about the responsibilities of parenting an adopted child. They are able to provide a secure and loving home for a child. They have a strong support network to whom they turn easily for advice and support.

Part 9: Recommendation

It is recommended that Robert and Angela Sherman be approved as candidates for the private adoption of a child.

Respectfully submitted,

Debbie Cattrello, M.S.W.
Adoption Worker

▼▼▼

CHAPTER FOURTEEN

The Fernandez Family: Supporting an Older Adult

Denise Gammonley
University of Central Florida

T he case study of the Fernandez family provides opportunities for you to learn about assessing a family with an older adult member, as well as to discuss family assessment and best practice interventions. Study questions and exercises may be done independently as a form of self-study or in peer group learning situations in your class. Some exercises are more relevant than others to the work of particular individuals and groups. Remember that different and creative responses are acceptable as your plan interventions, but ensure that you are following evidence-based practices for your client.

Study Activities

1. Learn more about the impact of substance abuse on older adults and their families at http://www.ncbi.nlm.nih.gov/books/bv.fcgi?rid=hstat5.chapter.48302.
   a. What assessment tools would you use to assess the alcohol severity problem of Jorge?
   b. Write a family assessment and include the presenting issues, strengths and problems in the family, and the role that culture plays in the family.
   c. Write the goals and intervention plan for this family.
2. Then use the Caregiver Well-Being Toolkit to identify one assessment instrument you could use to evaluate the success of your intervention with the Fernandez family. You can find the Caregiver Well-Being Toolkit at http://www.chcr.brown.edu/PCOC/family burden.htm.
3. Use the AgeLine database to locate an outcome study or an intervention study designed to help family caregivers of people with Alzheimer's disease. The AgeLine Research Database can be viewed at http://www.aarp.org/research/ageline/.
4. Look up the research on psychoeducation family groups. Do you think this intervention is suitable for families with a member who has Alzheimer's disease? Explain how this intervention helps, and outline the intervention group sessions.

Case Study: The Fernandez Family

Eighty-three-year-old widowed Yolanda Fernandez resides in a single-family home in an upper-middle-class neighborhood with her 62-year-old (single, never married) son Jorge. Yolanda suffers from moderate Alzheimer's disease and has recently been declared legally incapacitated to make personal decisions or to control her finances. She is still able to do some activities of daily living independently and has not exhibited significant agitation or incontinence yet. She needs supervision during the day, however, because she has a tendency to wander away from home if left alone. Most nights she is less active and sleeps through the night, thanks to a prescription for a psychotropic medication.

Jorge has lived in the family home for his entire life and serves as the primary caregiver for his mother. He is a gay man and a recovering alcoholic who experiences frequent relapses. He is employed sporadically as a waiter but often loses jobs due to recurrent problems with addiction. Mostly, Jorge relies on Yolanda's substantial income for financial support.

Fifty-two-year-old Wanda is Yolanda's daughter and guardian of person and property. She resides in the same neighborhood as Yolanda and Jorge with her spouse, Eduardo, and their two teenage sons, Carlos and Miguel. Yolanda is deeply involved in her faith community, the Catholic Church, and works part-time in the rectory office. Fifty-three-year-old Eduardo, an investment banker, struggles to accept the sexual orientation of Jorge and prefers that Jorge not interact with his two sons.

You have received a referral from Adult Protective Services for this case requesting a comprehensive family assessment and possible family therapy intervention for Jorge, Yolanda, and Wanda. Neighbors made the report of neglect to Adult Protective Services after witnessing Yolanda wandering around in the front yard in her pajamas on more than one occasion. According to the neglect report, Jorge reportedly left his mother for extended periods on several occasions. There have also been reports that he frequently brings home male companions who may stay for days or weeks in the home. Adult Protective Services has agreed to close the case if Jorge and Wanda agree to purchase daily respite care for Yolanda and seek family counseling to resolve their differences.

Conflict between Wanda and Jorge remains high and is exacerbated by the fact that Wanda had Jorge involuntarily committed for inpatient alcohol treatment earlier in the year. Wanda would like Yolanda to move into a life care residence or rest home, but Jorge is dead set against it. The Fernandez family is Cuban American. Yolanda first moved to the United States in 1960 at the age of 37, accompanied by Wanda, who was 7, and Jorge, who was 15. Yolanda's spouse, Francisco, emigrated to the United States along with Yolanda and the children in 1960 and established himself in a successful career as an accountant but struggled with alcohol addiction most of his adult life. He died in a motor vehicle accident in 1986.

▼▼▼

CHAPTER FIFTEEN

The Jacques Family: Assessment and Intervention in Family Violence

Jennifer Becker
Florida International University

The case study of the Jacques family provides opportunities for you to learn about assessing a family suffering from domestic violence, as well as to discuss family assessment and best practice interventions. Study questions and exercises may be done independently as a form of self-study or in peer group learning situations in your class. Some exercises are more relevant than others to the work of particular individuals and groups. Remember that different and creative responses are acceptable as your plan interventions, but ensure that you are following evidence-based practices for your client.

Study Activities

Activity 1: Assessment

1. Find at least one empirically based measure to assess the risk of family violence presented by the father in this case. Discuss the properties and limitations of this measure.
2. Research the "cycle of violence" within relationships impacted by domestic violence. Describe how this cycle is evident in the Jacques family.
3. Assess and discuss current risk and protective factors present within the family system.
4. Find at least two empirical studies addressing the impact of exposure to domestic violence on children. Considering the unique developmental stages and behavioral and emotional problems evidenced by the Jacques children, discuss the apparent impact of exposure to domestic violence on each child.
5. Research the relationship between domestic violence, mental health disorders, and substance abuse. Report your findings.
6. Explore the available literature regarding parenting self-efficacy of mothers who are victims of domestic violence. How would you assess Marie Jacques's perceptions of her parenting abilities? Refer to Chapter 12, Activity 2, for parenting references in the Foxx

family and determine what type of evidence-based parenting program Marie may be best suited for. What parent, child, or family factors were the basis for your decision?

Activity 2: Intervention

1. Based on what you have learned from the empirical literature about the risks and deleterious effects associated with domestic violence, what intervention(s) would you recommend for the Jacques family?
2. What strategies would you employ to effectively engage the mother and children in treatment?
3. What resources can you provide to assist the family in identifying and accessing support for improved individual and family functioning at this time?

Activity 3: Cultural Issues

1. What is the influence of cultural traditions, rituals, and transitions in the Jacques family system?
2. How would you employ culturally competent assessment and intervention strategies in assisting Marie Jacques and her children?

Case Study: The Jacques Family

Reason for Referral

The Jacques family was referred for individual and family therapy by a Child Protective Services (CPS) caseworker, following Marie Jacques' hospitalization for injuries sustained during a domestic violence dispute. Her husband, Jean Jacques, reportedly physically assaulted Marie with a baseball bat, resulting in a compound fracture to her arm and severe bruising and cuts to her face. The Jacques' 11-year-old son, Joshua, called 911 during the dispute. When the police arrived, they arrested Jean. An ambulance brought Marie to the hospital. CPS obtained temporary custody of the children. The Jacques' five children were placed in an emergency shelter during the 10 days Marie was hospitalized. The CPS caseworker was unable to locate relatives to care for the children. When Marie was discharged from the hospital, the children returned home to her care. CPS assessed the family to be at minimal risk of harm and has closed their case with referrals to therapeutic services, including family therapy and individual counseling for all five children. At the time of referral, Jean was still incarcerated, pending charges of domestic violence and aggravated assault.

Presenting Problems

The Jacques family presents with an extensive history of domestic violence disputes and family dysfunction. All five of the Jacques children—Samuel, age 12; Joshua, age 11; Valerie, age 9; Miranda, age 6; and Matthew, age 4—demonstrate behavioral and emotional problems, as reported by shelter staff, the CPS caseworker, and their mother. Marie is unemployed. She reports feelings of depression and pain from her injuries, which inhibit her motivation to seek employment, perform household chores, and maintain parenting abilities. Marie fears her husband will be released from jail and will return to the home to kill her. The children also express fear of their father's return.

Family History

Family history is based on an intake interview with Marie Jacques.

Marie is a 31-year-old woman, born in Freeport, Bahamas. She reports being physically abused by her father but having a positive relationship with her mother throughout her childhood. Marie completed high school with honors. At the age of 19 she gave birth to her oldest son, Samuel. Marie states that Samuel's biological father sexually assaulted her, and although she considered an abortion, she chose to give birth due to her religious beliefs. Just after Samuel was born, Marie met her current husband, Jean Jacques. At the age of 20, the Jacques married and moved to the United States with Samuel. According to Marie, her husband was "a wonderful man who took care of me and my new baby." She states, "He promised us the good life and we all moved together to Florida. He said he would raise Sammy as his own."

Shortly after moving to Florida, Marie gave birth to Joshua. Despite her desire to enroll in a nursing program, Marie agreed with her husband to stay home and take care of the children. Marie's mother reportedly encouraged her to "be a good mother and wife. Stay home with the children and keep up the house." Within two years, she had three children, including Valerie. Marie reports that just after Valerie's birth, Jean began "acting really crazy and sometimes violent." He prohibited Marie from visiting her mother in the Bahamas and would not allow her family to visit. Marie states, "He started drinking a lot. He became very possessive, and wouldn't let me go anywhere or say anything." Marie expresses her desires to be supportive of her husband and take care of her children. She states she felt it was her "duty."

In an attempt to improve their relationship, Marie planned another pregnancy and gave birth to Miranda. "She was his baby and things got better for a while." But soon thereafter, Marie reports that Jean became increasingly violent. "He would just hit me for no reason. He would yell at the kids and call Sammy names. He also started having a hard time sleeping. He said he heard voices and would tell me he's sorry, someone told him to hit me. Sometimes he seemed scared of himself. He had to stop working and then he really drank a lot. He would be gone for days sometimes. I always thought he was doing drugs."

Marie reports feeling "trapped" and did not know what to do. She sought the help of a social worker she met through a neighbor. Marie convinced her husband to be evaluated by a psychiatrist, who diagnosed him with bipolar disorder and psychotic symptoms. "He seemed to feel better knowing what was wrong. They gave him medication and he promised everything would be better again. And it was for a while. He was happy, good to the kids, and good to me like the old days." Marie became pregnant with their youngest son, Matthew. Jean was hired as a store manager, and they moved to a bigger home. Marie began planning to enroll in the nursing program she had always hoped for.

Two years ago, Marie's husband gave her permission to take her children to visit her mother for three weeks in the Bahamas. She states, "I wanted them to know their grandmother and cousins, to see the island I grew up on. It was the worst thing I could have done." Marie reportedly returned to find her husband "passed out on the sofa. There were liquor bottles everywhere and I found a crack pipe. He stopped taking his medication. And then it all started again." Marie reports that Jean became increasingly violent. He lost his job, and they were evicted from their home. The family spent months "in and out of homeless shelters" until they were repeatedly denied services due to Jean's violent outbursts. After a severe physical altercation, a social worker assisted Marie and her children in admission to a domestic violence shelter.

After three months in the shelter, Marie and her children moved into a transitional housing program and then secured Section 8 housing. She had no contact with Jean for about one year. "And then he found me. He begged us back. He cried and said it would all be different. He was back on his medication and was applying for jobs. The kids missed him. I missed him. I let him in and he stayed." Marie reports that less than six months later, he discontinued his medications and quit his job. The most recent domestic violence incident was the first since his return and, according to Marie, the most severe she has ever experienced. She states, "The children have seen too much violence." Samuel attempted to intervene while his stepfather assaulted his mother with a baseball bat. Jean threw Samuel across the room and ignored the screams and cries of Valerie and Miranda.

Since returning home from the hospital, Marie reports that she is "always tired," unable to get out of bed, and has little to no appetite. She states she has not cleaned or done laundry in weeks, which is evidenced by sinks full of dishes, food and utensils on the floor, and clothing and toys strewn all over the home. She states the children often cook for themselves and "take care of each other." Marie states that school personnel and neighbors have called and attempted to help, but she has resisted their efforts. "I just can't see anybody right now. I don't know what to do." Marie has a cast on her arm and surgical pins inserted in her elbow. She reports frequent pain but does not take prescribed pain medication. She has contacted her mother, who has agreed to come to Florida and stay with the family in a few weeks.

Samuel Jacques   Samuel "Sammy" Jacques is a 13-year-old male, presenting as tall and thin. His stepfather, Jean, has raised him since birth. However, Sammy states, "I don't feel like he's my dad anymore." Sammy has darker skin than his family and states he is often teased by his siblings and also his stepfather "for being black." He was diagnosed with attention-deficit hyperactivity disorder and learning disorder at the age of 7. He is currently placed in the sixth grade, receiving Cs and Ds. He has been attending a special education school since failing the third grade and being suspended several times in mainstream elementary school. His behavioral problems in school have reportedly escalated over the past three years. He gets into fights, usually with younger peers at school, as many as three times per week. He states he has no friends at school "because they all hate me."

Sammy is also physically and verbally aggressive with his younger siblings. He recently slapped his mother during an argument. His mother reports that "he is obsessed with fire" and has set several small fires in the backyard and kitchen, none of which resulted in major damage. Sammy presents with a blunted affect and is difficult to engage. He states he enjoys drawing and demonstrates artistic skills. He has also participated in a karate program every summer, for which he expresses pride in his accomplishments. One of Sammy's teachers, Mrs. Johnson, has taken a special interest in Sammy and has offered to provide after-school tutoring.

Joshua Jacques   Joshua Jacques, age 11, presents as a quiet, reserved child. He is obese and has asthma, which requires frequent nebulizer treatments. He presents as disheveled, and his fingernails are bitten down so far that most fingers are encrusted with blood. He is in the fifth grade at the local elementary school, where he receives Bs and Cs. Joshua rides his bike to school every day with a neighborhood friend, Joseph, and often spends the night at his home. He states, "Joe is my best friend and I really like his family, too. They are like normal people. I wish they were my family." Joshua states he called the police while his father assaulted his mother. He reports, "I didn't want him to kill her. I know if he comes back he will. I dream about it every night. But then I worry about what they are doing to him in jail."

Joshua reports frequent nightmares and difficulty sleeping. He states he frequently visualizes his mother being beaten and is distracted by these thoughts while at school. Joshua's mother recently received a progress report from school stating that he is at risk of failing two classes. She also reports Joshua has hygiene problems and "refuses to bathe." Joshua states he likes to play video games and fish in the canal behind his house. Other than Joseph, he states he has no "real" friends and prefers to be alone. Joshua gets along well with his sister Valerie and sometimes takes on responsibilities around the house, such as taking out the trash and watching his youngest brother. He states he usually does well in school and is worried about failing.

Valerie Jacques   Valerie Jacques, age 9, is a small, thin female. She also presents as quiet and withdrawn, yet kind and eager to please. Valerie is in the fourth grade at the local elementary school, where she receives straight As. She has made the honor roll and had perfect attendance since the first grade. She is reportedly well liked by peers and teachers, although she does not socialize with friends outside of school. Valerie walks her younger brother and sister home from school every day. She packs their lunches, prepares dinner, and picks up their toys. Valerie's mother reports, "Valerie is very meticulous and a big help around the house." Valerie gets along well with her brother Joshua, but frequently argues with Samuel. She states she enjoys reading and writing. Valerie has a stack of neatly kept journals, which she writes in every day.

Miranda Jacques   Miranda Jacques is a 6-year-old girl who presents with a happy yet distant affect. She is enrolled in kindergarten at the local elementary school. Her mother reports, "Her teacher is always calling saying she is concerned about her. She says she doesn't pay attention or follow directions." According to her mother, Miranda "spaces out" at both home and school. Her mother states, "She has a very active imagination. She will be playing with dolls for hours and not even notice anything is going on. I will call her name 10 times before she stops talking to her doll and looks up." Her mother also reports daily bed-wetting and enuresis. Miranda often wakes her mother in the middle of the night due to nightmares. Lately she has been waking her sister Valerie following nightmares and sleeps in bed with her. She enjoys coloring and watching cartoons.

Matthew Jacques   Matthew Jacques is a 4-year-old boy who is small for his age and very physically active. He attends the Head Start preschool program at the local elementary school. He has trouble saying the alphabet and identifying colors and numbers. Matthew's mother describes him as "fearless." He recently jumped off the second story balcony of their townhouse, sprained his ankle, and had stitches in the back of his head. His mother reports, "He pulled the stitches out. It's like he feels no pain." He plays roughly with his siblings and the family dog, often pulling his tail and biting him. Matthew does not follow his mother's directions, but he responds well to Valerie, seeking her attention and affection. He enjoys playing with trucks and toy cars, but his play often becomes so aggressive his toys are taken away. The assistant principal at Matthew's school has contacted his mother several times to offer help with food and respite child care services.

▼▼▼

CHAPTER SIXTEEN

La Torre Family: A Young Adult with Mental Illness

Marian Dumaine
Florida International University

The case study of the La Torre family provides opportunities for you to learn about assessing a family with a young adult member with a chronic and persistent mental illness, schizophrenia, as well as to discuss developmental, clinical, and sociocultural issues and best practice interventions. Study questions and exercises may be done independently as a form of self-study or in peer group learning situations in your class. Some exercises are more relevant than others to the work of particular individuals and groups. Remember that different and creative responses are acceptable as your plan interventions, but ensure that you are following evidence-based practices for your client.

Study Activities

Activity 1: Psychoeducation Workshop Role-Play

As a basis for this study activity you can prepare by going to a Web site by SAMAHA, the National Mental Health Information Center. This Web site provides a complete manual of family psychoeducation and is developed as a six-step workshop.

Read the La Torre family case. Based on this case, the class will form a psychoeducation group. This role-play requires one week to plan. The task requires that you conduct one psychoeducation workshop session on schizophrenia. Two class members should facilitate the workshop, and others are to role-play families with a member who has this mental illness. The workshop leaders prepare for the educational component, and the family members should prepare question for the workshop session. Family members should not share their planning with others role-playing. The facilitators need to be prepared to answer the questions.

Use 40 minutes to carry out the workshop session, and then discuss how this intervention helps families. What would additional workshop and group meetings look like? What strategies are best to engage and maintain families in the group?

Activity 2: Case Activities for Written Assignments or Class Discussion

1. What is the impact of Celia's developmental stage on the problems she has been experiencing in her family environment, school adjustment, and social relationships?
2. Write a family assessment based on the strengths and resources of this family. Assess strengths and problems of the whole family system, marital system, parent–child system, sibling subsystem, and individual (Celia's) system.
3. What role does culture play in the family?
4. Obtain a copy of the Hudson assessment instruments identified in the case study and practice administering them to a colleague. Summarize your findings.
5. Using library and Internet search techniques, how would you assess changes in levels of expressed emotion?
6. Research has suggested that psychotropic medication and social skills training are important interventions for clients diagnosed with mental illness. How would you add these interventions to your existing treatment plan?
7. What obstacles would you anticipate to client and family involvement in treatment? How would you work with the family system to help the family members overcome these treatment barriers?
8. Different students groups will complete the following activities:
    a. Develop a genogram to examine the family history and to assess intergenerational relationships, cultural identity, conflicts, and family themes. Special attention should be given to any mental health issues that have been identified in the family through the generations.
    b. Construct an ecomap to examine family relationships, social supports, resources, and conflict areas.

Case Study: La Torre Family

Referral Information
The La Torre family was referred to Family Connections by a school guidance counselor who was concerned about Celia's sudden decline in her grades and avoidance of social contacts with her peers.

Family Data

- Father: Pedro La Torre, age 42.
- Mother: Luisa La Torre, age 40.
- Children of the La Torre marriage: Angel, age 21; Celia, age 14.

Presenting Problem
Celia attends the eighth grade at Century Middle School and has been at the top of her class every year, active on the student council, and busy with after-school activities. Celia had many friends, and the house was often active with her comings and goings. She was particularly interested in gymnastics and competed for the state championship for three years in a row.

Recently she has begun to isolate herself and reject any visits or telephone calls from friends. She has appeared sad, crying, unable to sleep, and disinterested in her homework. Celia has received failing grades in mathematics and English. She responds with angry retorts when her parents have inquired about her distress.

Family History

Celia's brother, Angel, age 21, recently returned to the home. Angel was first hospitalized at age 14 at Help Hospital due to auditory hallucinations, bizarre behaviors, suicidal ideations, and reduced impulse control. In the next four years he was hospitalized four times. Angel experiences auditory, visual (evil spirits), and tactile ("weird" body sensations) hallucinations, as well as paranoid delusions with a religious content (reads the Bible throughout the day). At times he is delusional about his medications or questions their effectiveness. He is easily agitated and responds to internal stimuli frequently, often laughing inappropriately. He is prone to tangential thoughts and ideas of reference, manifesting grandiose thoughts at times. Periodically Angel travels across the country "to escape the devil," and his whereabouts are unknown for several months. The family has received telephone calls from mental health agencies in California about Angel being homeless, wandering the streets.

Pedro and Luisa have been married 22 years, having married subsequent to Luisa's pregnancy with Angel. They migrated to New York from Puerto Rico 15 years ago with Luisa's mother after the sudden death of Luisa's father, which was attributed to a cerebral hemorrhage. Pedro's family continues to reside in Puerto Rico. Pedro and Luisa's marriage became strained after Angel began exhibiting signs of mental illness. Pedro began staying away from the home for several nights at a time, and they argued frequently about how to cope with Angel's erratic behavior. Pedro believed that Luisa was being too lenient with Angel, that Angel was "weak" and needed to "begin acting like a man." Pedro threatened to leave the home after Luisa permitted Angel to return. Luisa is often preoccupied about the welfare and whereabouts of her son, and she has begun to show little interest in her own appearance.

Assessment and Intervention Information

Sources of Information

The primary family issues initially identified are Celia's behavioral changes, Angel's mental illness, and the strain on the marriage. The family has moved from another culture and has no extended family support nearby. Additional information about these areas will be obtained from family members, school officials at Century Middle School, and mental health agencies treating Angel in recent years. The social worker plans to schedule interviews with the family and has asked the family to sign releases of information to grant permission to contact the school and mental health agencies.

Assessment Instruments

1. A genogram will be developed with the family to examine the family history and to assess intergenerational relationships, cultural identity, conflicts, supports, and family themes. Special attention will be given to any mental health issues that have been identified in the family through the generations.
2. An ecomap will also be constructed with the family's input to examine family relationships, social supports and resources, and conflict areas.
3. Assessment evaluation tools will include the Index of Clinical Stress (Hudson, 1992), the Index of Marital Satisfaction (Hudson, 1992), and a nonstandardized questionnaire. The Index of Clinical Stress measures the family's level of stress as they perceive it and will be administered to family members before and after the intervention. The Index of Marital Satisfaction measures the presence and magnitude of problems in the couple's relationship and will be administered before and after the intervention. The nonstandardized questionnaire will be administered prior to treatment to assess family knowledge about mental illness, levels of guilt, and stigma. The questionnaire will be re-administered after treatment to measure changes in knowledge and attitudes toward mental illness.

4. Efforts will be made to engage the family in treatment, recognizing potential barriers related to culture and beliefs about mental illness, and exploring their perception of the present family difficulties. The social worker will observe the family interaction patterns, alignments, roles and power, and conflict resolution strategies in the interviews.

5. Additional psychosocial information will be sought from the family:
   a. *Information about Celia*, to include developmental history; school performance and attendance; any alleged history of abuse or neglect; medical history; peer relationships; interests, hobbies, and club affiliations; spiritual supports; substance use; risky behaviors; attempts at injury to self or others; and acculturation.
   b. *Information about Angel*, to include the same areas as for Celia with the addition of information about the onset of his mental illness, treatment history, medication compliance, financial support, employment, and ability to function.
   c. *Information about the parents, Pedro and Luisa*, to include information about their education and employment history; acculturation; legal status; parenting practices; marriage; living situation; financial stressors; medical history; spiritual supports; substance use; extended family relationships; and social activities.
   d. *Assess strengths and problems* of the whole family system, marital system, parent–child system, sibling subsystem, and individual (Celia's) system, utilizing the theoretical formulation presented in this book.

Intervention Selection

Meetings with the family revealed that Celia and her parents were fearful that she would get schizophrenia. In addition, Angel was talking to himself at night, was not taking care of his personal hygiene, and had almost set the house on fire due to smoking in bed. Celia verbalized shame about bringing her friends to the house.

The social worker then consulted the notes from her family intervention class and conducted a literature search for evidence-based interventions for families with a member diagnosed with mental illness. The evidence-based intervention of psychoeducation for families was chosen because of its focus on brief therapeutic interventions and its use of group support and education to counter the stigma and self-blame verbalized by Angel's parents. It was hoped that this intervention would also improve Celia's functioning and lessen marital strain by helping the family cope with the stress related to Angel's mental illness.

Evidence-Based Intervention Strategy

Two theoretical models used in psychoeducation interventions for families, the Dynamic Vulnerability Formulation (Zubin & Spring, 1977) and Expressed Emotion (Yank, Bentley, & Hargrove, 1992), provide an explanation to families about relapse, as well as positive steps, to help families cope with the behavior of the ill family member. The Dynamic Vulnerability Formulation views relapse as an accumulation of coping failures in an individual with a vulnerability to coping breakdown. Therefore, treatment is focused on restoring adaptation and raising tolerance thresholds by increasing an individual's coping ability, ameliorating the effects of stress, and enhancing support networks. Expressed emotion (EE) is an empirically derived operational construct that relates to the propensity of family members or significant others to become overly critical or involved with the mentally ill family member, resulting in the erosion of the ill person's coping abilities despite medication compliance (Dumaine, 1997).

Psychoeducational approaches educate individuals diagnosed with persistent mental disorders such as schizophrenia and their significant others about stress, vulnerability, and protective factors. The goal is to lessen environmental stress and expressed emotion, increase collaborative problem solving, and teach communication and problem-solving skills. Families attend survival skills workshops where they learn about the nature and etiology of schizophrenia; antipsychotic medications; the role of genetics in the development of schizophrenia; specific measures to help the individual diagnosed with schizophrenia; strategies to cope with the illness; aftercare issues, the availability of vocational rehabilitation programs, and ways to promote social integration for the client (Hogarty et al., 1991). Therefore, psychoeducation seeks to improve coping skills and minimize stresses related to family life.

Studies of controlled outcome research indicate evidence of the effectiveness of psychoeducational approaches with families with a mentally ill family member (deGroot, Lloyd, & King, 2003; Falloon et al., 1985; Hogarty et al., 1991; Kopeikin et al., 1983). In addition, a manual outlining the specific curriculum was available for use (Anderson, Reiss, & Hogarty, 1986). A final rationale for the selection of the family psychoeducational approach was the existence of other families at the agency who were also struggling with caring for a mentally ill family member. Clearly an opportunity existed to apply this approach.

Based on the evidence for psychoeducation groups, the intervention included the following:

1. *Assessing the need for similar services by other clients and their families in the community:* Assessment of need for similar services entailed providing a description of the client target group: families coping with members diagnosed with severe mental illness. The rationale for services was outlined, underscoring the stress and guilt often experienced by family members; the need for families to be educated about the illness; and the need to develop strategies to lower the emotional climate in the home (Anderson, Reiss, & Hogarty, 1986).

2. *Determining the frequency and duration of each group meeting:* The frequency and duration of each group meeting would depend on the curriculum, scheduling constraints, and clinical judgment regarding the optimal time needed to present and process the material. The model outlined by Anderson, Reiss, and Hogarty in their 1986 text was chosen because this model is frequently referenced in the literature, and the program content is presented in detail. Five days are recommended for the training, but the training could also be conducted in smaller blocks of time over a longer period. Ten four-hour sessions were chosen to lengthen the program and promote group sharing, questioning, and processing of the material.

3. *Providing information to the community about the upcoming family psychoeducation groups:* An information packet about the program was developed specifying the following topics: the experience of schizophrenia; the principles of psychoeducation; information about coping with schizophrenia; connecting strategies; treatment contracts; vocational issues; social integration; and emancipation (Anderson, Reiss, & Hogarty, 1986). The social worker attended the local NAMI chapter meetings, as well as mental health coalition meetings, to inform potential group members about the program. In addition, the local newspaper printed an article about schizophrenia and mentioned the possible benefits to family members of attending the program, now called Be Informed. Finally, clients in the psychiatric crisis unit were asked for permission to contact their family members to inform them about the program.

4. *Engaging with families:* The worker then began connecting with clients and their families, utilizing the principles of the model: being immediately available in a crisis, focusing on the present crisis, avoiding treating the family as the patient, attending to family supports and stressors, preparing for the treatment contract, and solidifying the treatment relationship. The worker was careful to avoid blaming and to provide support and clarification about expectations for group membership.

5. *Facilitating family psychoeducation sessions:* The worker planned to arrange specialized training for the trainers. All trainers were asked to read the book *Schizophrenia and the Family* (Anderson, Reiss, & Hogarty, 1986) and were given homework. The homework entailed reviewing the material on a specific section and providing up-to-date handouts and PowerPoint presentations for the section. The trainers then trained each other and utilized feedback from the training group to enhance their final presentations.

Measuring and Evaluating Change
The effectiveness of the family psychoeducation intervention would be measured by three "before-and-after" measures: the Index of Clinical Stress, the Family Emotional Involvement and Criticism Scale (FEICS) (Shields, Franks, Harp, McDaniel, & Campbell, 1992), and a nonstandardized

questionnaire about the curriculum. The Index of Stress would be administered to the client diagnosed with mental illness prior to the training and upon graduation. The FEICS would be administered to the parents prior to the training and upon graduation. The nonstandardized questionnaire about the curriculum would be administered before and after each training section and would focus on family changes in knowledge and attitudes toward mental illness. In addition, Angel's progress would also be assessed on the following dimensions for one year before the training and one year after the training: crisis episodes, medication compliance, substance use, and vocational activities. These dimensions were chosen because of their frequent use in empirical studies of interventions with people diagnosed with mental illness.

Family psychoeducation was also intended to improve Celia's functioning, and the La Torre marital relationship, by reducing the family stress level and replacing fears about mental illness with facts. Celia's levels of socialization and depression will be assessed, as well as her sleep pattern, academic grades, and interest in gymnastics. Changes in marital strain would be assessed by administering the Index of Marital Satisfaction (Hudson, 1992) before and after the intervention.

Some of the challenges anticipated in implementing the intervention were (1) involving all family members; (2) ensuring a high quality of training; and (3) coordinating treatment with other service providers.

Involving All Family Members   The clients diagnosed with mental illness and their siblings, age 12 and above, are included in sessions, sometimes with their family members and sometimes in separate groups. The material must be presented in a nonthreatening, clear way to each group. It is also necessary to repeat the information, check for comprehension frequently, and help participants apply the information to their own situations.

Quality of Training   It is important that correct information is imparted to family members and that a caring, nonjudgmental attitude is conveyed by the trainer. Therefore, continued monitoring of the training should occur, as well as opportunities to process the group experiences.

Coordination with Other Service Providers   The families are likely to be involved in other treatment services. For example, the La Torre family is involved with Celia's school and Angel's psychiatrist and case manager at the mental health center. Angel might also become involved in social skills training or vocational rehabilitation. The social worker coordinating the family psychoeducational intervention will want to inform Angel's case manager about progress and be involved in case planning. The social worker will need to obtain permission from family members to exchange treatment information.

References

Administration on Aging. (2004). *Older Americans 2000: Key indicators of well-being*. Washington, DC: Federal Interagency Forum on Aging Related Statistics. Available [online]: http://www.agingstats.gov/chartbook2000/default.htm.

Alexander, J. F., & Parsons, B. V. (1982). *Functional family therapy*. Monterey, CA: Brooks/Cole.

Alexander, L. B., & Luborsky, L. (1986). The Penn Helping Alliance Scales. In L. S. Greenberg & W. M. Pinsof (Eds.), *The psychotherapeutic process: A research handbook* (pp. 325–366). New York: The Guilford Press.

Allender, J., Carey, K., Garcia-Castanon, J., Garcia, B., Gonzalez, B., Hedge, G., Herrell, A., Kiyuna, R., Rector, C., & Henderson-Sparks, J. (1997). *Interprofessional collaboration training project*. California State University, Fresno. Available from Teaching Research Division, Western Oregon State College, Monmouth, Oregon 97361.

American Psychiatric Association. (1994). *Diagnostic and statistical manual of mental disorders* (4th ed.). Washington, DC: Author.

Ammerman, R. T., & Hersen, M. (Eds.) (1999). *Assessment of family violence. A clinical and legal sourcebook*. (Second Edition). NY: John Wiley & Sons.

Anderson, C., Reiss, D. J., & Hogarty, G. (1986). *Schizophrenia and the family*. New York: Guilford.

Baird, S. C., & Wagner, D. (2000). The relative validity of actuarial- and consensus-based risk assessment systems. *Children and Youth Services Review, 22*(11/12), 839-871.

Bandura, A. (1977). *Social learning theory*. Englewood Cliffs, NJ: Prentice-Hall.

Barth, R., Landsverk, J., Chamberlain, P., Reid, J., Rolls, J., Hurlburt, M., Farmer, E., James, S.,

McCabe, K., Kohl, P., & Wood, P. (2005). Parent training programs in child welfare services: Planning for a more evidence-based approach to serving biological parents. *Research on Social Work Practice,15*, (5), 353–371.

Bavolek, S. J. (1984). *Handbook for the Adult–Adolescent Parenting Inventory*. Eau Claire, WI: Family Development Associates.

Bazron, B., Dennis, K., & Isaacs, M. (1989). *Toward a culturally competent system of care*. Washington, DC: CASSP Technical Assistance Center, Georgetown University.

Beavers, W. R., & Hampson, R. (1990). *Successful families: Assessment and intervention*. New York: Norton.

Beier, E. G., & Sternberg, D. P. (1977). Marital communication. *Journal of Communication, 27,* 92–100.

Bengston, V. L., & Allen, K. R. (1993). The life course perspective applied to families over time. In P. Boss, W. J. Doherty, R. LaRossa, W. R., Schumm, & S. K. Steinmetz (Eds.), *Source book of family theories and methods: A contextual approach* (pp. 469–499). New York: Plenum.

Botsford, A. & Rule, D. (2004). Evaluation of a group intervention to assist aging parents with permanency planning for an adult offspring with special needs. *Social Work, 49*(3), 423-431.

Buri, J. R., Misukanis, T. M., Mueller, R. A. (1989). Parental Nurturance Scale [PNS]. In K. Corcoran & J. Fischer (Eds*.) Measures for clinical practice: A sourcebook*. (3rd ed.), (2 vols.) 427–428. New York: Press.

Bronfenbrenner, U. (1986). Ecology of the family as a context for human development research perspectives. *Developmental Psychology, 22,* 723–742.

Burns, B. J., Hoagwood, K., & Maultsby, L. T. (1998). Improving outcomes for children and adolescents with serious emotional and behavioral disorders: Current and future directions. In M. H. Epstein, K. Kutash, & A. J. Duchnowski (Eds.), *Community-based programming for children with serious emotional disturbance and their families: research and evaluations* (pp. 685–707). Austin, TX: PRO-ED.

Burns, G. L., & Patterson, D. R. (1990). Conduct problem behaviors in a stratified random sample of children and adolescents: New standardization data on the Eyberg Child Behavior Inventory. *Psychological Assessment, 2,* 391–397.

Campis, L. K., Lyman, R. D., & Prentice-Dunn, S. (1986). The parental locus of control scale: Development and validation. *Journal of Clinical Child Psychiatry, 15,* 260–267.

Carstensen, L. L., Isaacowitz, D. M., & Charles, S. T. (1999). Taking time seriously: a theory of socioemotional selectivity. *American Psychologist, 54,* 165–181.

Carter, B., & McGoldrick, M. (1998). Overview of the family life cycle. In B. Carter & M. McGoldrick (Eds.), *The expanded family life cycle: Individual, family and social perspectives* (3rd ed.). Boston: Allyn & Bacon.

Carter, B., & McGoldrick, M. (2005). Expanded family life cycly, The: individual, family, and social perspectives. Boston: Allyn & Bacon.

Chambless, D., & Hollon, S. (1998). Defining empirically supported therapies. *Journal of Consulting and Clinical Psychology, 66*(1), 7–18.

Cicchetti, D., & Lynch, M. (1993). Toward an ecological/transactional model of community violence and child maltreatment: Consequences for children's development. Children and violence [Special issues]. *Psychiatry: Interpersonal and Biological Process, 56,* 96–118.

Colapinto, J. (1982). Structural family therapy. In A. Horn & M. Ohlsen, *Family counseling and therapy* (pp. 112–140). Itasca, IL: F. E. Peacock.

Corcoran, K. (1992*). Structuring change: Effective practice for common client problems.* Chicago: Lyceum Books Inc.

Corcoran, J. (2000). *Evidence-based social work practice with families. A lifespan approach.* New York: Springer Series on Social Work.

Corcoran, J. (2003). *Clinical applications of evidence-based family interventions.* New York: Oxford.

Corcoran, K. (in press). What is evidence-based practice? In B. Thomlison & K. Corcoran (Eds.), *Evidence-based internships: A field manual.* New York: Oxford Press.

Corcoran, K., & Fischer, J. (2000). *Measures for clinical practice: A sourcebook volume: Couples, families, and children* (3rd ed.). New York: Free Press.

Corcoran, K., & Gingerich, W. (1992). Practice evaluation: Setting goals, measuring change. In K. Corcoran (Ed.), *Structuring change: Effective practice for common client problems* (pp. 255–272). Chicago, IL: Lyceum Books.

Corcoran, K., Gorin, S., & Moniz, S. (2005). Managed care and mental health. In S. Kirk (Ed.), *Mental disorders in the social environment. Critical perspectives for social work knowledge* (pp. 430–442). New York: Columbia University Press.

Corcoran, K., & Vandiver, V. (2004). Implementing best practice and expert consensus procedures. In A. R. Roberts & K. R. Yeager (Eds.), *Evidence-based practice manual: Research and outcome measures in health and human services* (pp. 15–19). New York: Oxford University Press.

Corcoran, K., & Videka-Sherman, L. (1992). Some things we know about effective clinical social work. In K. Corcoran (Ed.) *Structuring change: Effective practice for common client problems* (pp. 15–27). Chicago: Lyceum Books Inc.

Cross, T., Bazron, B., Dennis, K., & Issacs. M. (1989). *Towards a culturally competent system of care. A monograph on effective services for minority children who are severely emotionally disturbed (Vol. I).* Washington, D.C.: Georgetown University Child Development Center, National Technical Assistance Center for Children's Mental Health.

Cournoyer, B. (2004). *The evidence-based social work skills book.* Needham Heights, MA: Allyn & Bacon.

DeGroot, L., Lloyd, C., & King, R. (2003). An evaluation of a family psychoeducation program in community mental health. *Psychiatric Rehabilitation Journal, 27*(10), 18–23.

DeMaria, R., Weeks, G., & Hof, L. (1999). *Focused genograms. Intergenerational assessment of individuals, couples, and families.* Philadelphia, PA: Brunner/Mazel.

Dishion, T. J., & Kavanagh, K. (2003). *Intervening in adolescent problem behavior. A family-centered approach.* New York: The Guildford Press.

Dumaine, M. L. (1997). *An evaluation of coping ability as a guide to the treatment of persons diagnosed with schizophrenia and substance abuse.* Michigan: UMI Dissertation Services, (pp. 35–36).

Elder, G. (1977). Family history and the life course. *Journal of Family History, 2*(4), 279–304.

Elkind, D. (1994). *Ties that stress: The new family imbalance.* Cambridge, MA: Harvard University Press.

Eggeman, K., Moxley, V., & Schumm, W. R. (1985). Assessing spouses' perceptions of Gottman's Temporal Form in marital conflict. *Psychological Reports, 57,* 171–181.

Ehrensaft, M. K., Wasserman, G. A., Verdelli, L., Greenwald, S., Miller, L. S., & Davies, M. (2003).

Maternal antisocial behavior, parenting practices, and behavior problems in boys at risk for
antisocial behavior. *Journal of Child and Family
Studies, 12*(1), 27–40.

Epstein, N., Baldwin, L., & Bishop, D. (1983). The
McMaster Family Assessment Device. *Journal of
Marital and Family Therapy, 9,* 171–180.

Falloon, I. R. H., Boyd, J. L., McGill, C. W., Williamson,
M., Razani, J., Moss, H. B., Gildreman, A. M., &
Simpson, G. M. (1985). Family management in
the prevention of morbidity of schizophrenia.
Archives of General Psychiatry, 442, 887–896.

Fantuzzo, J., McDermott, P., & Lutz, M. N. (1999).
Clinical issues in the assessment of family vio-
lence involving children. In R. T. Ammerman &
M. Hersen (Eds.), *Assessment of family violence.
A clinical and legal sourcebook* (2nd ed., pp. 10–23).

Fine, M. A., & Schwebel, A. I. (1983). Long-term
effects of divorce on parent–child relationships.
Developmental Psychology, 19, 703–713.

Fischer, J., & Corcoran, K. (2000). *Measures for clinical practice. Volume 2: Adults* (3rd ed.). New
York: Free Press.

Fisher, P. A., & Chamberlain, P. (2000). Multidimensional treatment foster care: A program for
intensive parenting, family support, and skill
building. *Journal of Emotional and Behavioral
Disorders, 8*(3), 155–164.

Franklin, C., & Jordan, C. (1992). Teaching students
to perform assessments. *Journal of Social Work
Education, 28*(2), 222–241.

Franklin, C., & Jordan, C. (Eds.). (1999). *Family
practice: Brief systems methods for social work.*
Pacific Grove, CA: Brooks/Cole.

Fraser, M. (Ed.). (2004). *Risk and resilience in childhood. An ecological perspective.* (2nd ed.).
Washington, DC: NASW Press.

Fraser, M. W., Kirby, L., & Smokowski, P. R. (2004).
Risk and resilience in childhood. In M. W. Fraser
(Ed.), *Risk and resilience in childhood. An ecologi-
cal perspective* (2nd ed., pp.13–66). Washington,
DC: NASW Press.

Gambrill, E. (1997). *Social work practice: A critical
thinker's guide.* New York: Oxford University Press.

Gambrill, E., & Shlonsky, A. (2000). Risk assessment in context. *Children and Youth Services
Review, 22*(11/12), 813–837.

Gambrill, E., & Shlonsky, A. (2001).The need for
comprehensive risk management systems in
child welfare. *Children and Youth Services
Review, 23,* (1), 79–107.

Gammonley, D., & Thomlison, B. (2000). Peer
support models for relative caregivers. *Kinship
Care: A curriculum.* Unpublished manuscript.
Tallahasee, FL: Department of Family and
Children's Services.

Garner, J. W., & Hudson, W. W. (1992). Non-
Physical Abuse of Partner Scale and the Physical

Abuse of Partner Scale. In W. W. Hudson, *The
WALMYR Assessment Scales Scoring Manual.*
Tempe, AZ: WALMYR Publishing.

Gibbs, L. (2003). *Evidence-based practice for the
helping professions: A practical guide with integrated multimedia.* Pacific Grove, CA: Brooks/
Cole.

Gibbs, L., & Gambrill, E. (1999). *Critical thinking
for social workers* (Rev. ed.). Thousand Oaks:
Pine Forge Press.

Goldenberg, I., & Goldenberg, H. (2000). *Family
therapy: An overview* (5th ed.). Belmont, CA:
Wadsworth.

Goldner, V., Penn, P., Sheinberg, M., & Walker, G.
(1990). Love and violence: Gender paradoxes in
volatile attachments. *Family Process, 29,*
348–364.

Goodman, H. (2004). Elderly parents of adults with
severe mental illness: group work interventions.
Journal of Gerontological Social Work, 44(1/2),
173–189

Green, R. J., & Werner, P. D. (1996). Intrusiveness
and closeness caregiving: Rethinking the concept of family enmeshment. *Family Process, 35,*
115–136.

Gurman, A. S. & Kniskern, D. (1981) (Eds.). *Handbook of family therapy.* New York: Brunner/Mazel.

Haggerty, K. P., Fleming, C., B., Lonczak, H. S.,
Oxford, M. L., Harachi, T. W., & Catalano, R. F.
(2002). Predictors of participation in parenting
workshops. *The Journal of Primary Prevention,
22*(4), 375–387.

Henggeler, S. W., Schoenwald, S. K., Bordin, C. M.,
Rowland, M. D., & Cunningham, P. B. (1998).
*Multisystemic treatment of antisocial behavior in
children and adolescents.* New York: Guilford
Press.

Hepworth, D. H., Rooney, R., Dewberry Rooney,
G., Strom-Gottfried, K., & Larsen, J. A. (2006).
Direct social work practice: Theory and skills (7th
ed.). Belmont, CA: Wadsworth.

Herr, J. J., & Weakland, J. H. (1979). *Counseling elders and their families: Practical applications for
applied gerontology.* New York: Springer.

Hiebert, B., & Thomlison, B. (1996). Facilitating
transitions to adulthood: Research and policy
implications. In B. Galaway & J. Hudson (Eds.),
*Youth in transition: Perspectives on research and
policy* (pp. 54–60) Toronto: Thompson Educational Publishing.

Hogarty, G., Anderson, C., Reiss., D., Kornblith, J.,
Greenwald, D., Ulrich, R., & Carter, M. (1991).
Family psychoeducation, social skills training,
and maintenance chemotherapy in the aftercare
treatment of schizophrenia. *Archives of General
Psychiatry, 48,* 340–347.

Hooyman, N., & Kiyak, H. A. (2005). *Social gerontology: A multi-disciplinary perspective* (7th ed.).
Boston: Allyn & Bacon.

Horowitz, M. J., Wilner, N., & Alvarez, W. (1979). Impact of event scale: A measure of subjective stress. *Psychosomatic Medicine, 41,* 209–218.

Hudson, W. W. (1982). *The clinical measurement package.* Pacific Grove, CA: Brooks/Cole.

Hudson, W. W. (1990a). *The WALMYR Assessment Scales Scoring Manual.* Tempe, AZ: WALMYR Publishing.

Hudson, W. W. (1990b). *The MPSI Manual.* Tempe, AZ: WALMYR Publishing.

Hudson, W. W. (1992). *The WALMYR Assessment Scales Scoring Manual.* Tempe, AZ: WALMYR Publishing.

Hudson, W. W., & Garner, J. W. (1992). Index of Alcohol Involvement. In W. W. Hudson, *The WALMYR Assessment Scales Scoring Manual.* Tempe, AZ: WALMYR Publishing.

Huffman, L., Mehlinger, S., & Kerivan, A. (2000). Risk factors for academic and behavioral problems at the beginning of school. *Off to a Good Start.* Washington, DC: Department of Health and Human Service. Retrieved January 30, 2006 *http://www.ce-credit.com/articles/ riskfactorsacademic.pdf*

Hughes, R. (1999, May). The meaning of "evidence based" services in PSR. *International Association of Psychosocial Rehabilitation Services (IAPSRS), 2,* 1–10.

Imber Coppersmith, E. (1983). The place of family therapy in the homeostasis of larger systems. In M. Aronson and R. Wolberg (Eds.). *Group and family therapy: An overview.* New York: Brunner/ Mazel, 1983, 216–227.

Ivanoff, A., & Stern, S. B. (1992). Self-management interventions in health and mental health settings: Evidence of maintenance and generalization. *Social Work Research & Abstracts, 28*(4), 32–38.

Janzen, C., Harris, O., Jordan, C., & Franklin, C. (2006). *Family treatment: Evidence-based practice with populations at risk* (4th ed.). Belmont, CA: Wadsworth.

Jordan, C., & Franklin, C. (Eds). (2003). *Clinical assessment for social workers. Quantitative and qualitative methods* (2nd ed.). Chicago: Lyceum Books.

Kirkpatrick, A. C., & Holland, T. (2006). *Working with families: An integrative model by level of need.* (4th edition). Needham Heights, MA: Allyn & Bacon.

Kopeikin, H. S., Marshall, V., & Goldstein, M. J. (1983). Stages and impact of crisis-oriented family therapy in the aftercare of acute schizophrenia. In W. R. McFarlane (Ed.), *Family therapy in schizophrenia* (pp. 69–97). New York: Guilford.

Kumpfer, K. L., Molgaard, V., & Spoth, R. (1996). The Strengthening Families Program for the prevention of delinquency and drug use. In R. D. Peters & R. J. McMahon (Eds.), *Preventing childhood disorders, substance abuse, and delinquency* (pp. 241–267). Thousand Oaks, CA: Sage.

Lecroy, C. W. (1994). *Handbook of child and adolescent treatment manuals.* New York: Free Press.

Lieberman, M.A., & Fisher, L. (1999). The effects of family conflict resolution and decision making on the provision of help for an elder with Alzheimer's disease. *The Gerontologist, 39,* 159–166.

Magura, S., & Moses, B. (1986). *Rating form for Child Well-Being Scales.* Washington, DC: Child Welfare League of America.

Magura, S., Moses, B. S., & Jones, M. A. (1987). *Assessing risk and measuring change of families: The family risk scales.* Washington, DC: Child Welfare League of America.

Mattaini, M. (1999). *Clinical interventions with families.* Washington, DC: NASW Press.

McCubbin, H. I., Boss, P. G., Wilson, L. R., & Dahl, B. B. (1991). Family Coping Inventory. In H. I. McCubbin and A. I. Thompson (Eds.), *Family assessment inventories for research and practice.* Madison, WI: University of Wisconsin.

McCubbin, H. I., Patterson, J. M., Bauman, E., & Harris, L. H. (1991). Adolescent–Family Inventory of Life Events and Changes. In H. I. Mccubbin and A. I. Thompson (Eds.), *Family assessment inventories for research and practice.* Madison, WI: University of Wisconsin.

McCubbin, M. A., McCubbin, H. I., & Thompson, A. I. (1991). Family Hardiness Index. In H. I. McCubbin and A. I. Thompson (Eds.), *Family assessment inventories for research and practice.* Madison, WI: University of Wisconsin.

McGill, D. (1992). The cultural story in multicultural family therapy. *Families in Society: The Journal of Contemporary Human Services,* 339–349.

Minuchin, S. (1974). *Families and family therapy.* Cambridge, MA: Harvard University Press.

Morrow-Howell, N., Hinterlong, J. , Rozario, P., & Tang, F. (2003). Effects of volunteering on the well-being of older adults. *Journals of Gerontology(b), Psychological Sciences, 58*(3), 137–145.

Mulvey, E., Arthur, M., & Reppucci, D. (2000). The prevention of juvenile delinquency: A review of the research. *The Prevention Researcher Online.* http://tpronline.org/articles/.

McNeece, C. A., & Thyer, B. A. (2004). Evidence-based practice and social work. *Journal of Evidence-Based Social Work, 1*(1), 7–25.

National Center on Women & Aging (1997). *The MetLife juggling act study.* Waltham, MA: Author.

Nichols, M. P., & Schwartz, R. C. (2005). *The essentials of family therapy* (2nd ed.). Needham, MA: Allyn & Bacon.

Nuss, W. S., & Zubenko, G. S. (1992). Correlates of persistent depressive symptoms in widows. *American Journal of Psychiatry, 149,* 346–351.

Okun, B. (1996). *Understanding diverse families. What practitioners need to know.* New York: The Guilford Press.

Olds, D. (2002). Prenatal and infancy home visiting by nurses: From randomized trials to community replication. *Prevention Science, (3)2,* 153–172.

Parker, G., Tupling, H., & Brown, L. B. (1979). A parental bonding instrument. *British Journal of Medical Psychology, 52,* 1–10.

Paul, R. W., & Binker, A. J.(Eds.). (1990). *Critical thinking: What every person needs to survive in a rapidly changing world.* Rohnert Park, CA: Center for Critical Thinking and Moral Critique, Sonoma State University.

Paul, R., & Elder, L. (2004) *Critical thinking concepts and tools* (4th ed.). Dillon Beach, CA: Foundation for Critical Thinking. http://www.criticalthinking.org.

Qualls, S. H. (2002). Therapy with aging families: Rationale, opportunities, and challenges. *Aging & Mental Health, 4*(3), 191–199.

Reamer, F. G. (1995). Ethics and values. *Encyclopedia of Social Work* (19th ed., pp. 893–902). Washington, DC: NASW Press.

Reimer, M., Thomlison, B., & Bradshaw, C. (1999). *The clinical rotation handbook.* Albany, NY: Delmar.

Robbins, M. S., Alexander, J. F., Turner, C. W., & Perez, G. A. (2003). Alliance and dropout in family therapy for adolescents with behavior problems: Individual and systemic effects. *Journal of Family Psychology, 7*(4), 534–544.

Roberts, A. R., & Yeager, K. R. (Eds.) (2004). *Evidence-based social work practice.* New York: Oxford Press.

Rothery, M. (1999). The resources of intervention. In F. J. Turner (Ed.), *Social work practice: A Canadian perspective* (pp. 34–47). Scarborough, ON: Prentice-Hall.

Rothery, M., & Enns, G. (2001). *Clinical practice with families. Supporting creativity and competence.* New York: Haworth Press.

Rycus, J. S., & Hughes, R. C. (2003). Issues in risk assessment in child protective services: Policy White Paper. Available from the North American Resource Centre for Child Welfare. Retrieved February 2, 2006 from http://www.narccw.com

Sackett, D. L., Strauss, S. E., Richardson, W. S., Rosenberg, W., & Haynes, R. B. (2000). *Evidence-based medicine: How to practice and teach EBM.* New York: Churchill-Livingstone.

Sargent, G. A. (1985). *The use of rituals in family therapy: When, where, and why.* Presented at the AFTA Conference in San Diego. Unpublished.

Sattler, J. (1998). *Clinical and forensic interviewing of children and families: Guidelines for the mental health, education, pediatric, and child maltreatment fields.* San Diego, CA: Jerome M. Sattler, Publisher.

Scharlach, A. E. (1987). Relieving feelings of strain among women with elderly mothers. *Psychology and Aging, 2,* 9–13.

Shields, C. G., Franks, P., Harp, J. J., McDaniel, S. H., & Campbell, T. L. (1992). Development of the family emotional involvement and criticism scale (FEICS): A self-report scale to measure expressed emotion. *Journal of Marital and Family Therapy,* 18(4), 395–407.

Steketee, G. (1999). *Overcoming obsessive compulsive disorder: A behavioral and cognitive protocol for the treatment of OCD.* Oakland, CA: New Harbinger Publications.

Stiffman, A. R., Orme, J. G., Evans, D. A., Feldman, R. A., & Keeney, P. A. (1984). A brief measure of children's behavior problems: The Behavior Rating Index for Children. *Measurement and Evaluation in Counseling and Development, 16,* 83–90.

Stormshak, E. A., Kaminski, R. A., & Goodman, M. R. (2002). Enhancing the parenting skills of Head Start families during the transition to kindergarten. *Prevention Science,* 3(3), 223–234.

Straus, M. A., & Gelles, R. J. (1990). *Physical violence in American families: Risk factors and adaptations to violence in 8,145 families.* New Brunswick, NJ: Transaction.

Taylor, T., & Biglan, A. (1998). Behavioral family interventions for improving child-rearing: A review of the literature for clinicians and policy makers. *Clinical Child and Family Psychology Review,* 1 (1), 41–60.

The Campbell Collaborative. (n.d.). *What helps? What harms? Based on what evidence?* Retrieved April 27, 2005, from www.campbellcollaboration.org/FraAbout.html.

The National Commission on Children. (1991). *Speaking of Kids: A National Survey of Children and Parents* (ASI Publication No. 15528-2). Washington, DC: U.S. Government Printing Office.

Thomlison, B. (2004). Child maltreatment. In L. Rapp-Paglicci, C. Dulmus, and J. Wodarski (Eds.), *Handbook of preventive interventions for children and adolescents* (pp. 381–415). New York: John Wiley & Sons.

Thomlison, B., & Bradshaw, C. (2002). Clinical practice evaluation. In F. J. Turner (Ed.). *Social work practice: A Canadian perspective,* (2nd ed.) pp. 340–353. Scarborough, ON: Prentice Hall, Allyn & Bacon.

Thomlison, B., & Corcoran, K. (in press). Evidence-based internships: A field manual. New York: Oxford Press.

Thomlison B., & Craig, S. (2005). Ineffective parenting. In C. Dulmus and L. Rapp-Paglicci (Eds.), *Handbook of preventive interventions for adults* (pp. 327–360). New York: John Wiley & Sons.

Thomlison, B., & Thomlison, R. (1996). Behavior theory and social work treatment. In F. J. Turner (Ed.), *Social work treatment: Interlocking theoretical perspectives* (4th ed.). New York: The Free Press.

Thomlison, R. J. (1984). Something works: Evidence from practice effectiveness studies. *Social Work, 19*, 51–57.

Thornton, T., Craft, C., Dahlberg, L, Lynch, B., & Baer, K. (2000). *Best practices of youth violence prevention: A sourcebook for community action.* Atlanta: Centers for Disease Control and Prevention, National Center for Injury Prevention and Control.

Thyer, B. A. (Ed.). (1989). *Behavioral family therapy.* Springfield, IL: Charles C. Thomas.

Thyer, B. A. (1994). Social work theory and practice research: The approach of logical positivism. *Social Work and Social Services Review, 4*, 5–26.

Thyer, B. A., & Wodarski, J. S. (Eds.) (1998). *Handbook of empirical social work practice* (Vol. 1). New York: John Wiley & Sons.

Tomm, K. (1984). One perspective on the Milan systemic approach: 2. Description of session format, interviewing style, and interventions. *Journal of Marital and Family Therapy, 10*(3), 253–272.

Tomm, K. (1988). Interventive interviewing: III. Intending to ask lineal, circular, strategic, or reflexive questions? *Family Process, 27*(1), 1–15.

Tomm, K., & Sanders, G. (1983). Family assessment in a problem oriented record. In J. C. Hansen and B. F. Keeny (Eds.), *Diagnosis and assessment in family therapy* (pp. 101–122). London: Aspen Systems Corporation.

Toseland, R. W., McCallion, P., Smith, T. & Banks, S. (2004). Supporting caregivers of frail older adults in an HMO setting. *The American Journal of Orthopsychiatry, 74*(3), 349–364.

Tracy, E. M., & Whittaker, J. K. (1990). The social network map: Assessing social support in clinical social work practice. *Families in Society, 71*, 461–470.

Tremblay, R. E. (2000). The development of aggressive behaviour during childhood: What have we learned in the past century? *International Journal of Behavioral Development. 24*, 129–141.

Tripodi, T. (1994). *A primer on single-subject design for clinical social workers.* Washington, DC: NASW.

Tutty, L. (1995). Theoretical and practical issues in selecting a measure of family functioning. *Research on Social Work Practice, 5*(1), 80–106.

U.S. Public Health Service (1999). Older adults and mental health. In *Mental health: A report of the Surgeon General.* Washington, DC: Author.

Available online: http://www.surgeongeneral.gov/library/mentalhealth/chapter5/sec1.html.

Vandiver, V. (2002). Step-by-step practice guidelines for using evidence-based practice and expert consensus in mental health settings. In A. R. Roberts & G. J. Greene (Eds.), *Social workers' desk reference* (p. 131). New York: Oxford University Press.

Webster-Stratton, C. (1992). Individually administered videotape parent training: "Who benefits?" *Cognitive Therapy and Research, 16*, 31–52.

Webster-Stratton, C. (1997). From parent training to community building. *Families in Society, 78*, 156–171.

Webster-Stratton, C. (1998). Preventing conduct problems in Head Start Children: Strengthening parenting competencies. *Journal of Consulting and Clinical Psychology, 66*, 715–730.

Webster-Stratton, C., & Taylor, T. (2001). Nipping risk factors in the bud: Preventing substance abuse, delinquency and violence in adolescence through interventions targeted at young children (0–8 years). *Prevention Science, 2*(3), 165–192.

Weisz, J. R., & Kazdin, A. E. (2003). Present and future of evidence-based

Weiss, C. H. (1995). Nothing as practical as good theory: Exploring theory-based evaluation for comprehensive community initiatives for children and families. In J. P. Connell (Ed.), *New approaches to evaluating community initiatives: Concepts, methods, and contexts.* Washington, DC: The Aspen Institute.

Whittaker, J., Schinke, S., & Gilchrist, L. (1986). The ecological paradigm in child, youth, and family services: Implications for policy and practice. *Social Service Review 60*, 483–503.

Williams, J., & Ell, K. (1998*). Advances in Mental Health Research. Implications for Practice.* Washington, DC: NASW Press.

Wright, L., & Leahey, M. (1994). *Nurses and families: A guide to family assessment and intervention* (2nd ed.). Philadelphia: F. A. Davis.

Wright, L., Watson, W., & Bell, J. (1996). *Beliefs; The heart of healing in families and illness.* New York: Basic Books, HarperCollins.

Yank, G. R., Bentley, K. J., & Hargrove, D. S. (1992). The vulnerability-stress model of schizophrenia. *American Orthopsychiatric Association, 63*(1), 55–69.

Zastrow, C. (1995). *The practice of social work* (5th ed.). Pacific Grove, CA: Brooks/Cole.

Zinn, M., & Eitzen, D. (1990). *Diversity in families* (2nd ed.). New York: Harper Collins.

Zubin, J., & Spring, B. (1977). Vulnerability—New view of schizophrenia. *Journal of Abnormal Psychology, 86*(2), 103–126.

Index

P

Parental Bonding Instrument, 99
Parental Locus of Control Scale, 99
Parental Nurturance Scale, 99
Parent-child management, 125–129
Parent-Child Relationship Survey, 98
Parent/family-based strategies, 90–91
Parenting, 98–99. *See also* Del Sol family
    case study
Partner Abuse Scale, 99
Paternalism, 10
Paul, R. W., 26–27
Personal beliefs, 4–5
Physical abuse, 99, 125–129, 141–145
Physical Abuse of Partner Scale, 99
Practice models, 5
Practice-setting beliefs, 8–10
Preferences, 4
Professional beliefs, 6
Protective factors, 20, 36, 62, 90
Psychoeducation, 58, 131, 139, 147, 150–152

R

Rapid assessment instruments (RAI), 96–97
Rating scale, 77
Reamer, F. G., 8
Reframing, 86
Retirement, 53
Risk factors, 20, 36, 62, 84, 90
Rituals, 88
Role change, 113–117
Role-playing, 77–78, 80, 106–107, 113–114,
    120–121, 147
Rothery, M., 18
Rycus, J. S., 99

S

Self-assessment, 25–31
Self-Report Family Inventory (SFI), 96, 98
Self-report tools, 75, 77
Sherman family case study, 131–138
Shlonsky, A., 99
Social network map/grid, 21
    constructing, 74–75
    Del Sol case study and, 107
    function of, 67
    intergenerational families and, 57
    learning activities on, 29, 81
    McCoy case study and, 113
Stereotypes, 52

Strengths, family, 85–86
Stressors, 34–36
Substance abuse, 100, 139–140
Substance Abuse and Mental Health Services
    Administration (SAMHSA), 92
SAMHSA National Mental Health Information
    Center, 58
Symmetrical alliance, 47

T

Taking Care of Families Program, 128
Teaching, 86–87
Therapeutic alliance, 15–16, 19
Thomlison, B., 96–97
Thompson Educational Publishing, 120
Time lines, 21
Trajectories, 54
Transition to independent living, 119–124
Triangle, 48
Tutty, L., 96

V

Values, 3–4. *See also* Beliefs
Vandiver, V., 89
Videka-Sherman, L., 89
Violence, family, 99, 141–145

W

Websites
    on adolescent behavior problems, 92
    on domestic violence, 126
    on evidence-based information, 83
    on genograms, 70
    on intergenerational families, 58
    on parenting skills, 126
    on psychoeducation, 58, 147
    on substance abuse, 92
    on substance abuse and older adults, 139
    on youth in transition, 120
Weeks, G., 44–45
Widowhood, 53, 55

Y

Yellowbird family case study, 119–124

Z

Zastrow, C., 101